The Law and Practice of Extradition

The Law and Practice of Extradition provides an in-depth overview of extradition law and practice, providing students with an understanding of how key elements have been shaped by the state, the fugitive and the international community.

The process of globalisation has offered huge opportunities for organised crime, both in terms of expansion of operations and the possibility to evade justice, confronting states with considerable challenges. *The Law and Practice of Extradition* addresses all key topics in this fast-evolving area, including extradition and international crimes, terrorism and human rights.

This textbook is particularly suitable for master's and post-doctoral students with a basic background knowledge of international law, criminal law and international relations, and will interest legal practitioners who seek a better understanding of extradition.

Harmen van der Wilt is a professor of International Criminal Law at the University of Amsterdam, the Netherlands, and an ad-litem judge in the Special Chamber on International Criminal Cooperation in Criminal Matters of the District Court of Amsterdam.

The Law and Practice of Extradition

Harmen van der Wilt

Routledge
Taylor & Francis Group
LONDON AND NEW YORK

Cover image: Galina Shafran (Getty Images)

First published 2022
by Routledge
4 Park Square, Milton Park, Abingdon, Oxon OX14 4RN

and by Routledge
605 Third Avenue, New York, NY 10158

Routledge is an imprint of the Taylor & Francis Group, an informa business

British Library Cataloguing-in-Publication Data
A catalogue record for this book is available from the British Library

Library of Congress Cataloging-in-Publication Data
A catalog record has been requested for this book

ISBN: 978-1-138-59042-7 (hbk)
ISBN: 978-1-032-25773-0 (pbk)
ISBN: 978-0-429-95668-3 (ebk)

DOI: 10.4324/9780429956683

Typeset in Sabon
by Deanta Global Publishing Services, Chennai, India.

Contents

Preface

Different from the ever-increasing avalanche of publications on the background and functioning of the International Criminal Court and international criminal tribunals, comprehensive works on the concept and significance of extradition are scarce. That is not surprising. Apart from being less 'spectacular,' extradition has a definitely local character. While it stems from an agreement between states and its natural legal source is found, therefore, in a treaty, the legal procedure preceding the actual surrender of a person to another state and the parameters within which the state is prepared to oblige are laid down in national law. This state of affairs reflects the idea that extradition is basically a sovereign act. It is the state's privilege to decide what should happen with persons who reside in its territory and who are, therefore, within its jurisdiction.

A respectable number of excellent legal treatises address the law and practice of extradition from a specifically national angle.[1] Few works have attempted the daunting task of probing the generic features of extradition as a concept that combines elements of (international) politics, international law, criminal law and human rights.[2] This monograph aims to make

1 To the best of the author's knowledge, most works hail from European or American scholars, but that finding may well be blurred by his limited linguistic capacities. Without any pretension of giving a comprehensive survey, and rather by way of example, I would like to mention M. Ch. Bassiouni, *International Extradition: United States Law and Practice*, 6th ed., Oxford University Press: Oxford 2014; Claude Lombois, *Droit Penal international*, Precis Dalloz: Paris 1979; Th. Hackner & Chr. Schierholt, *Internationale Rechtshilfe in Strafsachen: Ein Leitfaden für die Praxis Taschenbuch*, 3e Auflage, C.H. Beck: Munich 2017; H. Schultz, *Das Schweizerische Auslieferungsrecht*, Verlag für Recht und Geselschat: Basel 1953; W. Schomburg & O. Lagodny, *Internationale Rechtshilfe in Strafsachen = International Cooperation in Criminal Matters*, 6e Auflage, C.H. Beck: Munich 2020; V.E. Hartley Booth, *British Extradition Law and Procedure*, Samson: Alphen aan den Rijn 1980; A.H.J. Swart, *Nederlands uitleveringsrecht*, Tjeenk Willink: Zwolle 1986; P.E. Trousse & J. Vanhalewijn, *Uitlevering en internationale rechtshulp in strafzaken*, Larcier: Brussel 1970.

2 M. Ch. Bassiouni, *International Extradition and World Public Order*, Sijthoff: Leiden, 1974; Geoff Gilbert, *Transnational Fugitive Offenders in International Law: Extradition and Other Mechanisms*, Martinus Nijhoff: The Hague 1998; I.A. Shearer, *Extradition in*

a contribution to that literature. It starts from the hypothesis that the legal institute of extradition – its possibilities and limitations – is the outcome of the interaction of several interests, to wit, those of the cooperating states, the fugitive and the international community. The aim to present a panoramic view of extradition in a concise monograph of some 200 pages requires making a number of hard choices.

First, I would like to say a few words about the intended readership. This is not a textbook for first-year university students. It presupposes a basic knowledge of international law, criminal law and international relations. I therefore surmise that advanced (master's) students, doctoral students and legal practitioners with an interest in the deeper layers of extradition might be expected to benefit from reading it.[3]

Second, and closely related to the former, it should be emphasised that this work does not present a complete and exhaustive survey of all aspects of extradition law. The focus is on those doctrines of extradition law that are shaped by and owe their existence to the interplay between the competing interests of the stakeholders just mentioned, such as the non-extradition of nationals, the dual criminality rule and the political offence exception. Some topics, like statutory limitations as impediment to extradition and the, now obsolete, tax offences exception, are not addressed in the book. Likewise, formalities of extradition procedure are hardly touched upon. Analysis of the details of procedure and – sometimes minute – interstate differences, besides producing boring reading, rarely prove illuminating for a deeper understanding of the nitty-gritty of extradition. An exception is made if procedural differences potentially reveal a shift in the weighing of the interests involved.

Finally, and this is probably the most delicate point, it is obvious that the predominant attention paid to European and, to a lesser extent, US doctrine and case law comes to the detriment of other jurisdictions. It is especially to this point that the author must show his colours. One of the reasons is trivial. Being a Dutchman, the author is obviously most familiar with Dutch law and practice on extradition.[4] Moreover, as a member of the European Union, the Netherlands has ample experience with processing European

International Law, Manchester University Press: Manchester 1971. Of more recent date: David A. Sadoff, *Bringing International Fugitives to Justice: Extradition and Its Alternatives*, Cambridge University Press: Cambridge 2016.

3 It is worth mentioning that the author used his students of the special Master of International and Transnational Criminal Law course at the University of Amsterdam as 'guinea pigs' to test the correctness of this assumption.

4 The author's first encounter with extradition law was his meticulous study of the *magnum opus* of one of his intellectual godfathers, Bert Swart's *Nederlands uitleveringsrecht*, mentioned in footnote 1. The author serves as a part-time judge in the International Rechtshulpkamer (Special Chamber for International (Criminal) Cooperation) of the District Court of Amsterdam that deals nearly exclusively with extradition and European Arrest Warrants.

Arrest Warrants, the system that since 2002 prevails in the European Union, as a substitute to extradition. Predicated on the principle of mutual recognition, the system aims to expedite the surrender of fugitives and make the procedure less cumbersome. One important way to achieve this is to abolish most grounds for refusal, which are considered redundant in a cooperation configuration of like-minded states. Paradoxically, the concern for the protection of the human rights of the fugitive has considerably increased. The dialectics between the interests of the states involved and the international institution of the EU and the rights of the fugitive come prominently to the fore. From the perspective of the central thesis of this work, the European system, therefore, deserves close attention. The frequent references to US statutes, literature and case law should be understood against the backdrop of the different approach taken by the common law on several topics, including the extradition of nationals, dual criminality and unorthodox renditions.

While the author admits therefore that analysis of European and US positions and practice of extradition is lopsided, case law and legal instruments hailing from Africa, Asia, Latin America and Oceania are scattered throughout the book. A systematic analysis of regional law and practice is, however, not intended. That choice can be defended based on the inductive methodology that is followed in this book. Legal opinions on certain doctrines of extradition law are scrutinized in search of patterns and common ground. They either corroborate the general findings on the appropriateness of – say – the political offence exception or qualify it, which requires an adaption or refinement of the doctrine or at least an explanation of a different view. An exhaustive inquiry of all opinions on the issue is not needed. The method neither pursues nor promises scientific truth. If the reader discovers a hiatus that would shed new light on an issue, the author would truly appreciate it if the individual could inform him.

Acknowledgements

This book is the outgrowth of a career as lecturer at two academic institutions spanning 30 years. In 1991, I was appointed an assistant professor of (international) criminal law at the University of Maastricht, which enabled me to develop a course on international criminal law. At the time, so-called supranational criminal law was still in its infancy or, perhaps better labeled, in hibernation, so I decided to focus entirely on the law and practice of extradition as the paradigm of international cooperation in criminal matters. The late Professor Bert Swart was my leading intellectual guide. His *Nederlands uitleveringsrecht* ("Dutch extradition law") served as an inexhaustible source of inspiration. I cherish the good memories of our manifold discussions.

In 2000, we – my wife and our three children – moved from rural Belgium to Hoorn as I obtained a position of associate professor and, from 2004 on, full professor at the University of Amsterdam (UvA). In the meantime, supranational criminal law had risen to prominence through the activities of ad hoc tribunals and the establishment by the Rome Statute of the International Criminal Court. The faculty allowed me to concentrate on both sub-disciplines of international criminal law, which were divided into separate courses. During those 20 years at UvA, scores of master's students followed these courses and I have greatly benefited from their dedication and acumen. Over the last two years, I (ab)used my master's students as guinea pigs, challenging them in considering issues raised in the chapters of this volume. It is a privilege to act as a teacher to such gifted young people. I owe special gratitude to Anivesh Bharadwaj, Doireann McCarthy, Julio Ramos Pirez, Nicola Campbell and Fiona de Vries who took the trouble of really reading the manuscript and making useful comments. Additionally, Fiona served as my student-assistant and suggested invaluable literature.

In 2004, I applied for a position as ad-litem judge at the *Internationale Rechtshulpkamer* (Special Chamber for International Cooperation in Criminal Matters) of the District Court in Amsterdam. The IRK has gradually evolved into a pioneering court that has contributed immensely to the legal understanding and practical application of the European Arrest Warrant. While technical problems – passwords, entrance passes – sometimes raised obstacles and spoilt my mood, as soon as I was 'in court' I benefited from the warm welcome and interest of my colleague judges. It is always tricky to mention particular names, but I would like to single out Yolanda de Vries, Marjan van Mourik, Karin Glerum, Cees Klomp and Hans Kijlstra with whom I had the most frequent – and pleasant! – exchanges of opinion. With court clerks Luberta Werkman, Sander van Munster and Vincent Glerum, the last mentioned also an academic colleague, I often had inspiring conversations on literature, music and legal doctrine.

While I succeeded in publishing articles in journals and in edited volumes, the intellectual academic harvest remained somewhat dispersed and fragmented. In 2019, the acting chair of the criminal law department, Denis Abels, granted me a generous sabbatical of three months. My wife and I spent about eight weeks in Mieussy, France, with our lifelong friends Dorine van Teeseling and Jaap Schep. They created the perfect, inspiring atmosphere for an academic writer and provided much-needed diversion in our birdwatching strolls in the mountains. Next, we moved to Maximilian University in Munich, where we enjoyed the warm hospitality of my doctoral student Nicolai von Maltitz and my colleague Professor Dr. Helmut Sätzger.

Family always comes last, because the author, like an opera composer, aims to build up tension and they are the most important. My brother Gert Jan and our three children, Martje, Femke and Bram always have an open ear for the multifarious reflections of their brother/father. I love them very much. Joke is the love of my life. She supports me in good times and in bad times and is responsible for me having reasonably succeeded in life (until now).

Table of cases

1 Introduction

Situated on the crossroads of criminal and international law, extradition has a mixed pedigree. Its criminal law features are obvious. The essence of extradition is the return of a person (from one state to another) who has been charged with having committed an offence or has already been convicted for the purpose of bringing that person to trial or the execution of a sentence. The purpose of criminal law enforcement defines the concept of extradition. Any other aim that is sought by the surrender of a person means that the procedure can be legally and properly qualified as extradition.[1] Its international law aspect is apparent from the fact that, in principle, two states are involved, namely, the requesting and the requested state.[2]

Since the 20th century, and especially after World War II, extradition has increasingly been considered as serving broader purposes, like sustaining world public order and furthering peaceful relations between nations.[3] A vigorous advocate of this point of view was the late M. Cherif Bassiouni.[4] His ideas have found resonance in the judgments of the European Court of Human Rights which has emphasised the need for closer cooperation, in reaction to international crime: 'As movement about the world becomes

1 Marjorie M. Whiteman, *Digest of International Law*, Volume 6, US Department of State 1968, 727.

2 'In principle' because surrender of persons for criminal enforcement purposes is conceivable and takes place between states and international criminal tribunals and courts. The procedure is governed by different legal rules and principles, allowing states less leeway to invoke grounds for refusal.

3 Although the germs of this conception were already discernible in the classic treatises on the international community as a *civitas maxima* by Wolff and Grotius. On the several depictions of international relations, see for instance, Hedley Bull, *The Anarchical Society: A Study on Order in World Politics*, Columbia University Press: New York 1977; with a particular interest for the connection between concepts of international order and extradition: M. Ch. Bassiouni and Edward Wise, *Aut Dedere, Aut Judicare; The Duty to Extradite or Prosecute in International Law,* Martinus Nijhoff Publishers: Dordrecht 1995, especially pp. 26–42 ('The Principle Aut Dedere, Aut Judicare and the Hypothesis of a *Civitas Maxima*').

4 Compare M. Ch. Bassiouni, *International Extradition and World Public Order*, Sijthoff: Leiden, 1974.

DOI: 10.4324/9780429956683-1

easier and crime takes on a larger international dimension, it is increasingly in the interest of *all* nations that suspected offenders who flee abroad should be brought to justice.'[5]

1.1 Stakeholders (i): the requesting and the requested state

Although this perception of extradition as a stairway to 'eternal peace' should not be dismissed forthwith, we will start with the more modest proposition that extradition (at least) serves the interests of the states involved. This idea has been easily taken for granted, but it deserves further scrutiny. For the requested state it is not self-evidently advantageous to surrender fugitives from justice to another state. It may be a convenient method to get rid of unwanted individuals who may yield a danger to a state's own society, but that benefit dwindles whenever these persons do not (or no longer) persist in their harmful behavior. Moreover, the requested state may harbor different opinions on whether the conduct is criminal at all or whether the fugitive is a menace to society. Scores of conditions and grounds for refusal in extradition conventions, like the principle of dual criminality and the political offence exception, owe their existence to the fact of life that conceptions on criminal justice are not universally shared and underscore that the willingness of states to engage in extradition is qualified at best. Arguably the strongest incentive for the requested state to comply with an extradition request is the prospect of obtaining a similar favour from the requesting state if the tables are turned. While reciprocity – *do ut des* – is generally a strong motive and principle in international relations and international law, its relevance in extradition is indeed overwhelming. That takes us directly to the interests of the requesting state.

At first blush, the benefits for the requesting state are rather obvious. After all, its powers of criminal law enforcement are obstructed by the suspect's flight abroad. Why would it lodge an extradition request in the first place if it would have no interest in obtaining custody over the fugitive? The logic is flawless, but it starts from the premise that the state has actually initiated an extradition and does not explain the utility of the institution in general. It is argued that the urgency or 'sense' of extradition at least partially depends on the nature of the offence and the theory of punishment to which one is inclined to subscribe. For the moment, some observations on both aspects will suffice.

From a *retributive* point of view, extradition is arguably an indispensable instrument. If one considers punishment as a Kantian imperative, a response that of necessity must follow the crime, it is simply unacceptable that the culprit will get away with it by escaping to another country. The

5 ECHR, 12 May 2005, Appl. No. 46221/99, *Gran Chamber (Öcalan v. Turkey (Merits))*, 37 EHRR 10, section 88. Emphasis added.

'injured' state might ponder cajoling the state of refuge to start criminal investigations and, if accepted, transfer criminal proceedings. However, this is usually considered as a second-best solution because the legal order and society of the state where the crime has been committed have suffered a blow and that state is authorised to act in kind. Moreover, *rehabilitative* objectives, incidentally siding with retributive theory, are served only if the offender will stand trial and face the consequences thereof in his or her home country. Similarly, those who favour *general deterrence* as the major aim of punishment will defend the concept of extradition as well because it sends the message that escape does not render the offender immune from the long arm of the law. Any potential wrong-doer might reconsider his evil intentions, if (s)he realises that the chances of being caught are not diminished by going abroad. On the other hand, the advocates of *special prevention* who defend trial and criminal punishment as a means of incapacitating the offender and precluding that (s)he relapses into his criminal behavior will not directly be convinced by the necessity of returning the fugitive to his home country. They will argue that society is at least temporarily protected against new onslaughts by the offender as long as (s)he stays abroad. Such was probably the general feeling in ancient times when travel was cumbersome and offenders generally remained in their home country. If criminals succeeded in escaping, their 'exile' was tantamount to social death and the harshest form of punishment because no one was capable of vouchsafing for his/her good (or bad!) behavior. Such social and geographical contingencies obviated the need for extensive extradition arrangements.[6] In modern times, such propositions are obviously entirely outdated. Offenders benefit from the digital revolution – cybercrime being a scholarly example. They use the most sophisticated means of communication, can travel when and where they wish, and can inflict harm to a wide array of states and societies, including the one from whence they fled. Nevertheless, some crimes are by their very nature more 'transnational' or 'international,' and these require concerted action by states or even the response of the international community as a whole.

6 Nonetheless, as Blakesley has demonstrated, extradition has been practiced since antiquity; see Christopher Blakesley, 'The Practice of Extradition from Antiquity to Modern France and the United States: A Brief History,' 4 *Boston College International and Comparative Law Journal* (1981), p. 39. See also Geoff Gilbert, *Transnational Fugitive Offenders in International Law: Extradition and Other Mechanisms*, Martinus Nijhoff: The Hague 1998, pp. 17–22, who attributes the emergence of a 'modern extradition system' in the 18th and 19th centuries, primarily based on international treaties, to the rise of the nation-state and the increased attention to the rights of individuals. On the history of extradition, see also Peter D. Sutherland, 'The Development of International Law of Extradition,' 28 *Saint Louis University Law Journal* (1940), pp. 33–40; and Jan H. Verzijl, *International Law in Historical Perspective, Volume 5*, Martinus Nijhoff: Leiden 1972, chapter 7, section 2.

1.2 Stakeholders (ii): the international community

The second half of the previous century witnessed the establishment of a score of multilateral treaties that were concluded with the aim of addressing the challenges of specific transnational crimes. Different from their bilateral predecessors, these treaties were not only concerned with extradition, but also included a comprehensive 'package' of measures, including the obligation of states-parties to criminalise conduct, establish adequate criminal jurisdiction, consider either extradition or prosecution whenever a suspect was found on their territory (*aut dedere, aut judicare*) and render each other the widest measure of mutual assistance in criminal matters.[7] Conventions on terrorism were structured along the same lines.[8] These initiatives demonstrate that states are obviously inclined to cooperate more intensively whenever they are apprehensive of an increased (and shared) vulnerability, either caused by the intrinsic volatility of the crimes or because offenders have opted to consider the entire world (or part of it: the infidels, Western, secularised society) as its enemy. A similar sentiment underlies the approach towards supranational crimes *stricto sensu* (aggression, crimes against humanity, genocide, war crimes), the perpetrators whereof are often qualified as *hostes humani generis* (enemies of mankind).[9] Apart from the well-known initiatives to hold these international criminals accountable before a supranational forum, states are increasingly active in creating a watertight network of interstate cooperation, which includes extradition and mutual assistance in criminal matters, in order to bring the culprits to justice. The point that I wish to make is that the determination of states to engage in extradition may well depend on the nature of the crime and is by no means static.

1.3 Stakeholders (iii): the requested person

So far, only the interests of states – and, in passing, the international community – in the establishment and practical application of extradition have been addressed. Assuredly, that is an unwarranted and highly one-sided

7 Typical examples include the UN Convention against the Illicit Traffic in Narcotic Drugs and Psychotropic Substances, Vienna, 20 December 1988, UNTS, vol. 1582, p. 94; and the (categorical) UN Convention on Transnational Crime (UNCTOC), New York, 15 November 2000, UNTS, vol. 2225, p. 209, with two Protocols (on Human Trafficking and Smuggling of Human Persons).

8 Compare, for example, the Convention for the Suppression of Unlawful Seizure of Aircraft (Hague Hijacking Convention, The Hague, 16 December 1970, UNTS, vol. 12325, p. 205; and the International Convention for the Suppression of Terrorist Bombings, New York, 9 January 1998, UNTS, vol. 2149, p. 251.

9 David Luban, 'The Enemy of all Humanity', *Netherlands Journal of Legal Philosophy* (2018), pp. 112–137. For a critical response: Marc de Wilde, 'Enemy of Humanity: The Dehumanizing Effects of a Dangerous Concept,' *Netherlands Journal of Legal Philosophy* (2018), pp. 158–174.

representation. After all, it is the individual suspect that is confronted with detention and the prospect of forceful removal by a state that usually bears no grudge against him.[10] One may object that aliens usually have no unrestricted title to remain on the territory of a foreign country. To be sure, most statutes on aliens condition their rightful residence on their not having been convicted of a serious offence. Apart from being inapplicable in case of the extradition of nationals, the argument does not relieve the state from giving a proper explanation for using enforcement powers against the requested person. The extradition procedure precisely serves that purpose and can be considered from that perspective as offering legal protection to the individual.

While human rights have made enormous headway since World War II, Bassiouni could still write in 1974 that 'Extradition is still regarded, with some variations in application but not in substance, as an institutional practice.' And he continues by holding that

> States are the subjects of its regulation, while individuals are objects of its outcome. The individual who is contemplated by extradition proceedings is not the primary party contemplated by extradition law and practice. Restrictions, limitations, or defenses which exist under extradition law are not, with a few exceptions, primarily designed for the benefit of the individual, instead they are designed to inure to the benefit of the states involved.[11]

Bassiouni's assertions remind us of the broader problem of how international law can accommodate the rights of individuals that are by definition 'third parties' under any treaty. His representation correctly reflects the state of the art in 1974, but it appears to be slightly outdated today. Gilbert neatly captures the modern spirit in contending that 'Extradition itself is an element in the international protection of human rights.'[12]

Human rights pervade extradition law and practice at different levels and in a number of ways. First of all – the most conspicuous and well-known way – the requested state bears responsibility for the relator and must ensure that the latter is not exposed to a real risk of a flagrant violation of human rights in the requesting state. The European Court of Human Rights has emerged as a champion of this principle, starting with the landmark decision in the *Soering* case, in which the plaintive, after being extradited, faced an

10 It is my personal experience as a judge in surrender or extradition proceedings that the relator, while being informed by the chair that this court will not assess his guilt or innocence, often immediately and automatically starts to a give an account of the particulars of the offence.

11 Bassiouni, supra footnote 4, pp. 562–563.

12 Gilbert, supra footnote 6, p. 6.

imminent stay on death row, preceding probable capital punishment.[13] Later case law of the European Court of Human Rights and the European Court of Justice covered the prospect of potentially unfair trials and, more recently, inhumane detention conditions in the requesting state.[14] While states face the embarrassing situation that any dismissal of extradition implies a (negative) assessment of the administration of justice in the requesting state and runs counter to the rule of non-inquiry, they have generally followed suit on pain of being held responsible for human rights violations themselves.

Second, the forced removal to another country for the purpose of facing criminal justice may imply that the individual is severed from his family and loved ones, particularly if that person has built a living and has put down roots in the requested state. Now again one may remonstrate that this is the logical and expected fate of those who choose to commit crimes, but the consequences may be especially harsh, in particular in view of possible alternatives (like prosecution and trial in the state of sojourn). Extradition may thus involve the right to family life (Article 8 European Convention on Human Rights).

Last but not least, because extradition procedure renders the requested person the opportunity to be apprised of the reasons for the restriction of his liberty, it should, in principle, be the exclusive route for states to obtain custody over fugitives of justice. The issue is a matter of great controversy, especially since the US Supreme Court in *Alvarez Machain* has (in)famously denied that extradition excludes other methods, thus effectively condoning the abduction of a Mexican national from Mexican territory by US police officials, with a view to standing trial before a US court.[15] The notorious *male captus, bene detentus (or: judicatus* doctrine, entailing that a court's jurisdiction is not affected by the (unlawful) method applied for bringing the suspect before the court) has been much criticised and (more rarely) defended.[16] The topic will be addressed in more depth later in this work. Suffice to observe at this point that, according to this author, the maxim can be reconciled neither with international law nor with (international) human rights law. Foreign police officials crossing a border to seize fugitives lack the authority to do so and impinge on both the sovereignty of the state and the habeas corpus rights of the individual. No single rule of international law even remotely allows for such conduct. Less intrusive methods, like luring or 'disguised extradition,' may not invade the sovereignty of a state,

13 ECtHR 7 July 1989, Appl. No. 14038/88 (*Soering v. United Kingdom*).

14 See on fair trial, amongst many others, ECtHR, 20 February 2007, Appl. No. 35865/03 (*Al-Moayad v. Germany*). On prison conditions: European Court of Justice (ECJ), 5 April 2016, C-404/15 and C-659/15 PPU, (*Aranyosi and Căldăraru*).

15 US Supreme Court, *United States v. Alvarez Machain*, 504 U.S. 655 (1992).

16 See, for instance: Christophe Paulussen, *Male captus, bene detentus? Surrendering Suspects to the International Criminal Court*, Intersentia: Antwerp 2010; and David A. Sadoff, *Bringing International Fugitives to Justice: Extradition and Its Alternatives*, Cambridge University Press: Cambridge 2016, *passim*.

but they contradict the principle of fair warning and should be ostracised whenever the lawful alternative of extradition is available.

1.4 Summary of content and approach

These introductory remarks serve to demonstrate that extradition is a fascinating and increasingly complex topic. This work intends to shed light on the phenomenon, from the perspective of states, the (wider) international community and the individual(s) involved, as briefly expounded above. While legal analysis is predominant, the work does not stop there, and it includes excursions into international relations and political philosophy whenever appropriate. This may, at first blush, appear a daunting task that cannot be accomplished in a succinct monography of barely 200 pages. However, the chosen perspective(s) allows the author to make some hard choices. This is not a textbook for undergraduate students in which all aspects of extradition law are meticulously explained. Nor is it a comprehensive compilation of treaties, domestic statutes and case law (if that would be feasible in the first place) and even a more or less complete survey and discussion of these sources is not intended.[17] The work is structured according to the well-known sub-doctrines of extradition law, such as dual criminality, political offence, double jeopardy and (non-) extradition of nationals. At each step, inquiry is made into why these principles or exceptions have come to fruition, set against the backdrop of the legal interests of the three categories of stakeholders identified above. Chapter 2 addresses the distinct approaches of common law and civil law countries on the extradition of nationals, against the background of the alternative of prosecution by the nation-state. Chapter 3 deals with the underlying rationales and practical application of the dual criminality rule. Chapter 4 discusses the rule of specialty. Chapter 5 starts with a discourse on the sensitive issue of extradition of political offenders, while Chapters 6 and 7 follow with an analysis of the efforts to exclude respectively war crimes and terrorism from the ambit of the political offence exception. Chapter 8 addresses the 'eternal practice' of abductions and disguised extradition. Chapter 9 completes with an extensive discussion of the relationship between extradition and human rights.

One of the more difficult issues is whether and to what extent a monography on international extradition should take into account regional differences in law and practice. The bifurcated nature of extradition may point in different directions. Being an instrument of international law, extradition may well induce states to reach compromises and find some

17 To the author's best knowledge, M. Ch. Bassiouni's *International Extradition: United States Law and Practice*, 6th ed., Oxford University Press: Oxford 2014, is unrivalled in completeness and detail, although, as the title indicates, the book takes an American perspective.

common denominator. Extradition is governed and regulated by treaties, while national legislation is often enacted to implement those treaties in the domestic legal order and reflects treaty provisions. The international legal component of extradition thus reinforces uniformity, obviating a meticulous analysis of all regional treaties and national legislation.[18] The criminal law dimension of extradition, however, is indicative of a richer diversity in legal position and practice. Any nation's criminal law bears the hallmark of its historical traditions and culture, its victories and defeats. Attempts to harmonise criminal law turn out to be notoriously difficult, as the efforts within the European Union have demonstrated.[19] Each state will insist on safeguarding its own legal and moral conceptions of crime and criminal law in its dealings with other states, and extradition is the perfect place where opposite opinions may collide. States are naturally drawn towards politically and culturally like-minded states and will more easily engage with them in mutual cooperation in criminal matters. Patterns of affinity and hostility between states are obviously always reproduced in treaty configurations, but the notion that criminal law expresses a nation's essence implies that the stakes are particularly high. Extradition may thus not be a 'one size fits all' device, but rather may display regional differences, reflecting geographically and politically distinct customs and traditions.

In view of these observations, pulling in contrary directions, it is indispensable to strike a balance between presenting extradition as a monolithic, universally accepted and practiced phenomenon and a more or less parochial affair to which states willy-nilly resort and that reveals a nigh unlimited variety in substance and procedure. Instead of aiming at a structural analysis of distinct regional approaches of the mainstays of extradition, the discussions of the several aspects of extradition law refer to the law and practice of specific states or regions whenever this is suitable to grasp the essence of a specific doctrine or to illustrate a deviant approach. As will appear throughout the book, however, this even-handed approach is set aside by the special attention given to, and emphasis placed on, European legal practice. While this preference, admittedly, reflects the provenance of the author, it is also warranted by the relatively recent enactment of the European Arrest Warrant. Practical experience with the application of this instrument within the European Union displays in a fascinating way the intricacies of, and the possibilities held out by, international cooperation in criminal matters between kindred states that have reached a high level of political integration.

18 Gilbert, footnote 2, 2 emphasises this uniforming trend: 'In comparative terms, extradition laws are very similar. Since the extradition system in all States is designed to achieve the same ends, then there is no problem of dysfunctional comparison between the laws of different States.'

19 See the contributions in André Klip & Harmen van der Wilt (eds.) *Harmonisation and Harmonising Measures in Criminal Law,* Proceedings of the Colloquium, Amsterdam, 13–14 December 2001, Royal Netherlands Academy of Arts and Sciences: Amsterdam 2002.

2 On the (non-) extradition of nationals

2.1 Different approaches of countries with common law and civil law legal systems

States that hail from a civil law tradition generally do not extradite their own nationals. For some states, like Germany and Poland, the exemption of nationals from extradition counts as an article of faith, having constitutional status.[1] Common law states have no problem with surrendering their own nationals. From their perspective, this position makes sense, as it is mainly inspired by the organisation and design of the adversarial criminal procedure that draws these systems towards a clear preference for the principle of territorial jurisdiction. Within this configuration, crime is considered a local affair that should be assessed in and by the community that is most directly affected by it. Consequently, common law states have no qualms in exposing their nationals to foreign jurisdiction. As early as 1901, the US Supreme Court held:

> When an American Citizen commits a crime in a foreign country, he cannot complain if required to submit to such modes of trial and to such punishment as the laws of that country may prescribe for its own people, unless a different mode be provided by treaty stipulation between that country and the United States.[2]

The principle that citizens of common law countries are not immune from extradition to another state has been corroborated by subsequent findings of US courts.[3] Why then do civil law systems so doggedly adhere to the non-extradition of their nationals? It is generally held that this predilection derives from the idea that the state and its subjects are mutually bound by bonds of allegiance (*Treupflicht*). This notion translates into the state's duty to render its citizens the protection of its laws and a corresponding right of the citizen

1 See Michael Plachta, '(Non-) Extradition of Nationals: A Never-Ending Story,' 13 *Emory International Law Review* (1999), pp. 77, 109, with other examples.
2 US Supreme Court, 14 January 1901, *Neely v. Henkel*, 180 U.S.109, 110 (1901).
3 See, for instance, *Quinn v. Robinson*, 783 F.2d 776, 782 (9th Dir. 1986).

DOI: 10.4324/9780429956683-2

not to be withdrawn from his 'natural' (indigenous) judge that is obviously best equipped to apply those laws (*ius de non evocando*).[4] The refusal to surrender nationals is arguably fueled by the fear that a foreigner (*any* foreigner) would be prejudiced at a trial in the state *locus delicti*,[5] but that is probably only an auxiliary argument because, carried to its logical extreme, it would imply an unwarranted discrimination between nationals and others who face a similar predicament.[6] The comprehensive rationale is that the national law of the requested state is not necessarily superior to any other state's law, but that it is the best for the citizen standing trial. And because the sovereign is able and capable of affording his citizens the protection of that law, he is under a duty to do so. Implicit in this understanding is the notion that the requested state has an alternative to alleviate the qualms of the requesting state, to wit the application of its own criminal law on the basis of the active nationality principle. We will later treat the pros and cons of this alternative.

As already indicated, such sentiments are completely foreign to the common law mind. They consider this as a whim, a relic of feudal times. Characteristic is the declaration in 1968 by the Chairman of the English House of Commons: 'We don't feel outraged honour at the thought of delivering an Englishman into the hands of foreign judges. He is, first of all, a criminal and only after that an Englishman.'[7] To bridge the gap between the two traditions, it might be beneficial to present the conundrum as a conflict of obligations, one the requested state owes to its own citizens, the other towards the requesting state. One might object that such a representation is far-fetched, if not improper, as the obligations derive from and are rooted in different bodies of law. The first one belongs to the realm of national, constitutional law, the second one is predicated on international law. However, at least from the perspective of lawyers belonging to the civil law tradition, there is a conflict nonetheless.

2.2 Legal and moral bonds between states and citizens

That the state owes obligations to its citizens is not controversial. Any social contract theory will subscribe to that notion. As John Locke writes in his Second Treatise:

4 I.A. Shearer, *Extradition in International Law*, Manchester University Press: Manchester 1971, p. 118.

5 Compare Zsuzsanna Deen-Racsmány, 'Modernizing the Nationality Exception: Is the Non-extradition of Residents a Better Rule?' 76 *Nordic Journal of International Law* (2006), pp. 29–30, who points out that it is 'disadvantageous to be tried in a foreign language, separated from friends, resources and character witnesses.'

6 M. Ch. Bassiouni, *International Extradition: United States Law and Practice*, 6th ed., Oxford University Press: Oxford 2014, p. 440: 'The rationale for this exemption rests on the notion that the requested national is likely to receive ill treatment or an unfair trial in the requesting state. To that extent, it is a discriminatory practice which differentiates between nationals and non-nationals.'

7 Quoted by Plachta, supra footnote 1, p. 94.

> Whoever has the legislative or supreme power in any commonwealth, therefore, is bound (1) to govern by established standing laws, promulgated and known to the people (and not by on-the-spot decrees), with unbiased and upright judges appointed to apply those laws in deciding controversies; and (2) to employ the force of the community at home only in the enforcement of such laws, or abroad to prevent or correct foreign injuries and secure the community from attack. And all this is to be directed *to the peace, safety, and public good of the people*, and to nothing else.[8]

It is interesting that Locke refers to the state's relations with other states in connection with the protection of its citizens. The well-being of 'the people' is the state's prime responsibility and should prevail over all other interests. There is already the suggestion that, in case of conflict between the claims of a foreign state and the rights of citizens, the latter should take precedence. Moreover, Locke stresses the importance of a well-functioning judicial system, implying that the rule of law can thrive only if the citizen has recourse to the courts. Obviously, Locke does not exhibit any opinion on whether *foreign* courts would equally be capable of dispensing true justice, as his discourse concerns a closed, national system.

Certain claims of citizens towards the state enjoy a particular elevated status because the concomitant obligations of the state can be invoked against all (*erga omnes*). In the *Barcelona Traction* case, the International Court of Justice famously held that *erga omnes* obligations comprise, inter alia, the prohibition of genocide, slavery and apartheid.[9] The concept of *erga omnes* obligations is often considered as a device to pierce the realm of sovereign prerogative, allowing other states to interfere whenever a state tramples the basic rights of its citizens. However, equally it implores foreign states to forbear any trespassing of those rights of citizens by other states.

For sure, the right not to be withdrawn from one's natural judge can be by no means considered as an essential privilege that can be invoked against all under international law. It is not (even) recognised as a human right at all by international instruments. The right to a fair trial implies the adjudication by an independent and impartial court, without further specification of the features of such a court vis-à-vis the plaintive. More difficult is the connection between (non-) extradition of nationals and the right of citizens to remain on the territory and move freely within the boundaries of their own state. Article 3, paragraph 1 of the Fourth Additional Protocol to the European Convention on Human Rights provides that 'No one shall be expelled, by means either of an individual or of a collective measure, from the territory of the State of

8 https://fs2.american.edu/dfagel/www/Philosophers/Locke/LockesSecondTreatiseSmaller.pdf. Chapter IX, section 131. Italics added.

9 International Court of Justice, *Barcelona Traction, Light and Power Company Limited*, Judgment, 5 February 1970, *ICJ Reports* (1970), p. 3.

which he is a national.' The provision raises the question of whether it would equally serve as a bar against extradition of nationals. In *X v. Austria*, the European Commission on Human Rights answered the question in the negative, explaining that expulsion implied that 'a person is obliged permanently to leave the territory of the State of which he is a national without being left the possibility of returning later.'[10] Domestic courts have similarly relied on the distinction between expulsion, being in principle permanent and irreversible in nature, and extradition in denying that the latter would impinge on citizens' rights to remain in their home country, even if the alternative of criminal prosecution 'at home' was available.[11] Any symmetry between the non-extradition of nationals and their right to remain in their home country is thwarted if national constitutions do not acknowledge the latter in the first place. Our interim conclusion can only be that the non-extradition of nationals has no backing in collateral rights of fair trial or rights of residency, neither at an international nor at a domestic level.

2.3 On the right to refuse extradition of nationals

That does not imply, however, that a state has no leeway or discretion to refuse the surrender of its nationals. Under international law, there is no absolute duty to extradite fugitives from justice, as Wheaton has famously observed, adding that 'if a state wishes to ensure that it secures the return of its own criminals it must enter into treaties with other states.'[12] Although international law does not prescribe that extradition can be granted only on the basis of a treaty, it is prevalent practice and most states require a treaty, sustaining extradition, under national law.[13] The international law perspective of extradition reflects the maximum sovereign freedom, implying that no state can, in principle, be bound without its consent. And that freedom implies that a state can enter into mutual obligations on the terms and conditions that its contracting partners are willing to accept. Treaties are thus the ultimate yardstick to ascertain whether the non-extradition of nationals is acceptable under international law. Whenever the treaty refers in general terms to the mutual obligation to extradite 'all persons,' without explicitly exempting nationals of the requesting state from that obligation, there is no room for refusing the surrender of nationals.[14] Such treaties are, however,

10 *X v. Austria*, App. No. 6189/73, 46 Eur. Commission on Human Rights Decisions & Reports, 214 (1974).

11 See, for instance, the Supreme Court of Canada in *United States v. Cotroni* [1989] 48 C.C.C. 3d, 193.

12 Wheaton's, *Elements of International Law*, 5th ed., revised, enlarged and rewritten by Coleman Phillipson, Stevenson and Sons: London 1916, p. 188.

13 See, for instance, the Netherlands, where the requirement is even incorporated in the Constitution, Article 2(3).

14 US Supreme Court, *Charlton v. Kelly*, 229 U.S. 447–457 (1912).

extremely rare. Most of them include provisions allowing parties to refuse the extradition of their nationals, in particular as a 'gesture' towards civil law states that insist on protecting their nationals for the reasons expounded above. Bassiouni has pointed out that such treaties oftentimes suffice by providing that 'neither of the contracting parties shall be bound to deliver up its own citizens or subjects under the stipulations of this convention,'[15] while others add that 'the executive authority of each shall have the power to deliver them up if, in its discretion, it be deemed to do so.'[16] It is questionable whether these treaties, except for acknowledging the right to refuse the extradition under international (treaty) law, offer the maximal flexibility as envisaged. In *Valentine v. United States, ex rel. Neidecker*, the United States Supreme Court has held that such treaties do not grant the executive the authority to surrender a citizen of the United States because that power is intrinsically connected to the obligation to surrender. As the treaty with France denied an obligation on the part of the contracting parties to deliver up their own nationals, it 'failed to grant the necessary authority.'[17]

Equally dependent on the action of the national legislator are individuals who wish to invoke their 'right' to non-surrender before the courts. Even in 'monistic' countries that consider international treaties as 'the law of the land,' requiring no implementation in domestic law, mere reference to the treaty would be of no avail because the provisions just mentioned are not self-executing in nature. The mere fact that they offer discretionary power to the executive implies that they do not serve to grant directly applicable rights and prerogatives to individuals.[18] The only exception would be a treaty that unconditionally prohibits the extradition of nationals.[19]

Such technicalities of municipal law need not further detain us here. For the present purpose, it suffices to ascertain that international treaty law accommodates both common law and civil law positions, allowing states enough room to maneuver and attune their performances to their respective convictions. Neither treaties nor state practice corroborates rigid assertions that the non-extradition of nationals is outdated and should be abandoned,

15 He mentions bilateral treaties between the United States and Venezuela, Italy and Iraq as examples.

16 Bassiouni, supra footnote 6, pp. 435–436, mentions treaties with Argentina, Japan and Mexico.

17 US Supreme Court, *Valentine v. United States, ex rel. Neidecker*, 29 US 5, 13 (1936).

18 Ironically, one might argue that the dictum of the US Supreme Court *in re Valentine* indirectly confers treaty rights on American citizens that they can invoke before the Court. But in this case it is probably more correct to hold that they benefit from an absence of statutory legislation, conferring the necessary powers, than from a substantive right granted by the treaty.

19 An example being the Benelux Treaty on Extradition and Mutual Assistance in Criminal Matters, Brussels, 27 June 1962, Trb. 1982, 8, Article 5(1) that has been superseded by the Framework Decision on the European Arrest Warrant.

or, reversely, that the non-extradition of nationals is a rule of international law.[20]

2.4 The concept of 'national' for the purpose of (non-) extradition

While the (non-) extradition of nationals may for the states involved be rather satisfactory and workable, from the perspective of other 'stakeholders' – individual citizens and the international community – it still raises several issues.

Starting with the former category, one may wonder who actually qualifies as a 'national' and at what moment that question should be determined. In view of the rational of the non-extradition of citizens, it would be reasonable if permanent residents of a state were to benefit from the protective rule as well. Refugees, in particular, should arguably be spared the traumatizing experience of being surrendered to (yet) another country in order to stand trial. The European Convention on Extradition makes allowance for an extension of the concept of 'nationals' by states parties.[21] After having acknowledged the states parties' right to refuse the extradition of its nationals (Article 6, paragraph 1, sub a), the provision continues: 'Each Contracting Party may, by a declaration made at the time of signature or of deposit of its instrument of ratification or accession, define as far as it is concerned the term "nationals" within the meaning of this convention.' Geoff Gilbert observes that the Nordic states (Denmark, Finland, Iceland, Norway and Sweden) harbour the most liberal and expansive interpretation of the term 'national': they have indicated by declaration that it would include nationals of other Nordic states and domiciled aliens, including refugees.[22] Initially, under Dutch extradition law, the executive had discretion to refuse the extradition of an alien who had integrated into Dutch society, provided that he or she could be prosecuted in the Netherlands. While this final condition obviously served to preclude impunity, it was somewhat self-defeating. After all, the Netherlands will usually lack jurisdiction for offences committed abroad by a non-national. The Netherlands was, in other words, dependent on the initiative of the foreign state to transfer criminal proceedings to the Netherlands, thus 'creating' vicarious jurisdiction. The inconsistency

20 For the latter point of view, see the remarkable finding of the Austrian Supreme Court in 1961: 'It may be observed that in criminal matters there is a generally recognised rule of international law (Article 9 of the Austrian Federal Constitution) that a State's own nationals must never be extradited to another state in whose territory they have committed a criminal offence.' *Service of Summons in Criminal Proceedings (Austria) Case*, translated and reprinted in 38 *Int. L. Rep.*, 133, 134.

21 European Convention on Extradition, Paris 13 July 1957, ETS 24, 1957.

22 Geoff Gilbert, *Transnational Fugitive Offenders in International Law: Extradition and Other Mechanisms*, Martinus Nijhoff: The Hague 1998, p. 177.

has been repaired by the amendment of the active nationality principle on 1 January 2015 in Dutch law, considering permanent residents on the same par as Dutch nationals for the purpose of criminal prosecution in the Netherlands of criminal offences committed abroad.[23]

2.5 New developments within the European Union

The European Council Framework Decision on the European Arrest Warrant (EAW), adopted in 2002, has taken the equalisation of residents with nationals a step further.[24] Article 4(6) of the Framework Decision qualifies as one of the optional grounds for refusal 'if the European arrest warrant has been issued for the purposes of execution of a custodial sentence or detention order, where the requested person is *staying in*, or is a national *or a resident* of the executing Member State *and that State undertakes to execute the sentence or detention order in accordance with its domestic law*.'[25] The provision qualifies the execution of the foreign judgment as an alternative obligation, thus integrating another form of international cooperation in criminal matters into the matrix of international legal assistance. Furthermore, Article 5(3) of the Framework Decision allows the executing member state 'to subject the surrender of a national *or resident* for the purposes of prosecution to the condition that the person, after being heard, is returned to the executing Member State in order to serve there the custodial sentence or detention order passed against him in the issuing Member State.'[26] While the Framework Decision on the EAW has, on the one hand, effectively abolished the nationality exception in the context of surrender for the purpose of prosecution, it has, on the other hand, expanded the scope of the exception by equalizing residents – and, in the case of surrender for the purpose of execution, even persons staying in the requested state – with nationals.[27]

It is remarkable that these initiatives, developed in the context of the European Arrest Warrant, are primarily inspired by the consideration that the prosecution, or, at least, the detention, of both nationals and residents in their home country serves the purpose of rehabilitation and are in line

23 Dutch Penal Code, Article 7, paragraph 3.

24 Council Framework Decision of 13 June 2002 on the European Arrest Warrant and the Surrender Procedures between Member States (2002/584/JHA), OJ L 190, 18 July 2002, p. 1.

25 Emphasis added.

26 Emphasis added.

27 As correctly observed by Zsuzsanna Deen-Racsmány, *Active Personality and Non-extradition of Nationals in International Criminal Law at the Dawn of the Twenty-First Century*, PhD thesis Boekenreeks van het E.M. Meijers Instituut voor Rechtswetenschappelijk Onderzoek van de Faculteit der Rechtsgeleerdheid, Universiteit Leiden, 2007, p. 185.

with the aims of modern criminal law.[28] Swart makes a convincing argument that the equalisation of nationals with permanent residents is based on this rational:

> The traditional objections against extradition of nationals that I personally would consider valid are not so much based on nationality in the legal sense. Rather the emphasis is on the fact that a person has his social roots and residence in a given society, that his social rehabilitation seems best ensured there and that he will have to continue his life within that society after having stood trial and served his sentence. If there are valid reasons not to extradite a national on occasion, the same objections might be relevant to aliens who have their ordinary residence in the requested state.[29]

In spite of Swart's ardent plea, the introduction of the European Arrest Warrant initially did not contribute to a uniform state practice, as Deen-Racsmány has demonstrated in a comprehensive analysis of implementing legislation, displaying considerable diversity.[30] She predicted that 'the EAW is not likely to bring uniformity into this picture in the short term.'[31] In this respect, her expectations have proven to be too pessimistic. Perhaps surprisingly, the European Court of Justice has, by way of preliminary rulings, succeeded in further developing the concepts of 'residency' and 'staying in,' thus contributing to their uniform application.

In *Kozlowski*, the court started by pointing out that the terms 'residency' and 'staying in' had indeed to be defined uniformly, as they concerned autonomous concepts of European Union law.[32] The court explained the background of this point of view in terms of the aim of the Framework Decision to put in place a system of surrender of persons, based on the principle of mutual recognition, that allowed the executing judicial authority to refuse only on the grounds provided in that Framework Decision. The court continued by holding that 'residency' implied that the person 'had established his actual place of residence in the executing Member State or has acquired, following a stable period of presence in that State, certain connections with that State, which are of a similar degree to those resulting from residency.'[33] And it completed its discourse by finding that, for 'staying' it

28 See the Explanatory Report to the European Convention on the Transfer of Proceedings in Criminal Matters, 1972, ETS 73.

29 A.H.J. Swart, 'Refusal of Extradition and the United Nations Model Treaty on Extradition,' *23 Netherlands Yearbook of International Law* (1992), p. 195.

30 Deen-Racsmány, supra footnote 27, pp. 196–199.

31 Deen-Racsmány, supra footnote 27, p. 199.

32 ECJ, Judgment of the Court (Grand Chamber), 17 July 2008 (*Kozlowski)*, C-66/08, section 43.

33 *Kozlowski* case, section 46.

is 'necessary to make an overall assessment of the various objective factors characterizing the situation of that person which include, in particular, the length, nature and conditions of his presence and the family and economic connections which he has with the executing Member State.'[34]

In *Wolzenburg* the requested person sought to rely on the specific privileges of European Union citizens to move and reside freely within the boundaries of the European Union.[35] His plea was only partially successful. While Article 18(1) of the Treaty of the European Communities does indeed confer such rights on European Union citizens, Article 12 of the EC Treaty – containing the prohibition of discrimination on the basis of nationality – did not preclude member states from making a distinction between their own nationals and nationals of other member states, requiring that the latter had already lawfully resided on the territory of that state for a continuous period of at least five years.[36] It is interesting that the court twice stressed that the objective of Article 4(6) and of Article 5(3) was to enable the executing member state to give particular weight to the possibility of increasing the requested person's chances of reintegrating into society when the sentence imposed on him has been served.[37] A prior residency of five years was apparently considered by the court as an appropriate yardstick to gauge the connections between the requested person and the executing state, being a precondition for any reintegration. While the court emphasised that the ultimate assessment of the degree of integration rested with the member state, it simultaneously put limits to that discretion by pointing out that a state would not be allowed to make any application for optional non-execution of the EAW conditional on supplementary administrative requirements, like the possession of a residence permit of indefinite duration.[38]

The equalisation of nationals and residents for the purpose of (non-) surrender is an inevitable consequence of the creation of an area in which citizens can move and settle freely. The European Union member states have consulted the European Court on the issue and have gradually implemented the court's guidelines and principles. It is my own experience as a judge in the Amsterdam Court on International Criminal Cooperation that the court dutifully investigates whether residents qualify to be considered on the same par as Dutch nationals, for the purpose of obtaining both the guarantee that they are allowed to serve a sentence in the Netherlands and the execution of a foreign sentence in the Netherlands. Wage slips and insurance papers are scrutinised and the Amsterdam court strictly adheres to the five-year period of permanent residency, which obtained the fiat of the European Court in

34 *Kozlowski* case, section 48.
35 ECJ, Judgment of the Court (Grand Chamber), 6 October 2009 (*Wolzenburg*) Case C-125/08.
36 *Wolzenburg* case, section 74.
37 *Wolzenburg* case, sections 62 and 67.
38 *Wolzenburg* case, section 53.

Wolzenburg. Beyond the realm of the European Union, the equalisation of permanent residents with nationals has not materialised. We therefore fully agree with Deen-Racsmány's observation that the subject has not become a rule of customary international law.[39] The general reluctance of states in this area is fueled by the concern that fugitives will go unpunished. That takes us to our final topic.

2.6 'Judicare' as an appropriate alternative?

The crucial question emerging from the non-extradition of nationals (and permanent residents) is what compensatory measures should be taken lest the fugitive escapes trial and punishment and remains scot-free. The most eligible and elegant solution is the prosecution and trial by the home state on the basis of the active nationality principle that authorises the state to prosecute its own nationals for offences committed abroad. A closed system of (international) criminal law enforcement would indeed require the requested state to choose between two options: surrender the fugitive or prosecute itself. This maxim of *aut dedere, aut judicare* has old credentials and has been discussed by Hugo Grotius. In his magnum opus *De Jure Belli ac Pacis,* Grotius addresses the principle as follows:

> The State therefore, or Governour of the State, where the Delinquent is, ought to bring no Obstacle to the Right which belongs to the other Power.
>
> IV. 1. But since for one State to admit within its Territories another foreign Power upon the Score of exacting Punishment is never practised, nor indeed convenient, it seems reasonable, that that State where the convicted Offender lives or has taken Shelter, should, upon Application being made to it, either punish the demanded Person according to his Demerits, or else deliver him up to be treated at the Discretion of the injured Party. This is that delivering up so commonly to be met with in History.[40]

The purport of this principle, as understood by Grotius, has been a matter of some controversy. First of all, the insertion of the sentence 'upon Application being made by it,' appears to indicate that the obligation to choose between rendition and prosecution is triggered only by an initiative of the injured state. The duty to start criminal proceedings does, in other

39 Deen-Racsmány, supra footnote 27, p. 199.

40 Hugo Grotius, *The Rights of War and Pace, Book II*, Edited and with an Introduction by Richard Tuck; From the edition by Jean Barbeyrac*; Major Legal and Political Works of Hugo Grotius*, Liberty Fund: Indianapolis, Chapter 21, p. 1062 (footnotes omitted); file:///F:/1032-02_LFeBk.pdf.

words, not exist in a void, but emanates from a prior request from another state.[41] Second, Grotius seems to envisage only the punishment of an already convicted person. Hence, the original wording of the maxim as *aut dedere, aut punire*, which would, in modern parlance, amount to the enforcement of a foreign judgment. However, Grotius did not intend to limit the alternative of rendition to this situation and would protest against any punishment without a proper judicial investigation of the guilt of the fugitive. Finally, it has been debated whether Grotius considered the maxim as a logical sequel of the emergence of a *civitas maxima*, which would prompt states to assist one another, out of a sense of solidarity, in a common endeavor to counter crime.[42] As Wise has convincingly demonstrated, such representation is far-fetched, as Grotius did not impute the same importance to the concept of *civitas maxima* as did his successors Wolff and Pufendorf. As the maxim of *aut dedere aut judicare* is commonly incorporated in multilateral conventions on the repression of international crimes, one might perhaps conclude that it is gradually recognised as a general principle that applies to crimes that affect human society as a whole.[43]

The *aut dedere, aut judicare* maxim has a wider relevance and we will have the opportunity to revisit it when we discuss extradition in respect of war crimes and the like. For the moment, it suffices to discuss its ramifications in the context of the non-extradition of nationals.

Article 6(2) of the European Convention on Extradition incorporates the *aut judicare* prong as a (mandatory) alternative to extradition of nationals. It stipulates that the party refusing the extradition of a national must, at the request of the requesting Party, 'submit the case to its competent authorities in order that proceedings may be taken if they are considered appropriate.' At first blush, the prosecution by the requested state may appear to be an adequate compensation, but that finding hinges on the assumption that *judicare* is indeed a full-fledged alternative. And that depends, in turn, on whether application of the active nationality principle can yield satisfactory results. Common law jurisdictions are likely to encounter the greatest problems in this respect. While these countries would naturally have no objections against extraditing their own nationals, rigid interpretation of reciprocity has inhibited them from doing so, leaving them no other option than to resort to the application of the active nationality principle, which is poorly developed in common law jurisdictions.[44] Indeed, common law

41 Similarly Plachta, supra footnote 1, p. 124.

42 See the seminal observations of Edward Wise in his co-production with M. Ch. Bassiouni, *Aut Dedere, Aut Judicare; The Duty to Extradite or Prosecute in International Law,* Martinus Nijhoff Publishers: Dordrecht 1995, pp. 26–42 ('The Principle Aut Dedere, Aut Judicare and the Hypothesis of a *Civitas Maxima*').

43 Bassiouni, footnote 6, p. 9.

44 Compare Dietrich Oehler, 'Recognition of Penal Judgments: The European System,' in: M. Ch. Bassiouni (ed.), *International Criminal Law* (2nd ed), Transnational: Ardsley, New

countries often restrict the active nationality principle to (very) serious offences that, moreover, also affect their own or their citizens' interests, which essentially implies that they require active nationality to be sustained by other principles of criminal jurisdiction, like passive nationality or the protective principle.[45]

However, more overall doubts have been expressed in respect of the desirability of applying the active nationality principle from the perspective of a sound administration of criminal justice. For one thing, its application is usually restricted by the requirement of dual criminality, a feature that it has in common with extradition and demonstrates its close connection with the latter, rather than that it serves as an obstacle. After all, in case of lack of dual criminality, the requesting state would not be able to obtain the surrender of the fugitive either. Plachta points additionally at the lack of certainty on the part of the requesting state that the requested state will, in fact, pursue investigations in view of discretionary powers of the public prosecutor, adding that such concerns may be alleviated if the requested state has adopted the system of compulsory prosecution (the so-called *Legalitätsprinzip*).[46] And finally, evidentiary problems may prevent the state from successfully accomplishing a criminal trial, as most evidence will usually be located in the place where the crime has been committed.[47]

Although these objections all make some sense, one should be careful not to give them undue weight. States may be inclined to shrink from delegating jurisdiction to another state because this robs them from exercising control over the result. But in the end, it betrays a lack of confidence, which can be mitigated by strengthening mutual commitments in treaties. The language of Article 6, section 2 suggests that the prosecutorial powers in the requested state have a margin of appreciation in deciding whether they will initiate investigations, but other treaties are more explicit in reminding the states of their alternative obligation, in case they decide not to extradite.[48] In essence, the gathering of evidence in case of prosecution of nationals hav-

York 1999, Volume 2, p. 611: 'countries which will extradite their own subjects, such as Great Britain or the U.S., on the basis of reciprocal treaty obligations, will, however, refuse to extradite their own subjects in the absence of reciprocity by the requesting state. These latter states do not usually prosecute for offences committed abroad; therefore, the danger that such offences will go unprosecuted is increased.'

45 Christopher L. Blakesley, 'A Conceptual Framework of Extradition and Jurisdiction over Extraterritorial Crimes,' 685 *Utah Law Review* (1984), pp. 704–706.

46 Plachta, supra footnote 1, p. 122.

47 Plachta, supra footnote 1, p. 123.

48 See, for instance, the UN Convention against Torture and Other Cruel, Inhuman or Degrading Treatment or Punishment, New York, 10 December 184, ILM, 1984, 1027. Article 7, section 1 stipulates: 'The State Party in territory under whose jurisdiction a person alleged to have committed any offence referred to in article 4 (torture etc. addition HvdW) is found, shall ... if it does not extradite him, submit the case to its competent authorities for the purpose of prosecution.' Section 2 continues in holding: 'These authorities shall take

ing committed offences abroad is not distinct from or more cumbersome than in other criminal proceedings having an extraterritorial component. The phenomenon is increasingly frequent due to the proliferation of transnational crime. For sure, such proceedings may be encumbered by a court's reluctance to allow evidence obtained abroad, by the difficulties to cajole foreign witnesses to bear testimony, in combination with judges' preferences to apprise themselves of 'fresh' evidence.[49] But a tightening network of multilateral assistance treaties remedies such erstwhile insurmountable problems. Law enforcement officials are often obliged to procure evidence 'on demand,' witnesses can be questioned by making use of video links, and search and seizures of real estate or bank accounts are increasingly conducted for the benefit of foreign trials.[50] Besides, criminal proceedings against nationals who are accused of having committed crimes in another country have at least one advantage: the court has custody over the major source of evidence, to wit the suspect.

In the opinion of this writer, a modern approach towards the 'problem' of extradition of nationals requires flexibility and tolerance by the states involved. Civil law countries might be persuaded to surrender their nationals, provided they obtain the guarantee that they are allowed to serve their sentence in their home country, a device that has been incorporated in Article 5(3) of the Framework Decision on the European Arrest Warrant. Common law countries might agree that a criminal trial on the basis of the active nationality principle can be successfully accomplished if they are prepared to render assistance in the production of evidence. Such positions are in line with the consideration that, in view of the process of globalisation, the 'best place of prosecution and trial' is not cast in stone.

On the basis of the preceding analysis, it is fair to conclude that prosecution (judicare) restores the balance of mutual obligations and is in line with the principle of reciprocity.[51]

---

their decision in the same manner as in the case of any ordinary offence of a serious nature under the law of that State,' thereby restricting the discretional powers of the prosecutor.

49 See for these problems, Michael Abell, *Obtaining Evidence Abroad in Criminal Cases, 2010*, Brill/Nijhoff: The Hague 2010; and Ethan E. Nadelmann, *Cops across Borders; The Internationalization of U.S. Criminal Law Enforcement,* Pennsylvania State University Press: University Park, Pennsylvania 1993.

50 Compare for the mandatory exchange of evidence the Directive of the European Parliament and of the Council of 3 April 2014 regarding the European Investigation Order in Criminal Matters, OJ of the EU, 1 May 2014, L 130/1; on witness interrogation by video link the European Convention on Mutual Assistance in Criminal Matters, 29 May 2000, OJ of the EU, 12 July 2000, C 197/3; and on search and seizure for the purpose of freezing and confiscation the UN against Transnational Organized Crime, New York, 15 December 2000, UNTS, vol. 2225, p. 209, Articles 12–14.

51 See Harmen van der Wilt, 'The Principle of Reciprocity,' in: Judge Rob Blekxtoon & Wouter van Ballegooij (eds.), *Handbook on the European Arrest Warrant*, TMC Asser Press: The Hague 2005, p. 73.

3 Dual criminality

3.1 Introduction to the concept

Extradition is usually granted only if the conduct for which the fugitive's surrender is requested constitutes a criminal offence under the law of both the requesting and the requested state.[1] Geoff Gilbert defines this 'rule of double (or dual) criminality' in negative terms, simultaneously emphasising its protective function vis-à-vis the individual: 'The essence of double criminality is that the fugitive should not be returned unless his actions could be prosecuted in either the requesting or, *mutatis mutandis*, the requested State.'[2] The rule is commonly adhered to, irrespective of whether extradition is predicated on treaty, reciprocity or comity.[3] It raises the question whether the rule can be qualified as customary international law. There is certainly authority for that position in academic writings and case law of older date.[4] Since the rule has partially been abolished within the framework of the European Arrest Warrant (see *infra*), that position may, however, no longer be tenable.

3.1.1 Dual criminality and extraditable offences

A close connection exists between the concept of 'extraditable offences' – that is, the category of offences for which states are prepared to surrender fugitives on the basis of reciprocity – and the rule of dual criminality.

1 See for interesting observations on the history, provenance and development of the doctrine, Jonathan O. Hafen, 'International Extradition: Issues Arising under the Dual Criminality Requirement,' 1 *Brigham Young University Law Review* (1992), pp. 191–199.

2 Geoff Gilbert, *Transnational Fugitive Offenders in International Law: Extradition and Other Mechanisms*, Martinus Nijhoff: The Hague 1998, p. 104.

3 M. Ch. Bassiouni, *International Extradition and World Public Order*, Sijthoff: Leiden, 1974, p. 313.

4 Compare Bassiouni, supra footnote 3, p. 326: 'It appears therefore that customary international law requires the condition of double criminality as to all basis for extradition.' See also the findings of the Swiss Federal Tribunal in *M v. Federal Department of Justice and Police* (75 *International Law Reports* (1979), p. 107 holding that 'double criminality is a tacit precondition for all extradition cases, even where the treaty is not express on the matter.' See also A.H.J. Swart, *Nederlands uitleveringsrecht*, Tjeenk Willink: Zwolle 1986, p. 135.

DOI: 10.4324/9780429956683-3

Whether they entirely conflate, however, depends on the way extraditable offences are identified in a treaty. Older, bilateral treaties used to follow the *enumerative* method, spelling out the offences for which both parties agreed to extradite. While the 'listed offences' usually constituted a common denominator of conduct, both punishable under the law of the requested and the requesting state, punishability under the law of the former was not implied, nor was it a prerequisite.[5] In modern (bilateral) treaties the rule of dual criminality is sometimes incorporated as a separate condition, apart from an enumeration of extraditable offences, which proves that the one does not automatically subsume the other.[6] Treaties that employ the enumeration method have fallen into disuse, as they are considered impractical, requiring adaption of the treaty each time the contracting parties wish to extend the scope of extradition with new offences. Multilateral extradition treaties have a preference for the *elimination* approach, which enables extradition for any offence, provided it is punishable in both the requesting and the requested state with a minimum prison sentence of a certain duration.[7] As the category of extraditable offences is defined in terms of dual criminality, both concepts are entirely fused. The minimum sentence requirement serves to preclude that extradition is requested in respect of conduct that is considered as a petty offence, either in the requesting or in the requested state. Extradition is a lengthy and often cumbersome affair and it would serve no useful purpose if the requested person would, after having been surrendered, have to be released forthwith.[8]

5 Compare Whiteman, 6 *British Digest of International Law* (1968), p. 774: 'It might be supposed that if two States agree in a treaty to a list of offences for which extradition shall take place, they would include only those acts which are crimes in both states. However, questions nevertheless may arise. Certain acts may, under the law of the requesting State, constitute a listed offence while under the law of the requested State, the same act may constitute no crime or, more frequently, one not listed in the treaty.'

6 Compare, for instance, the bilateral extradition treaty between the United States and Japan of 3 March 1978, 31 U.S.T. 892, Article I(1), which reads: '1. Extradition shall be granted in accordance with the provisions of this Treaty for any offense listed in the Schedule annexed to this Treaty, which forms an integral part of this Treaty, when such an offense is punishable by the laws of both Contracting Parties by death, by life imprisonment, or by deprivation of liberty for a period of more than one year; or for any other offense when such an offense is punishable by the federal laws of the United States and by the laws of Japan by death, by life imprisonment, or by deprivation of liberty for a period of more than one year.'

7 A good example is Article 2(1) of the 1957 European Convention on Extradition, Paris 13 December 1957, European Treaties Series No. 024: 'Extradition shall be granted in respect of offences punishable under the laws of the requesting Party and of the requested Party by deprivation of liberty or under a detention order for a maximum period of at least one year or by a more severe penalty. Where a conviction and prison sentence have occurred or a detention order has been made in the territory of the requesting Party, the punishment awarded must have been for a period of at least four months.'

8 It bears emphasis in this context that the time passed in detention, pending the extradition procedure, is usually deducted from the final sentence in the requesting state.

The double criminality rule raises two particular issues in which the interests of the individual, the states involved and the wider international community, directly or indirectly, come to the fore. For one thing, one may wonder what the rationale underlying the rule actually is. Second, case law displays a wide variety of opinions on how the rule must be applied in practice.[9] It is to these two topics that we will now turn.

3.2 Rationales

That the conduct in respect of which extradition is sought should be a punishable offence in both the requesting and the requested state is not self-evident. For sure, it is clear that the conduct must incur criminal responsibility under the law of the requesting state, in view of the purposes of extradition and the requirements of the *nullum crimen, nulla poena sine lege* principle. It is less obvious, however, why it should constitute a criminal offence in the requested state as well. Generally, three justifications are advanced.[10]

The first one, focusing on sovereign equality, holds that the rule warrants perfect symmetry in mutual obligations. No state, so the argument runs, would be willing to oblige, if its counterpart would not reciprocate in an analogous situation. Bassiouni subscribes to that position, although he correctly observes that one should distinguish between reciprocity as a general concept underlying extradition and the subsequent practice, honouring that reciprocity, of which the application of the dual criminality rule is a manifestation.[11] One might wonder, however, why sovereignty requires obligations to be perfectly symmetrical. As we have seen in the previous chapter, common law states are nowadays often inclined to accept the non-extradition of nationals by their civil law counterparts, provided they prosecute them instead. A substantive rather than a formal equality of performance is pursued in those cases.[12]

Perhaps a more convincing explanation is that the dual criminality rule releases the requested state from the obligation to render assistance in respect of conduct that it would be reluctant or even opposed to applying its criminal law. This approach, which has been dubbed the social (or

9 For a thorough analysis of the different approaches in – primarily – common law jurisdictions, see Sharon A. Williams, 'The Double Criminality Rule and Extradition: A Comparative Analysis,' 15(2) *Nova Law Review* (1991), pp. 581–624.

10 See Elies van Sliedregt, 'The Principle of Dual Criminality and the European Arrest Warrant,' in: Nico Keijzer & Elies van Sliedregt (eds.), *The European Arrest Warrant in Practice*, TMC Asser Press: The Hague 2009, pp. 52–54. See also Swart, supra footnote 4, pp. 131–133, who, however, mentions only two rationales, casting doubt on the relevance of the *nullum crimen* principle as a basis for the dual criminality rule. See discussion below in Section 3.2.1.

11 Bassiouni, supra footnote 3, pp. 314–315.

12 Swart, supra footnote 4, p. 130.

societal) rationale, celebrates, in essence, value pluralism.[13] States often exhibit considerable differences in their appraisal of human conduct that is potentially harmful to others or society as a whole. State reactions to, for instance, trade in soft drugs may vary from condoning to harsh repression. Such diversity, even within the European Union, has been noticed by the British Home Affairs Select Committee, on the occasion of a debate on international cooperation in criminal matters:

> Simple examples are the permissive attitude towards cannabis in the Netherlands, the greater tolerance to certain forms of pornography in Germany, the very tough stand taken by Greek courts against hooliganism. Even in those areas where there has been considerable international consensus, such as drug trafficking, there are differences in the extent to which they enforce the law and the manner in which they enforce the law.[14]

It is obvious that individuals may benefit from different perspectives between states on what conduct should be criminalised by seeking refuge in a state with a more liberal disposition (at least in respect of the conduct concerned). While states may have different opinions on the reprehensibility of certain forms of behavior 'on the fringes of the criminal law,' they are more likely to concur on crimes that, in a Durkheimian sense, strike at the core values of a community. It is in the realm of such crimes like murder, grave assault and rape that extradition is least problematic, as dual criminality is largely guaranteed. One might perhaps expect states to close ranks even tighter in respect of international crimes that affect the international community as a whole, but here the picture becomes blurred because of political cleavages. We will address the political offence exception and its relationship to the extradition of terrorists and war criminals in detail in subsequent chapters, but it requires little imagination to predict that clashes among the interests of individuals, states and the international community in this area will be particularly vehement. Multilateral conventions on the suppression of terrorism address the problem of divergent legal systems impeding international cooperation by obliging states parties to incorporate terrorist offences in their domestic legislation. An example is the Convention on the Suppression of Terrorist Bombings, article 2 of which starts by defining the offence:

> Any person commits an offence within the meaning of this Convention if that person unlawfully and intentionally delivers, places, discharges or detonates an explosive or other lethal device in, into or against a

13 It has been advanced by the Dutch Supreme Court, 16 January 1976, NJ 1973, 281 (*Pauksch*).

14 Home Affairs Select Committee, Seventh Report, Practical Police Co-operation in the European Committee, volume 2, section 96; as quoted by Gilbert, supra footnote 2, p. 104.

> place of public use, a State or government facility, a public transportation system or an infrastructure facility: (a) With the intent to cause death or serious bodily injury; or (b) With the intent to cause extensive destruction of such a place, facility or system, where such destruction results in or is likely to result in major economic loss.

Article 4 refers to this provision and enjoins states to

> adopt such measures as may be necessary: (a) To establish as criminal offences under its domestic law the offences set forth in article 2 of this Convention; (b) To make those offences punishable by appropriate penalties which take into account the grave nature of those offences.[15]

Such an obligation to adapt, if necessary, national substantive criminal law serves the dual purpose of enabling states parties to prosecute persons engaging in these crimes and extradite them on request, without being hampered by lack of double criminality. Conventions following a similar format have been established and have been widely ratified ever since the 1970s. Efforts to draft a comprehensive convention on terrorism, however, have been thwarted by a lack of international consensus on what the concept actually means, exacerbated by strong differences of opinion on whether and when political violence is permitted. Lodge eloquently expresses the quandary when, commenting on this lack of consensus, she argues that

> These problems highlight the dependence of law upon the political order in which it operates, for successful definition must be based upon agreement as to the nature of the phenomenon to be described, and at an international level there is widespread disagreement as to the circumstances in which it is lawful to use violence for political ends.[16]

Indeed, Lodge reminds us that lawyers are not only confronted with the normative challenge to navigate between (individual) political freedom and the exigencies of a safe and stable international order, but that we have to meekly avow that any legal aspirations find their limits in the political reality of a divided world. The rule of dual criminality reflects this state of affairs.

3.2.1 Dual criminality and **nullum crimen**

Whereas the societal rationale emerges from the notion of cultural/political diversity and addresses the interests of the (requested) state and the

15 Convention on the Suppression of Terrorist Bombings, New York, 15 December 1997, 37 ILM, 249 (1998).

16 Juliet Lodge, *Terrorism; A Challenge to the State*, Martin Robertson: London 1981, p. 195.

individual, the third rationale, postulating a connection between dual criminality and the *nullum crimen* principle, entirely focuses on the rights of the requested person. It is by no means self-evident that the *nullum crimen* principle would require the conduct for which extradition is sought to be a criminal offence in the requested state. After all, in that state the relator is not charged with a criminal offence.[17] However, one might argue that this state, albeit on the behest of another state, applies criminal enforcement measures, which it would not be authorised to do without proper title. Bassiouni seems to suggest that the rule of double criminality compensates for the fragmentation of criminal law systems that would deprive the itinerant 'law breaker' from fair notice as an inherent element of the *nullum crimen* principle. The fact that the conduct is also a criminal offence in the requested state would render the assertion that he is 'unpleasantly surprised' by the charge underlying the extradition request less credible.[18] There is an underlying hint that *nullum crimen* has a wider purport and implies that a person can be held accountable only if his conduct is criminal in a wider regional area that at least encompasses the states involved. In that respect, Bassiouni's proposition ignores the prevailing fragmented state system in which the *nullum crimen* principle is mandatory only in the state where the suspect is actually standing trial. The rule of dual criminality owes its existence to the fact that criminal systems are not identic, which nurtures the suspect's uncertainty about the criminal nature of his conduct. One can try to alleviate that concern by restricting extradition to the areas where the states have found common ground *in criminalibus* , but it offers no principled reason why the conduct – from the perspective of *nullum crimen* – should constitute a criminal offence in the requested state. The argument, although ingenious, is therefore not entirely persuasive because it shifts the responsibility from the situs of the problem, to wit, the requesting state, to another state and makes the remedy for an infringement of the legality principle contingent upon the suspect crossing borders. Moreover, the extent to which a person can invoke ignorance of the law as a defence may well depend on the principle of jurisdiction sustaining the requesting state's charges, territoriality always prevailing over weaker principles like passive personality. If the requesting state can present a strong claim, in particular that the crime has allegedly been committed on its territory, the fact that the conduct would also constitute a crime in the requested state does – from the perspective of *nullum crimen* principle – hardly make a difference. If, on the other hand,

17 A.H.J. Swart, 'Human Rights and the Abolition of Traditional Principles,' in: A. Eser & O. Lagodny, *Principles and Procedures for a New Transnational Criminal Law*, Freiburg im Breisgau: Max Planck Institut für ausländisches und internationales Strafrecht 1992, p. 520.

18 Bassiouni, surpa footnote 3, p. 319: 'Double criminality provides an implicit element of notice by analogy in that the individual is held to the same proscribed conduct known to the individual in his or her own legal system.'

the relator is understandably apprehensive of an unexpected move by the requesting state, suddenly presenting itself as the protector of its nationals being corrupted by narcotics dealers on the territory of the requested state, other means are at the disposal of the latter to refuse extradition.[19] In other words, from the perspective of the *nullum crimen* principle, lack of double criminality would not be appropriate to refuse extradition if the claims of the requesting state are strong and not necessary if the requesting state's claims are weak.

Elies van Sliedregt has advocated stronger attention for the *nullum crimen* dimension of the dual criminality rule in a critique on the partial abolition of the principle in the context of the European Arrest Warrant.[20] Article 2, section 2 of the Framework's decision on the European Arrest Warrant contains a list of 31 'categories of offences' in respect of which dual criminality need not be verified, provided that they are penalised in the requesting state by a maximum prison sentence of three years or more. The gist of van Sliedregt's argument is that these broadly defined categories (for instance 'computer-related crime') do not meet the requirements of strict construction that serve to inform the suspect for what conduct he is prosecuted. Under the dual criminality regime, the function of properly apprizing the suspect was performed by the requested state, as the court had to inquire whether the charge in the extradition request corresponded with a specific equivalent within its own penal code. Now that this regime has partially been abandoned, the relator is largely left in the dark in respect of the accusations against him and therefore the protective function of the dual criminality regime in the realm of *nullum crimen* is to be properly compensated at the European Union level.

To be sure, van Sliedregt has a point. Courts are not allowed to check whether the administering state has correctly indicated that the conduct under scrutiny qualifies as a 'listed offence' because, by doing so, it could apply only its own standards, which would amount to a reintroduction of dual criminality. The principle of mutual recognition demands that the executing state has to take the qualification by the administering state for granted. So, at the moment of his surrender, the requested person is left in abeyance of the charges that the requesting state holds against him. On closer scrutiny, however, the problem is more apparent than real. While the judgment indeed only mentions the listed offence in broad terms, for instance, 'illicit trade in narcotics,' the relator can learn from the European Arrest Warrant itself, for which specific criminal offences his surrender is sought, because the Arrest Warrant is accessible to him and his counsel. The issue boils down to the relator – like the court – being ignorant as to why the requesting state considered

19 Article 7(1) of the European Convention allows the state to refuse extradition, if the conduct can be located on its territory.

20 Van Sliedregt, supra footnote 10, pp. 67–69.

the offence to be outside the domain of dual criminality, rather than to the legal basis of the criminal prosecution (which *nullum crimen* demands). Like Bassiouni, van Sliedregt attempts to find a remedy for an irregularity that originates in the requesting state. Now I would not hold for a second that the requested state has no responsibilities for any infringements that already occurred or even may occur in the requesting state. The entire idea of human rights prevailing over extradition is predicated on that notion (see chapter 9). If the requested state has a reasonable suspicion that the requested state acts in contravention of the *nullum crimen* principle, it should refuse the extradition forthwith. But such an infringement is in principle not at hand. The issue is whether an adequate independent argument can be made for the contention that conduct must constitute a criminal offence under the law of the requested state, on pain of breaching the *nullum crimen* principle. And I am not convinced that this is possible. I do not deny that the dual criminality has a *nullum crimen* dimension, but only as a derivative of and compensation for certain deficiencies in the state of trial.

3.3 Application of the rule of dual criminality in practice

Any issues that arise in the context of the practical application of the rule of dual criminality in the requested state emanate from the incongruency of criminal law systems. The check of dual criminality requires a translation of factual and legal elements, prompting the court to assess the conduct 'as if' it had occurred within its own jurisdiction. The extent to which the court is allowed to do this is a matter of some controversy, as we will soon find out. Basically, the process consists of two steps, which are not always clearly distinguished in case law and academic literature.

3.3.1 Criminality according to the law of the requested state

The first prong consists of a rather solipsistic analysis whether the conduct would qualify as a criminal offence under the law of the requested state, if the conduct would have occurred within its jurisdiction Such assessment can take the form of three inquiries, differing in their degree of depth or thoroughness, as Bassiouni has helpfully elucidated.[21] The first, most marginal one, entails whether the acts are chargeable as an offence regardless of their prosecutability. The second one inquires whether the acts are chargeable and prosecutable. Generally, this requires an investigation into the jurisdictional basis of the prosecution. However, the court is not expected to determine whether the requested state can exercise jurisdiction itself, but whether, by analogy, it could have claimed jurisdiction had it been in the

21 Bassiouni, supra footnote 3, p. 324.

position of the requesting state.[22] As the requesting state will usually have territorial jurisdiction, this test will generally be easily met. However, if the requesting state seeks to prosecute on the basis of extraterritorial jurisdiction, treaty provisions often authorise the requested state to, optionally, refuse extradition, if, in a similar situation, it would have no jurisdiction to proceed.[23] It begs the question whether prosecutability (by analogy) is part and parcel of the dual criminality test, since now the lack of it features as a separate – but optional – ground for refusal. The answer is probably negative, but it is of theoretical more than of practical relevance, now that most of the extradition requests are predicated on prosecutions based on territorial jurisdiction.[24] The third, most exacting, approach inquires whether the acts are chargeable, prosecutable and could also result in a conviction. In this case, the court investigates whether the conduct would be subject to statutory limitations – under its own law – and whether the relator would be able to rely successfully on a justification or an excuse. Swart reserves for this approach the term dual criminality *in concreto*, in contradistinction to the dual criminality *in abstracto*, which suffices with the simple assessment whether the conduct meets the elements of a criminal offence under the law of the requested state.[25] The terminology is uncertain and confusing, though, as the terms *in concreto* and *in abstracto* are also used in another sense, as we soon will notice. No consensus exists whether one of the two approaches is to be followed.[26] Bassiouni makes mention of a

22 This process is generally known as 'analogue transformation' or, in Germany, as *Singemässe Umstellung des Sachverhalts*. It serves useful purposes for an inquiry whether extradition that seeks to protect specific legal interests of the requesting state, but that are as such not safeguarded under criminal legislation of the requested state, would still square with dual criminality, if, in the analogue situation, the requested state would consider infringement of similar legal interests of its own as a criminal offence. Examples are the bribing of civil servants or conscientious objection. For a solid explanation of the concept, see Christen Tinkl, *Die Rechtsstellung des Einzelnen nach dem Rahmenbeschluss über der Europäischen Haftbefehl*, Peter Lang: Frankfurt am Main 2008, pp. 145–146.

23 See, for instance, Article 7(2) of the European Convention on Extradition, footnote 7: 'When the offence for which extradition is requested has been committed outside the territory of the requesting Party, extradition may only be refused if the law of the requested Party does not allow prosecution for the same category of offence when committed outside the latter Party's territory or does not allow extradition for the offence concerned.' Largely similar: Article 4(7), sub b of the Framework Decision on the European Arrest Warrant.

24 Gilbert mentions an interesting Canadian case *Romania v. Cheng* [1997], NSJ No. 106, C.R. No, 129432, 6 March 1997, in which the court of Nova Scotia rejected a Romanian extradition request because 'Romania's only claim to jurisdictional competence was on the basis of the passive nationality principle, generally rejected by States as a valid ground on which to justify criminal competence to prosecute.'

25 Swart, supra footnote 4, pp. 145–151.

26 David A. Sadoff, *Bringing International Fugitives to Justice: Extradition and Its Alternatives*, Cambridge University Press: Cambridge 2016, p. 195, observing that 'Modern State practice is not uniform concerning whether justifications (e.g. self defence) or excuses (e.g. insanity) should be accounted for in determining whether a given offense is punishable.'

rather old case in which a Greek Court of Appeals decided that an extraditable offence was to be found *in concreto*, eliciting the criticism of the requesting state (the United States).[27] There are arguments sustaining both propositions. An assessment *in concreto* probably best corresponds with the philosophy underlying the rule of dual criminality, especially the social/societal rationale.[28] On the other hand, for practical reasons an assessment *in abstracto* is in most cases the only thing feasible. The court of the requested state has only a summary of the facts at its disposal. Not being authorised to adjudicate on the guilt of the suspect itself, and lacking the information to do so, it simply cannot assess whether he or she could successfully invoke a justification or an excuse. Moreover, in many cases the charges will not be sustained by all evidence required because the extradition is sought precisely for enabling the requesting state to pursue (further) investigations. Swart observes, in passing, that if an extradition treaty compels the requesting state to produce evidence, the inquiry into the factual course of events (including the feasibility of a justification or excuse) can be more thorough.[29] This remark is highly relevant, as it alludes to a conspicuous difference in extradition procedural practice between common law and civil law countries. Whereas the latter consider the submission of an exposition of the facts sufficient, without requiring further evidence of the possible involvement or guilt of the requested person, common law countries are more demanding. Indeed, the (UK) Fugitive Offenders act of 1967 and its successor, the 1989 Extradition Act, require that the evidence, sustaining the accusation by the requesting state, would be sufficient to warrant his trial for that offence if it had been committed within the jurisdiction of that court.[30] Although evidentiary rules in extradition proceedings and the dual criminality doctrine are formally distinct, they are conceptually related. After all, the (mandatory) production of evidence enables the court of the requested state to ascertain whether a criminal procedure would probably result in a conviction. That connection is acknowledged by Hartley Booth who observes that

> many of the submissions that there is insufficient evidence against the fugitive to establish a *prima facie* case might be regarded as examples

27 Greece Court of Appeals of Athens, *In re Insull*, 31 October 1933, 7 ILR 346. Bassiouni, supra footnote 3, p. 351: 'In effect, the court examined whether or not the relator could have been found guilty under Greek law which was tantamount to a finding of potential conviction than mere prosecutability.'

28 Swart, supra footnote 4, p. 148.

29 Swart, supra footnote 4, p. 147.

30 Compare the 1967 Act, s. 7(5), which is replicated in Article 9,s. 8, sub (a) of the 1989 Extradition Act. The committal for trial rule is often colloquially called the *prima facie* case, but that qualification has been criticised for being imprecise and ambiguous; see Lord Reid in *R v. Governor of Brixton Prison ex parte Armah* [1968] A.C. 192, pp. 229–230.

> of the proposition that the offence charged must have been committed according to a British understanding of the offence.[31]

One might conclude that common law countries – probably more than states belonging to the civil law tradition – are committed to a strict and literal assessment of the question whether the conduct for which the extradition is requested would incur criminal responsibility under their own law. This approach also surfaces in the standard procedure of British courts to inquire whether the conduct would qualify as a criminal offence under English law – and could have been prosecuted – at the time when it was performed (*tempore delicti*) rather than at the moment of the submission of the extradition request.[32] While civil law jurisdictions might object that such a rigid inquiry would be in contradiction to the hypothetical nature of the assessment, common law jurisdictions may retort that this scrupulous analysis does justice to the rationales, underpinning the doctrine (as expounded above).

3.3.2 *Similarity between the criminal law provisions in the requesting and the requested state?*

During the second phase of the assessment of dual criminality, the court of the requested state has to leave the comfort zone of its own legislation and engage in a comparison with the law of the requesting state. The purpose of this inquiry is to determine for which offence the extradition is requested. The conduct or factual course of events is the point of departure for such an investigation, but the legal qualification will often shed light on the intentions of the requesting state. For this process, Bassiouni makes, somewhat confusingly, *again* a distinction between a concrete (objective) and an abstract (subjective) method. The first method – in the words of Bassiouni – 'relies on the label of the offence and a strict interpretation of its legal elements. The second approach relies on the activity regardless of its specific label and full

31 V.E. Hartley Booth, *British Extradition Law and Procedure*, Samson: Alphen aan den Rijn 1980, p. 51.

32 Compare the assessment of the dual criminality rule in the Pinochet case per Lord Hope: 'Most of the allegations of torture and conspiracy to torture in Chile and elsewhere failed to satisfy the dual criminality test. While the torture of non-Spanish citizens outside of Spain (the requesting state, addition HvdW) had long been a crime in Spain, the torture of non-English citizens outside of England only became a crime in England on September 29, 1988, when England adopted § 134 of the Criminal Justice Act. ... As a consequence, the crimes of torture and conspiracy to torture allegedly committed by Pinochet prior to that date (which constituted the bulk of the alleged atrocities) did not meet the test of dual criminality.' House of Lords, 24 March 1999, Judgment – *Regina v. Bartle and the Commissioner of Police for the Metropolis and Others, Ex Parte Pinochet; Regina and Evans v. Others and the Commissioner of Police for the Metropolis and Others Ex Parte Pinochet (On Appeal from a Divisional Court of the Queen's Bench Division)*.

concordance of its elements in the respective laws of the two States.'[33] The strict, *in concreto* assessment is probably a legacy of the old enumerative method, practiced in bilateral treaties, that required a minute comparison of the translations of the list of offences as they had been incorporated in the respective domestic legislations in order to find out whether the parties indeed agreed that it was an extraditable offence. It is generally acknowledged that strict congruence of the elements of the offence in both jurisdictions is outdated and no longer required.[34] Many legal instruments corroborate the demise of the objective (legalistic) approach. Article 2 s. 1 sub (b) of the (bilateral) Extradition Treaty between the Kingdom of the Netherlands and the United States of America, referring to the dual criminality rule, stipulates:

> In this connection it shall not matter whether or not the laws of the Contracting Parties place the offense within the same category of offenses or denominate an offense by the same terminology.[35]

In a similar vein, the Second Protocol to the European Convention on Extradition, which seeks (amongst others) to expand the possibilities of extradition for fiscal offences, clarifies that inevitable interstate disparities of substantive criminal law provisions should not thwart international cooperation:

> Article 2. Extradition may not be refused on the ground that the law of the requested Party does not impose the same kind of tax or does not contain a tax, duty, customs or exchange regulation of the same kind as the law of the requesting State.[36]

The message is clear: if the requested state recognises tax fraud as a criminal offence under its own jurisdiction, it is bound to comply with a request for extradition.

Yet, the old-fashioned practice of enumerating extraditable offences has survived in many treaties, compounding the assessment of dual criminality. While the identification of extraditable offences and the dual criminality rule are not to be (entirely) conflated (as we discussed before in par. 3.1),

33 Bassiouni, supra footnote 3, p. 322. Compare also, in more detail, S.Z. Feller, 'The Significance of the Requirement of Double Criminality in the Law of Extradition,' 10 *Israel Law Review* (1975), p. 51.

34 Compare Williams, supra footnote 9, p. 607, who refers to the unreported Canadian case of *Caro-Payan* (Ontario District Court, 18 February 1988): 'The decision in *Caro-Payan*, which holds that for double criminality to be present there is no need for all the constituent elements of the offense to be the same in both the requesting and requested state, is non-controversial.'

35 Extradition Treaty between the Kingdom of the Netherlands and the United States of America, The Hague 24 June 1980, Treaty Series 1980, p. 111.

36 Second Additional Protocol to the European Convention on Extradition, Strasbourg, 17 March 1978, Trb. 1979, p. 120.

they are inextricably connected. Common law jurisdictions in particular have struggled to liberate themselves from the straitjacket of listed offences in (bilateral) treaties in an attempt to simplify international cooperation by giving a more liberal interpretation of the dual criminality requirement. Often the legal issues are complicated by the idiosyncrasies of the Commonwealth, creating a distinct surrender regime for the ' in-crowd,' or the federal political structure of the United States. The details of these arrangements are beyond the scope of this monography; we will keep to the main lines.[37]

In the United Kingdom, the objective *in concreto* assessment was abandoned quite a while ago. Already in 1896, an English court decided that inquiry into the dual criminality prerequisite did not require that the tags under which the conduct could be brought were identical.[38] It would suffice if the offences under both laws were substantially similar. The British court in the *Budlong* case confirmed this position by holding that the dual criminality requirement would be met if

(1) the crime for which extradition is demanded would be recognized as substantially similar in both countries, and
(2) there is a prima facie case that the conduct of the accused amounted to the commission of the crime according to English law.[39]

The *Budlong* decision was illuminating. For one thing, it neatly distinguished between the two prongs that were identified before. Moreover, it substituted the rigid 'complete identity' test for a more flexible standard, acknowledging that there should be at least a certain degree of congruence between the legal qualification of the conduct in both states. In the view of this author, such similarity arguably has a dual function. Not only does it reflect the common ground on which the states agree to cooperate on the basis of reciprocity, but it also serves as a shorthand, enabling the states to understand for what crime the extradition is actually requested.

Nonetheless, the *Budlong* finding was overturned shortly after. In the case of *Nielsen* the House of Lords argued that, in extradition proceedings, it was paramount to inquire whether the conduct qualified as a crime under the law of the requested state. The criminal nature under the law of the requesting state could be taken for granted and no heed should be paid to whether there was a more or less corresponding legal provision under that law:

37 See for comprehensive analyses, the works of Hafen, supra footnote 1, Williams, supra footnote 9 and Barbara Sicalides, 'Comment, RICO, CCE, and International Extradition,' 62 *Temple University Law Review* (1989), p. 1281.

38 *In re Arton* (No.2) [1896] 1 OB 509 at 517.

39 *R v. Governor of Pentonville Prison, ex parte Budlong*, [1980], 1 WLR 1110, 1122/1123 (quoted by Gilbert, supra footnote 2, p. 108).

> the magistrate must decide, whether such evidence (sustaining the request for extradition, addition added) would, according to the law of England, justify the committal for trial of the accused for an offence that is described in the 1870 list ... In making this decision it is English law *alone* that is relevant. The requirement that he shall make it does not give him any jurisdiction to inquire into or receive evidence of the substantive law of the foreign State in which the conduct was in fact committed.[40]

The complete disregard for the foreign law obviously precluded the court from a comparative inquiry into the congruence of the respective legal provisions in both states. I therefore entirely agree with Brabyn who contends that 'the Budlong requirement "that the foreign crime with respect to which extradition is requested must be substantially similar to a relevant offence in English Law" was forcefully rejected in Nielsen.'[41]

The disparaging qualifications of the double criminality rule by Lord Diplock in the cases of *Nielsen* and *McGaffery*,[42] who talks about the sobriquet of double criminality and 'so called double criminality,' reveal poor understanding of the concept. Obviously, the House of Lords in these cases applies the double criminality rule by investigating whether the conduct would yield a criminal offence under English law. After all, such an inquiry into the state of the art in the requested state is the gist of the concept, as punishability in the requesting state is self-evident. What the Lords chose to do in these cases, however, is to shift the emphasis entirely to the conduct, conveniently glossing over any legal qualification in the requesting state.[43] By concentrating exclusively on the application of their own domestic (criminal) law, the Lords effectively erased the second prong of the dual criminality assessment that is the topic of this subparagraph.

It is questionable whether ignoring the second step is fully in line with the philosophy underpinning the dual criminality rule. Subsequent case law shows that courts have continued to struggle with the issue. The Canadian case of *United States v. McVey*, discussed at some length by Sharon Williams, involved the interface between extraditable crimes and dual criminality.[44] The extradition request was predicated on the charge that the relator had submitted false statements to the United States Customs Service. This particular crime did not feature on the list of extraditable offences

40 *In re Nielsen* [1984] 2 WLR 737, 748–749, italics added.

41 Brabyn, 'Exceptional Accusation Cases under the Extradition Acts 1870 to 1935,' *Criminal Law Review* (1987), pp. 796, 798.

42 *United States v. McGaffery*, [1984] 2 Al E.R. 570, 573 (HL)

43 Compare, explicitly, Lord Diplock in the *McGaffery* case: '[the proper test under Nielsen] is whether the conduct of the accused, if it had been committed in England, would have constituted a crime falling within one or more of the descriptions included in the list.'

44 *United States v. McVey*, 33 B.C.L.R. 2d 28 (1989); Williams, supra footnote 9, p. 605.

in the Canada-United States Extradition Treaty, but forgery did and the Canadian court reasoned that the definition of forgery was wide enough to cover McVey's conduct. However, under United States law his acts did not constitute forgery. If the Canadian court would have sufficed to apply the Nielsen/ Mc Gaffery standard the outcome would have been straightforward: the conduct was a criminal offence under Canadian law and that offence – forgery – appears in the schedule to the treaty, enumerating extraditable offences. Ergo: extradition is to be granted. Interestingly, however, the court invoked a passage in the landmark work on Canadian extradition law of La Forest in order to sustain its decision.[45] La Forest had suggested a clever compromise, holding that, if the conduct would constitute different crimes in the respective states, the names of the crimes of *both* countries would have to be listed.[46] Whatever the merits of this construction, it fails to buttress the outcome in Mc Vey. After all, the US crime of 'submission of false statements' was absent on the list.

It is submitted that application of the 'substantially similar' test as advanced in *Budlong* would have yielded the same, positive result.[47] The offences of 'use of false statements' and 'forgery' are akin in that they serve to protect the same legal and moral interest, to wit the integrity and honesty of parties in trade relations. To be sure, the forgery is performed in order to cheat another person. A lenient interpretation of the standard would have prompted the court to conclude that the dual criminality requirement had been met and that extradition should therefore be granted.

The relevance of choosing between the rigid 'objective' and the liberal subjective method has been particularly acute in cases where courts of the requested state have been confronted with specific legal constructs of criminal liability that are known only in the requesting state. In the case of *Sudar v. United States,* the (Canadian) High Court of Ontario was seized to decide whether extradition of the relator who was charged with racketeering and conspiracy to racketeer would be allowed.[48] 'Racketeering' is a typically American legal construct that covers all kind of Mafia practices, like extortion and the use of front stores.[49] Addressing the dual criminality require-

45 G.V. La Forest, *Extradition to and rom Canada*, 2nd ed., Canada Law Book: Toronto 1977.

46 It follows from La Forest's definition of an extradition crime as 'an act ... that constitutes a crime in the (requesting) state and in the state where the person is found, and that is mentioned and described in an extradition treaty between those states under a name or description by which it is known in *each* state.' La Forest, supra footnote 45, p. 42 (italics added).

47 It might be observed that the United States Supreme Court favoured a similar approach in *Wright v. Henkel*, 259 U.S. 308 (1923). Noting that the elements of the crime of 'fraud' in the requesting state (Great Britain) and the requested state (United States) were (slightly) different, the Court held that the dual criminality requirement had been satisfied because the two were 'substantially analogous.'

48 *Sudar v. United States*, 39 N.R.433 (1981).

49 Compare the Racketeer Influenced and Corrupt Organizations Act, 18 U.S.C. sections 19611–1968 (1962).

ment, the court saw no impediments to extradition, despite the absence of a similar legal construct in Canadian law. It rather pierced the veil of the generic concept of 'racketeering' by identifying the underlying offences:

> The only real substantive components of the indictment against Sudar for the purposes of extradition are the conspiracy and the activities of murder, threats to murder etc. There is no doubt as to the criminality of these activities and of any conspiracy in relation thereto. They are recognized as such the world over.[50]

Similarly, an Australian court, confronted with an extradition request by the United States seeking the surrender of the fugitives on charges of participating in a continuing criminal enterprise (CCE), had no qualms in complying with the request, although the concept of CCE was unknown in Australian law.[51] The court followed the same approach as its Canadian counterpart in *Sudar* by unearthing the concrete offences, consisting of importing and possessing narcotics for the purpose of distribution, rather than focusing on the composite crime. While an *exact* parallel, according to the Court, did not exist under Australian law, the court held that 'because at least one act which formed an element of continuing enterprise, or an *equivalent* act, would have constituted an offence against a law if it had occurred in New South Wales, the offence itself is an extradition crime.'[52]

While in these cases the specific concepts that served to sustain collective liability of multiple perpetrators were skipped over, the courts interestingly pointed out that the requesting and the requested state were on the same page as to the criminality of the substantive conduct. The approach echoes the *Budlong* position that the legal provisions of both states, while not having to be identical, must at least serve to protect legal interests (*Rechtsgüter*) that are by and large the same. Courts in civil law jurisdictions have displayed a similar opinion. The Dutch Supreme Court has acknowledged that the conduct for which the extradition was requested need not be covered by exactly the same legal provisions in the requesting and the requested state. It sufficed that both provisions ' in essence protected the same legal interests'.[53] It should be emphasised that the Dutch Supreme Court has harboured a rather liberal interpretation in this respect. Confronted with a case in which Italian authorities had requested the extradition of an international civil servant who was accused of taking bribes, the Court held that the fact that the case pattern was covered by a corresponding provision in

50 Sudar, supra footnote 48, at p. 433.

51 *Riley v. Commonwealth*, 60 A.L.J.R., p. 106.

52 *Riley v. Commonwealth*, supra footnote 51, p. 109 (emphasis added).

53 Dutch Supreme Court, 30 August 2005, ECLI:NL:HR:2005:AT7564. See also Hanneke Sanders, *Handboek overleveringsrecht*, Intersentia: Antwerp 2011, p. 169.

Dutch law (art. 328*ter* DPC) that concerned passive corruption by non-civil servants. Classification under a legal tag that had a slightly different legal purport did, however, not preclude extradition because of lack of double criminality. Whereas the focus of the Italian provision was on the public law aspect of the contractual relation and the Dutch provision stressed rather the lack of loyalty of the employee *vis-à-vis* his employer, the disparity of the respective legal provisions was not of such a nature as to warrant such an outcome.[54]

Against the backdrop of the previous analysis, it is submitted that the *Nielsen* decision by the House of Lords, in its zeal to get rid of the over-formalistic and restrictive objective method, does not match the purpose and philosophy of the dual criminality rule. In the opinion of this author, one cannot completely disregard a certain degree of correspondence between the legal interests that the criminal law of the cooperating states serves to protect, as has been acknowledged in the *Budlong* decision and in subsequent case law of courts in several jurisdictions.[55] To be sure, not all rationales underpinning the dual criminality rule impel such a conclusion (see above par. 3.2). The abstract method, embraced by the House of Lords in the *Nielsen* case, does not vitiate the legality principle (*nullum crimen*). After all, the obligation on the part of the requesting state to submit the legal provisions that sustain the charges against the fugitive properly inform the latter and provide him/her with fair warning. Moreover, neither the *Budlong* nor the *Nielsen* approach thwarts the equilibrium of performances and would therefore militate against the principle of (full) reciprocity. The strongest case that can be made for the 'substantial similar' approach as favoured by the *Budlong* court is inspired by the societal (or social) rationale. A simple example suffices to illustrate my point. If a state were to request extradition of a person suspected of having desecrated religious symbols or political devices of a similar sacrosanct character and the requested (secular) state, lacking an equivalent provision in its criminal law, would classify it under the label of ' intentional destruction of property', one could hardly argue that the states involved share a common appreciation of the affected value. Any court of the requested state that takes cultural, religious and political pluralism seriously would be hard pressed to refuse extradition because of lack of dual criminality, especially if the criminal sanctions for the conduct in question would widely diverge. Whereas the self-indulgent and myopic approach of the Nielsen court would have no objections against the extradition, the ' substantial similar' interpretation of Budlong would rescue the court from its predicament.

54 Dutch Supreme Court. 4 January 2000, ECLI:NL:HR:2005:AT7564.

55 One might add that the process of *Singemässe Umstellung* can be explained only against the backdrop of a legal comparison of the criminal provisions in both countries, compare Swart, supra footnote 4, p. 152.

3.4 Dual criminality and harmonisation of criminal law

The rule of dual criminality is an instrument to measure the degree of states' willingness to engage in mutual assistance in criminal matters. After all, it not only indicates the limitations of such preparedness, but also, by implication, marks off the common ground in the area of criminal law that reflects their cultural, political and moral affinity. It is therefore to be expected that kindred states are inclined to mutually surrender fugitives from justice for a broader spectrum of criminal offences than states harbouring lukewarm relations. One might surmise that the evolution from the enumerative to the eliminative method of checking dual criminality – apart from being inspired by practical reasons – was fueled by a general tightening of international relations, enabled by states willing to sacrifice part of their sovereignty for the common good.

These assumptions are corroborated by developments in extradition law in (mainly) Europe. The Benelux Treaty on Extradition and Mutual Assistance augmented the ambit of extradition by lowering the threshold of the custodial sentence in the requesting and requested state to six months.[56] More radical and spectacular is the Nordic system of extradition and international cooperation, which is built upon mutual trust between countries that display strong linguistic, cultural and historical ties.[57] Mathisen explains how the system can function in the absence of treaties and (therefore) without any obligations to extradite. It is predicated on the adoption of uniform extradition provisions in domestic legislation in the late 1950s and the early 1960s, leaving the Nordic states maximal flexibility. With the exception of political offences and extradition of nationals, there is no 'general requirement that the conduct for which the suspect was wanted would have to be criminal under the laws of the requesting State.'[58]

3.4.1 Partial abolition of dual criminality in the European Arrest Warrant

The Nordic system has more or less served as a blueprint for the European Arrest Warrant. At the summit of the European Council's conference in Tampere in 1999, the principle of mutual recognition was presented as the device that was to govern international cooperation in criminal matters between the member states of the European Union. The European Arrest

56 Benelux Treaty Concerning Extradition and Mutual Assistance in Criminal Matters between the Kingdom of Belgium, the Grand Duchy of Luxembourg and the Kingdom of the Netherlands, Brussels, 27 June 1962, Trb. 1962, 97.

57 G. Mathisen, 'Nordic Cooperation and the European Arrest Warrant. Intra Nordic Extradition, the Nordic Arrest Warrant and Beyond,' 79 *Nordic Journal of International Law* (2010), pp. 1–33.

58 Mathisen, supra footnote 57, p. 9.

Warrant was proudly heralded as the first progeny of the principle. The transfer of suspects and convicts between the member states would henceforth be qualified as 'surrender,' a novel label that emphasised the distinction with time-worn extradition. Mutual recognition connotes the willingness of states to take differences in perspectives for granted and to move beyond the common ground, rendering mutual assistance in criminal matters irrespective of whether both parties agree that the conduct warrants criminal prosecution. It presumes therefore diversity in the realm of criminal law. Against this backdrop, it is both puzzling and surprising that Article 2(2) of the Framework Decision on the European Arrest Warrant restricts the abandonment of dual criminality for 32 categories of crimes, which have, for all intents and purposes, largely been harmonised throughout the European Union.[59] One is inclined to wonder whether abandoning dual criminality is not redundant, if offences are already criminalised 'across the board.' To be sure, this paradox has been acknowledged by the Advocate General in his opinion preceding the ECJ case of *Advocaten voor de Wereld*. In an interesting footnote, he observes:

> In fact, it is not the double criminality requirement which is set aside but rather the requirement of verification, because the nature of the acts listed – such as murder, grievous bodily injury, kidnapping, illegal restraint, hostage-taking, organised or armed robbery, and rape – is such that they are classed as offences in all the Member States.

And he observes a bit later on that 'They are offences where the verification of double criminality is regarded as superfluous because the acts concerned are punished throughout the Member States.'[60]

The abolition of the verification of dual criminality is meant to speed up the procedure, but would probably also serve to iron out technical legal differences that might indeed preclude cooperation in respect of crimes on which grosso modo all members of the European Union agree. Such considerations are sound (and legitimate), but they also reveal the deeper truth that mutual recognition and harmonisation cannot simply be presented as two, though opposite, strategies that obviate dual criminality.[61] Mutual rec-

59 For a minute analysis, tracing the listed offences to European instruments aiming at their harmonisation, see N. Keijzer, 'The Double Criminality Requirement,' in: R. Blekxtoon & W. van Ballegooij (eds.), *Handbook on the European Arrest Warrant*, T.M.C. Asser Press: The Hague 2005, p. 139.

60 Opinion by Advocate General Ruiz-Jarabo Colomber, delivered on 12 September 2006, ECJ (Grand Chamber), 3 May 2007 (*Advocaten voor de Wereld v. Council of Ministers of the European Union*), Case C-303/05.

61 On the relationship between mutual recognition, dual criminality and harmonisation, see also Lorea Bachmaier, 'European Arrest Warrant, Double Criminality and Mutual Recognition: A Much Debated Case,' 8(2) *European Criminal Law Review* (2018): pp. 152–159;

ognition and harmonisation are related in a dialectical way in that states are prepared to gloss over legal differences only if their legal systems are already sufficiently approximate.[62] In the absence of such rapprochement, the rule of dual criminality is an indispensable device in order to carve out the areas in which states, on the basis of a shared conviction that criminal law repression is necessary, are prepared to cooperate, but – probably more importantly – to identify the realm where such consensus is lacking. The rule precludes international cooperation that is not sustained by a substantive agreement on the reprehensibility of certain conduct and thus protects both states and individuals against the oppression of presumed equality.

---

and Ivan Turudic, Tanja Borzic & Ivana Bujas, 'Relation of the Principle of Mutual Recognition/Trust and Verification of Double Criminality' 36(2) *Zbornik Pravnog Fakulteta Sveucilista u Rijeci* (2015), pp. 1075–1098.

62 Compare A.H.J. Swart, who in his inaugural lecture in 2001 already pointed to this dialectic relationship. A.H.J. Swart, *Een ware Europese Rechtsruimte*, ACIL-publications: Amsterdam 2001.

4 The doctrine of specialty

4.1 Content

The rule of specialty stipulates that a surrendered person can be prosecuted only for the crime for which his extradition has been granted. It serves as an effective backstop for any ground for refusal because, in the absence of the rule, the requesting state could easily circumvent the restriction. It must therefore be considered as a rule of customary international law, implied in each and every extradition procedure, because the whole venture would be nugatory without the existence of the rule, rendering the requested state completely powerless.[1] It should be observed in this respect that assistance of the requested state is indispensable for the requesting state's exercise of criminal law enforcement, in respect of both prosecution (unless the requesting state allows for trials in absentia) and a fortiori for the imposition of sentences. However, that proposition should perhaps be qualified as it rests on the assumption that extradition is the only lawful method to obtain custody over a fugitive.

The presentation of the specialty doctrine as a preventative against a (potential) abuse of the process of the requested state suggests that this state can waive the restriction at will. And, indeed, Article 14 of the European Convention on Extradition, after spelling out the general doctrine on specialty, mentions the consent of the requested state as the first exception to the rule. It continues by adding that 'Consent shall be given when the offence for which it is requested is itself subject to extradition in accordance with the provisions of this Convention.'[2]

1 M. Ch. Bassiouni, *International Extradition and World Public Order*, Sijthoff: Leiden, 1974, p. 354: 'Without a doctrine of specialty, the surrendering state will not in effect determine whether the substantive requirements of extraditable offences and double criminality have been fulfilled. The doctrine is, therefore, concomitant of a requested state's right to determine the extraditability of the person sought for the offence specified.' On the specialty doctrine being a rule of (unwritten) customary international law, see Swart, footnote 1, p. 339.

2 European Convention on Extradition, Paris, 13 December 1957, European Treaties Series No. 024.

DOI: 10.4324/9780429956683-4

The arrangement stands to reason because the requesting state could simply follow up by issuing a new extradition request, which the requested state would not be allowed to refuse. Its consent is a time-saving measure. The wording is imperative (consent *shall* be given), but simultaneously exhaustive. The requested state would not be permitted to allow the prosecution in respect of an offence for which extradition is explicitly precluded (for instance, a political offence) because, by doing so, it would exceed the framework of the treaty. It raises the interesting question of whether the requested state can thwart the rule of specialty by allowing the requested state to pursue proceedings in case the requested state could have the option to refuse extradition. Neither the rationale underlying the specialty doctrine nor the express wording of Article 14 militates against that possibility, but the discretion works of course both ways. The state would equally be entitled to refuse consent in such a case, because it would be illogical, first, to allow a requested state to refuse extradition or surrender and, next, to press the state to give in when the requesting state moves to prosecute an offence that might have been subject to the (optional) refusal of the requested state.

Article 27, section 1 of the Framework Decision on the European Arrest Warrant (EAW) turns the tables by stipulating that

> 1. Each Member State may notify the General Secretariat of the Council that, in its relations with other Member States that have given the same notification, consent is presumed to have been given for the prosecution, sentencing or detention with a view to the carrying out of a custodial sentence or detention order for an offence committed prior to his or her surrender, other than that for which he or she was surrendered, unless in a particular case the executing judicial authority states otherwise in its decision on surrender.[3]

The last part of this long sentence is crucial because, had it been left out, the provision would have deprived the requested state of the possibility of considering the merits of an optional refusal in each and every case.

4.2 Protection of the individual?

The considerable discretion of the requested state to determine the scope of the specialty rule raises the question of whether the relator can invoke the protection of the rule in court in either the requested or the requesting state. The former option will usually not be available, as any incursion on the specialty rule is by definition bound to happen in the requesting state, after the relator has been surrendered. International instruments pay heed to the

3 Council Framework Decision of 13 June 2002 on the European Arrest Warrant and the Surrender Procedures between Member States (2002/584/JHA), OJ L 190, 18 July 2002, p. 1.

position of the relator. Article 27, section 2 of the Framework Decision on the EAW stipulates that the right of the requesting state to initiate prosecution for other offences than for which the surrender has been granted revives after the surrendered person has been offered a reasonable time (45 days) to leave the territory of that state.[4] The arrangement suggests that the relator during that period enjoys a temporal immunity. Moreover, Article 27(3) sub e (juncto Article 13) and f of the Framework Decision provides that the relator is entitled to renounce the specialty rule.[5] Gilbert has correctly qualified in this context 'the power of the requesting State to take into account any other offence with the consent of the fugitive, who may have an interest in wiping the slate clean' as 'another limitation on the strict understanding of specialty.' And he continues by observing that 'this development places the principle firmly in the list of those provisions designed *solely* to protect the fugitive, given that supporting consent from the requested State is not also required.'[6] While there is some truth in this contention, it overstates the case. After all, the power of the individual to renounce the specialty rule does not automatically imply a collateral right to invoke it before the courts of the requesting state. We tend to agree with the view of Bassiouni, who asserts: 'Implicitly, it (the specialty rule) protects the relator from unexpected prosecution, even though it is principally advanced as a means of protecting the requested state from abuse of its process.'[7]

Whether the defendant has a right to rely on the specialty rule is ultimately a question to be decided on the basis of the national law of the requesting state.[8] Courts in the United States are divided on the issue.[9] However, from

4 The rule of specialty does not apply 'when the person having had an opportunity to leave the territory of the Member State to which he or she has been surrendered has not done so within 45 days of his or her final discharge, or has returned to that territory after leaving it.' For a similar arrangement, see European Convention on Extradition, Article 14.

5 The possibility is incorporated in many extradition treaties, see, for instance, Article 18(4) of the Extradition Treaty between the Government of the United Kingdom and Northern Ireland and the Government of the United States of America with Exchange of Notes, Washington, 31 March 2007: 'If the person sought waived extradition pursuant to Article 17, the specialty provisions in this Article shall not apply.' However, remarkably, it is absent in the European Convention on Extradition.

6 Geoff Gilbert, *Transnational Fugitive Offenders in International Law: Extradition and Other Mechanisms*, Martinus Nijhoff: The Hague 1998, p. 198 (emphasis added).

7 Bassiouni, supra footnote 1, p. 354.

8 The Dutch Supreme Court has held the Prosecutor's Office inadmissible in its charges, when it sought to prosecute defendant for offences, different from the one for which extradition had been granted, Dutch Supreme Court, 27 September 1983, NJ, 1984, 96.

9 Compare the comprehensive review by Linda Friedman Ramirez, 'Legal Challenges in Extradition Cases,' in: Linda Friedman Ramirez (ed.), *Cultural Defences in Criminal Law* (3rd ed), Juris Penal Inc.: New York 2010, pp. 387–388, who contrasts *Shapriro Ferrandina*, 476 F.2n 894.906 (2. Cir. 1973), finding that specialty is a right of the asylum state rather than a right of the accused, with *US v. Martonak,* 187 F.Supp 2d, 117, 122 (S.D.N.Y. 2002) finding that defendant has standing to raise specialty issue.

the perspective of the defendant, the situation is grim because the United States is prepared to accept extradition outside the purview of a treaty, as an expression of an act of comity, simultaneously restricting the operation and applicability of the specialty doctrine to extradition treaties. The observance of cordial foreign relations reigns supreme and prevails over any recognition of relator's rights in this representation of extradition. If the foreign authorities, by way of friendly gesture, were willing to surrender fugitives, one should be careful not to push their tolerance, but if they did not balk at the prosecutorial vigour to subsequently charge other offences than initially had been agreed upon, the good understanding had apparently not been hurt. This approach glaringly surfaced in the *Ficconi and Kella* case.[10]

At first blush, it is surprising that the United States was willing to accept the surrender of a fugitive on the basis of comity – and that Italy was prepared to grant it! – because, in the reversed situation, the United States would not be capable of returning the favour, as it requires a treaty basis for extradition. The case of *Ficconi and Kella* paved the way for further examination of the specialty doctrine.

In the case of *U.S. v. Alvarez-Machain* the monopoly of extradition as the single means to obtain custody over a fugitive residing in a foreign country was discussed, and rejected, in the context of the forcible abduction of plaintive by DEA agents from Mexican territory.[11] Defendant moved to challenge the jurisdiction of American courts to try him on charges of being complicit in the murder of US government officials in Mexico by contending that his abduction violated the bilateral extradition treaty between the United States and Mexico.[12] The applicability of the specialty doctrine by analogy surfaces both in the infringement of the 'gentleman's agreement' that the fugitive will be prosecuted only for the offences and on the terms of the requested state – in fact, Mexico had vigorously protested the abduction – and in the incursion of relator's rights. Of course, the legal validity of these claims is predicated on the assumption that extradition is the sole and only method to obtain physical custody over a fugitive residing abroad. In fact, the relator forcefully captured the essence of such a monopoly – and the spirit of the specialty doctrine – by contending that 'all the processes and

10 *Ficconi and Kella v. Attorney General of the United States*, F. 2d, 464 (2. Cir. 1972. Compare Bassiouni, supra footnote 1, p. 355, who, commenting on the case at hand, contends: 'In the absence of any affirmative protest from Italy, the court did not believe that the government would regard the prosecution of appellants for subsequent offences of the same character as the crime for which they were extradited as a breach of faith by the United States.'

11 *U.S. v. Alvarez-Machain*, 504 U.S., 655 (1992). For an in-depth discussion, see Chapter 8.

12 Defendant could rely on a judgment of the Second Court of Appeals in *Verdugo Urquidez v. United States*, 939 F.2dm 1341, 1350 (A9 1991), which held that 'the forcible abduction of a Mexican national with the authorization or participation of the United States violates the Extradition Treaty between the United States and Mexico.'

restrictions on the obligation to extradite established by the Treaty would make no sense if either nation were free to resort to forcible kidnapping to gain the presence of an individual for prosecution in a manner not contemplated by the Treaty.'[13]

The ardent plea did, however, not convince the Supreme Court. First, it confined the operation of the specialty doctrine to extradition proceedings, quoting the landmark decision of the Supreme Court in *Rauscher* on the issue:

> [A] person who has been brought within the jurisdiction of the court *by virtue of proceedings under an extradition treaty,* can only be tried for one of the offences described in that treaty, and for the offence with which he is charged in the proceedings for his extradition, until a reasonable time and opportunity have been given him, after his release or trial upon such charge, to return to the country from whose asylum he had been forcibly taken under those proceedings.[14]

As Alvarez-Machain, different from the *Rauscher* case, was brought within US jurisdiction by way of abduction, the specialty doctrine as embedded in an extradition treaty did not apply as such. It would, however, apply by analogy, if the bilateral treaty prohibited any transfer of a fugitive beyond the terms of the treaty, as Alvarez-Machain claimed. The Supreme Court found, however, that 'the language of the Treaty, in the context of its history, does not support the proposition that the Treaty prohibits abductions outside of its terms.'[15] Ultimately, the Supreme Court addressed the defendant's contention, confirmed by a similar view, as expressed by the Second Court of Appeal in *Verdugo*, that the purpose of the bilateral treaty was violated by the forcible abduction. While the treaty indeed did not explicitly prohibit such practice, it was implicit in the essence of extradition wielding monopoly over and excluding all other means of transfer and corroborated by the prohibition of abductions under customary international law. The Supreme Court was not persuaded by this argument either, pointing at the inferential leap that was required to construe the interpretation of an extradition treaty in terms of general principles of international law that were not directly related to extradition practice.[16]

We have dwelled some time upon this case because it neatly demonstrates how the effect of the specialty doctrine can be curtailed if states are prepared to resort to measures beyond the context of extradition in order to bring fugitives to justice. In a later chapter on unlawful rendition/ alternatives to

13 *U.S. v. Alvarez-Machain*, supra footnote 11, at p. 664.
14 *U.S. v. Rauscher*, 119 US, 407, 411 (1886). Emphasis in the *Avarez Machain* case.
15 *U.S. v. Alvarez-Machain*, supra footnote 11, at p. 664.
16 *U.S. v. Alvarez-Machain*, supra footnote 11, at p. 669.

extradition, we will take the opportunity to comment in more detail on this (in)famous precedent.

Other jurisdictions have been more rigid in the application of the specialty doctrine, simultaneously acknowledging that a criminal suspect could rely on the principle before the criminal court of the requesting state. In the case of *Lahoria v. India*, the Supreme Court of India accepted the claim of the applicant who contested the jurisdiction of the Rajasthan High Court that had moved to try him for offences under the Terrorist and Disruptive Activities (Prevention) Act of 1987.[17] Lahoria had previously been extradited to India by the United States for another offence. The Supreme Court clarified that Article 21 of the (Indian) Extradition Act, which was in full consonance with Article 7 of the Extradition Treaty between the United States and the United Kingdom and Northern Ireland with the Government of the Republic of India, explicitly prohibited prosecution for an offence other than the extradition offence in relation to which he was surrendered or returned. The Supreme Court took pains to further elucidate its position. Emphasising the inalienable right to liberty of the individual, the court reminded the United States and the United Kingdom that they themselves prescribed that no fugitive could be extradited without a treaty. While such an approach would not qualify as a rule of international law, the reverse, implying that states would be bound to surrender fugitives in the absence of a treaty, would equally be untenable.[18] If the fugitive was surrendered by virtue of an extradition treaty, the terms of that treaty should be adhered to. Observing that the specialty doctrine had solidified into a rule of customary international law and was to be taken into account in the application of the treaty, it followed that

> when a person is extradited for a particular crime, he can be tried for only that crime. If the requesting State deems it desirable to try the extradited fugitive for some other crime committed before his extradition, the fugitive has to be brought to the status quo ante, in the sense that he has to be returned first to the State which granted the extradition and a fresh extradition has to be requested for the latter crime.[19]

Strictly spoken, the reference to customary international law was obiter and redundant, as the treaty itself in the strongest terms forbids the prosecution for another offence.[20] What the judgment extolls, however, is that

17 *Lahoria v. India, Original Writ and Special Leave Petition*, AIR 2001 SC 1716, ILDC 170 (IN 2001), 17 April 2001, India; Supreme Court, Reporter: Dr. Ravindra Pratap.

18 *Lahoria v. India*, supra footnote 17, par. 7: 'There is no rule of international law which imposes any duty on a State to surrender a fugitive in the absence of extradition treaty.'

19 *Lahoria v. India*, supra footnote 17.

20 Article 7 of the treaty reads as follows: 'A person surrendered can in *no case* be kept in custody or be brought to trial in the territories of the High Contracting Party to whom the

extradition treaties serve not only the interests of states, but are also concluded for the purpose of reinforcing legal certainty and foreseeability for the fugitive. As the specialty doctrine is the indispensable capstone of each extradition treaty, the finding of the Indian Court has a higher principled bearing than meets the eye.

4.3 Extradition to third states

A final topic that requires a brief discussion in this chapter concerns the prohibition of re-extradition of the fugitive to a third state without the consent of the requested state, as it is usually considered as a corollary of the specialty doctrine.[21] The arrangement makes sense, as, like the specialty doctrine *stricto sensu*, it warrants the requested state's enduring scrutiny over the fate of the relator, who, after all, is in the power of the requesting state as a consequence of the former's actions. It would for instance be inappropriate if the requested person would, by mediation of the requesting state, end up standing trial before the courts of a state with whom the initial requested state has no treaty. If, on the other hand, the third state could obtain the surrender of the requested person on the same terms as the requesting state, there is less need to be so circumspect. It is interesting in this respect to contrast the light procedure, modeled after Article 27(1) of the Framework Decision on the European Arrest Warrant, by which member states can renounce their entitlement to give consent with the strict regulation governing the relations with third States.[22] But even in that case, the initial requested state has an interest in sustaining direct contacts with the state that will ultimately put the relator on trial, lest it does not exceed the parameters of the charges for which the extradition is granted.[23] It demonstrates that the prohibition of re-extradition without the consent of the

surrender has been made for any other crime or offence, or on account of any other matters, than those for which the extradition shall have taken place, until he has been restored, or has had an opportunity of returning, to the territories of the High Contracting Party by whom he has been surrendered' (italics added).

21 See, for instance, Article 15 of the European Convention on Extradition (footnote 2) that reads: 'the requesting Party shall not, without the consent of the requested Party, surrender to another Party or to a third State a person surrendered to the requesting Party and sought by the said other Party or third State in respect of offences committed before his surrender.'

22 Article 28, section 4 of the Framework Decision provides that 'a person who has been surrendered pursuant to a European arrest warrant shall not be extradited to a third State without the consent of the competent authority of the Member State which surrendered the person. Such consent shall be given in accordance with the Conventions by which that Member State is bound, as well as with its domestic law.'

23 It is interesting in this context that Article 53 of the Riyad Arab Agreement for Judicial Cooperation subjects re-extradition to a third state to the further requirement that 'even then, the contracting party requested to extradite shall submit an application to the contracting party from which it had received such person to that effect, accompanied by the documents presented by the said third state.' Riyad Arab Agreement for Judicial Coopera-

requested state and the specialty doctrine *stricto sensu* is not only conceptually but also, in actual practice, closely related.

The risk of re-extradition to a third state recently surfaced in the protracted proceedings against Julian Assange. He had sought diplomatic asylum in the Ecuadorian Embassy in London, being sought for sexual assault in Sweden and for conspiracy to commit computer intrusion by the United States. The Swedish authorities had dropped rape charges but persisted in his surrender in respect of the offence of 'absconding by a person released on bail.' During extradition proceedings in the United Kingdom, Assange expressed his fear that he would be surrendered to the United States, which would probably expand the indictment against him with charges based on the Espionage Act for publication by Wikileaks of classified material.[24] The Westminster Magistrate's Court did not share Assange's anxiety. It was confident that, if the United States had approached Sweden with an extradition request, the latter state would have contacted the British court before proceeding with the request for surrender. The plaintiff would thus be allowed to raise all bars against any subsequent extradition to the United States before the Magistrate's Court.[25]

The ruling not only testifies to the requested state's judiciary's concern for the fate of the fugitive, but also demonstrates that the requesting state's abiding by the specialty rule is to a large extent a question of trust.

---

tion, 6 April 1983, Unofficial translation, endorsed by the Council of Arab Ministers of Justice, Refworld; https://www.refworld.org/docid/3ae6b38d8.html.

24 For a comprehensive survey of the background of the case, see Stephen P. Mulligan, *Frequently Asked Questions about the Julian Assange* Charges, Congressional Research Service, updated 9 June 2019; https://fas.org/sgp/crs/secrecy/LSB10291.pdf.

25 In the *Westminster's Magistrate's Court* (Extradition); An Application by Mr. Julian Assange, 13 February 2018, section 13; https://www.bailii.org/ew/cases/Misc/2018/B3.html.

5 The political offence exception

5.1 Introduction: provenance and rationales

One of the exceptions to extradition that is well-nigh universally acknowledged concerns the political offence. Article 3(1) of the European Convention on Extradition, for instance, stipulates that

> Extradition shall not be granted if the offence in respect of which it is requested is regarded by the requested Party as a political offence or as an offence connected with a political offence.[1]

The non-extradition for political offences is, from a historical perspective, by no means self-evident. Bassiouni, for example, points out that the rendition of political adversaries was, until the late 18th century, the rule rather than the exception, explaining this state of affairs against the prevailing political climate of interregional allegiances:

> Sovereigns obliged one another by surrendering persons who most likely affected the stability of their political order of the requesting state. Thus, the stronger the relationship between the sovereigns, the more interest and concern they had for each other's welfare and the more intent they would be on surrendering those political offenders who had created the greatest dangers to their respective welfare.[2]

Perhaps this general statement requires some qualification, as Bedi has observed that 'extradition of culprits was not limited to political crimes

1 European Convention, Paris, 13 December 1957, European Treaties. Article 41 of the Riyad Arab Agreement for Judicial Cooperation, 6 April 1983, Unofficial translation, endorsed by the Council of Arab Ministers of Justice, Refworld; https://www.refworld.org/docid/3ae6b38d8.html, decrees in nearly identical terms that 'No extradition no extradition shall be carried out … (a) If the crime for which extradition is requested is considered by the laws of the requested party as a crime of a political nature.'

2 M. Ch. Bassiouni, *International Extradition and World Public Order*, Sijthoff: Leiden, 1974, p. 4. In a similar vein, Arthur Nussbaum, *A Concise History of the Law of Nations*, Mac-

DOI: 10.4324/9780429956683-5

alone; not only political offenders but also such people charged with murder, theft, robbery, rape, abduction and other serious non-political crimes were surrendered.'[3] While authority is thus divided on the issue, the main trend was to ask and grant the extradition of political adversaries.[4]

What caused this major and spectacular reversal to occur? The impetus was no doubt that the rise of nationalism in the aftermath of the Peace of Westphalia prompted peoples, in their pursuit of self-determination, to break away from empires.[5] Offering political asylum was a statement of solidarity with 'fellow travelers' who equally resisted authoritarian regimes, but still had not succeeded in beating them.[6] It is no coincidence that the first country to incorporate the political exception to extradition in domestic legislation was Belgium, which in 1830 had separated from the Netherlands. While such heroic gestures were grist to the mill of politicians who sought to elicit public support from their constituencies, at the international level governments of smaller states had to move more cautiously in not antagonizing major powers. The political offence exception, when institutionalised and generally accepted, enabled states to keep aloof from internal power contests. Rather than evincing partiality with the course of insurgents, the political offence exception came soon to be considered as a token of neutrality, a precocious asset in unruly times. After all, the vanquished of today could be the victors of tomorrow.[7]

These political considerations were further buttressed by the humanitarian concern that the fugitive might, on return, face harsh, unfair and biased treatment, in view of the particular threat he posed to those in power. The

millan: New York 1961, p. 214: 'We have seen that there had been extradition of fugitives from foreign countries since antiquity; but those fugitives had been political adversaries or unlawful emigrants rather than criminals.'

3 S. Bedi, *Extradition in International Law and Practice,* Bronder-Offset: Rotterdam, 1966, p. 5.

4 Compare also Christopher Blakesley, 'The Practice of Extradition from Antiquity to Modern France and the United States: A Brief History,' 4 *Boston College International and Comparative Law Journal* (1981), p. 49, observing that 'Nevertheless, as late as the 1660's, the purpose of most major rendition agreements remained essentially political,' illustrating the point with many telling examples.

5 For the underlying social, psychological and economic drives, see Benedict Andersen, *Imagined Communities: Reflections on the Origins and Source of Nationalism*, Verso: London/New York 2006 (New and Revised Edition); and Ernest Gellner, *Nations and Nationalism*, Cornell University Press: Ithaca, New York 1983.

6 Compare Ivor Stanbrook & Clive Stanbrook, *The Law and Practice of Extradition*, Barry Rose (Publishers) Ltd./ Justice of the Peace Ltd.: Chichester and London 1980, p. 106: 'The democratic and revolutionary movements which swept through Europe during the late eighteenth and early nineteenth centuries produced a flood of political refugees who sought and received asylum in the West. Their enforced return to oppressive regimes was abhorrent to public opinion.... The modern custom of granting political asylum was thus established.'

7 It explains the popularity of the political offence exception in South America where regime change was all too frequent.

political offence exception owed its popularity in no small measure to the fact that contracting parties could suffice by formally invoking it, without having to reveal which particular reason fueled their apprehensions. The ideological, political and humanitarian rationale have all underpinned the political offence exception and together have contributed to its status as a resilient institution, having survived the wear and tear of time.[8]

Any complacency on its persistent relevance, however, is utterly simplistic, because it conceals the unfaltering controversies on the essence of the exception and its application in practice. The exception reflects all the tensions between the conflicting interests of a stable and peaceful world public order, political diversity and individual freedom that are at the core of this work.[9] As a prelude to the more detailed discussion of the conceptual categorisation and case law on the topic, it is useful to identify the major points of dispute.

From the outset, one of the greatest concerns has always been to exclude particularly heinous and detestable crimes from the protection that the exception aims to offer. One of the early manifestations of this objective is the so-called *clause d'attentat*, stipulating that the assault on the life of the head of state is not to be considered a political offence.[10] As the provision does not make any distinction between respectable sovereigns, elected by or at least enjoying widespread support of the people, and despicable tyrants, it purports to guarantee the stability of international relations rather than expressing universal outrage at the heinousness of the crime. Another device has been to single out international crimes that are committed on behalf of the state from the purview of the exception, by holding that the exception was available only to political offenders who were 'at odds' with the powers that be. In a British case concerning the extradition of a former SS-man accused of having committed several atrocities at concentration camps during World War II, the court held that at the time of the offence he was a servant of the State and not at odds with it. Chapman J. elucidated the concept of 'proceedings of a political character' as follows:

> I think the words postulate some sort of political behavior on the part of the accused prison which makes in the eyes of those in power desirable that he should be rendered silent or inactive. Again, I can see no basis

8 See on the three rationales more in detail: Chr. van den Wijngaert, *The Political Offence Exception to Extradition: The Delicate Problem of Balancing the Rights of the Individual and International Public Order*, Kluwer: Deventer 1980, pp. 4–18.

9 It is telling that Geoff Gilbert, *Transnational Fugitive Offenders in International Law: Extradition and Other Mechanisms*, Martinus Nijhoff: The Hague 1998, dedicates more than 130 pages (Chapter 6) of his seminal book to the 'political offence exemption.'

10 See, for instance, Article 3(3) of the European Convention on Extradition, supra footnote 1, which provides that 'The taking or attempted taking of the life of a Head of State or a member of his family shall not be deemed to be a political offence for the purposes of this Convention.'

for any suggestion that the accused are being prosecuted for political reasons of that kind.[11]

Apart from filtering out some of the most egregious crimes from the ambit of the exception, reserving the benefits of the political offence exception to those who are at loggerheads with the state corresponds, as the words of Chapman suggest, with its humanitarian rationale. A more comprehensive approach, taking into account that international crimes can be committed both at the behest of the state and against it, straightforwardly excludes some very heinous crimes from the protection of the political offence exception. Article VII of the Genocide Convention, for instance, stipulates that 'Genocide and the other acts enumerated in article III shall not be considered as political crimes for the purpose of extradition.'[12] Similarly, Article 11 of the Convention for the Suppression of Terrorist Bombings provides that 'none of the offences set forth in article 2 shall be regarded, for the purpose of extradition or mutual assistance, as a political offence or an offence connected with a political offence or as an offence inspired by political motives.'[13] We will address the extradition in respect of war crimes and terrorist offences in more detail in subsequent chapters. Suffice at this point to observe that the quandary of the political offence exception reaches its summit in the attempts to exclude from its scope those offences that are political par excellence.

A second challenge is to distinguish political from common crimes in order to preserve the integrity of the former. This is a hazardous affair because many crimes are of a mixed nature, displaying both common and political features. The textbook example of the bank robber who claims to fight the capitalist system and promises, as a modern Robin Hood, to distribute the loot among the poor, is an example in kind. The bottom line is that a political motive does not suffice.[14] Both courts hailing from the common and the civil law systems agree on this.[15] But beyond this common

11 *In re Gross and others ex parte Treasury Solicitor* [1968] 3 All E.R. 804, 807. Source: V.E. Hartley Booth, *British Extradition Law and Procedure*, Samson: Alphen aan den Rijn 1980, pp. 43–44.

12 Convention on the Prevention and Punishment of the Crime of Genocide, Paris, 9 December 1948, UNTS 1951, No. 1021.

13 Convention on the Suppression of Terrorist Bombings, New York, 15 December 1997, 37 ILM, 249 (1998).

14 Gilbert, supra footnote 9, p. 216.

15 See the British case of *Schtraks v. Government of Israël* [1964] AC 556, 591 in which Lord Radcliffe on behalf of the House of Lords expressed the opinion that '(the nature of a political offence would be lost sight of) if one were to say that all offences were political offences, so long as they could be shown to have been committed for a political object or with a political motive or for the furtherance of some political cause or campaign.' In the French case *Re Giovanni Gatti*, the court revealed a similar opinion: 'The offence does not derive its political character from the motive of the offender, but from the nature of the rights it injures' [1947] *Ann. Dig.* 145 (Case No. 70, 145–146).

ground, it is difficult to draw the line. Doctrine and case law have turned the concept of political offence into a grey area, encompassing not only pure political offences, but also (potentially) common crimes that facilitate political offences, as the anxiety of the just quoted provision in the Terrorist Bombing Convention to exclude all of them already demonstrates.

A third aspect of the political offence exception, related to but yet to be distinguished from the previous one, is that most legal systems require the offence to be both instrumental and proximate to the achievement of the ultimate political goal. In the United Kingdom, this idea probably sprang from the 'political incidence' doctrine that forged a link between the offence and a larger political struggle for power.[16] But it features in the authoritative Swiss predominance doctrine as well and constitutes the essence of it. *In re Nappi*, the Swiss court held that

> The political character of an offence is predominant only if the offence is in direct relation to the end sought. In order that such a relationship may exist, this offence must be a really efficacious method of achieving the end, or constitute an integral part of acts leading thereto, or represent an incident in a general political movement in which the parties have recourse to such methods.[17]

At first blush, it is not immediately clear why a political fugitive should only benefit from the exception if his actions are likely to yield success. Why should a person who – perhaps pathetically and like a Don Quixote – tries to withstand an oppressive government on which his feeble endeavours make no impression be denied the protection of the exception? Of course, it depends on how one defines a political objective – as a wholesale power turnover or in more modest terms – but it appears to offer a premium to brutal regimes that can easily choke all resistance. To a certain extent, the parameter serves a double purpose. First, it may be an appropriate method to weed out *prima facie* improbable claims and at this point it conflates with the effort to distinguish between political and common crimes. But at a deeper level it infers a balancing of the political act and the prevailing climate it seeks to change. It connotes a value judgment – not so much of the political objective as such but of the means that are used to accomplish that aim – in relation to the environment in which it takes place. Under the most exacting test, the political offence must be capable of achieving the final goal, is to be commensurate with (or at least not disproportionate to) the damage caused and should be the only method to realise the political

16 In his *History of the Criminal Law in England* (1883, Vol. 2, p. 70), Sir J.F. Stephen held that 'foreign criminals are not to be surrendered for extradition crimes if those crimes were incidental to and formed a part of political disturbances.'

17 *In re Nappi*, 19 *Int. L. Rep.* (1952), pp. 375 and 376.

objective. This final 'subsidiarity check' shifts attention to the context in which the offence is committed and turns the political offence exception into a variable of the democratic quality of the state against which it is directed. The somewhat simple and simplified argument runs that violence is both unwarranted and unnecessary if political change can be accomplished by peaceful means. It is one of the main rationales that underpinned the decision to abandon the exception entirely from conventions that are concluded between like-minded and democratic states.[18]

These preliminary observations demonstrate that the political offence exception in extradition law is a complex topic. The identification of the political nature of an offence is only the first step. Subsequently, courts have to decide whether the fugitive is entitled to benefit from the exception. That assessment, apart from obviously depending on the specifics of the case, hinges on temporal and political-geographical contingencies, like the degree of political affiliation between the cooperating states. Depending on such parameters, the scope of the exception can be expanded or reduced to the point of extinction (at least regionally). To be sure, these two prongs are not always distinguished, nor can they be as they are strongly intertwined. However, for analytical purposes, it makes sense to inquire first what a political offence, in contradistinction to a common crime, actually is and next what extra features it has to possess to qualify as a ground for exemption from extradition. This will hopefully provide us with a conceptual framework on the basis of which we can better appreciate and understand the malleability of the exception against the backdrop of historical and political developments and enable us, perhaps, to say something about its viability.

5.2 What is an offence of a political character? Some attempts at categorisation

It should come as no surprise that no commonly accepted definition of a 'political offence' exists. It is in the nature of politics that it breeds dissent.[19] We would therefore fully agree with Viscount Radcliffe's sober observation:

18 The European Union's 1996 Convention relating to Extradition between Member States (27 September 1996, OJ 96 C 3103/02), which has been replaced by the Framework Decision on the European Arrest Warrant, paved the way by putting the situation on its head. Article 5(1) of this convention provided that 'For the purposes of applying this Convention, no offence may be regarded by the requested State as a political offence, as an offence connected with a political offence or an offence inspired by political motives.' The Framework Decision on the European Arrest Warrant is completely silent on the political offence exception.

19 The intense antagonism that is inherent to the political realm has momentously been captured by Carl Schmitt, *The Concept of the Political*, expanded edition, translated, introduced and notes by George Schwelb, p. 26: 'The specific political distinction to which political actions and motives can be reduced is that between friend and enemy'; https://www.docdroid.net/cNhoLIH/the-concept-of-the-political-carl-schmitt-pdf#page=4.

> What then is an offence of a political character? The courts, I am afraid, have been asking this question at intervals ever since it was first posed judicially in 1890 and no definition has yet emerged or by now is ever likely to.[20]

States may generally concur, on the basis of the considerations expounded in the previous paragraph, that extradition should not be granted for political offences, but what this concept actually entails is inherently subjective. The very insertion of the words 'as regarded by the requested state' or 'in view of the requested state' in extradition treaties implies that opinions on the matter might – and often will – differ.

On a more abstract, conceptual level, the consent is (obviously) larger. At the apex of the categorisation of political crimes stands the *pure* or *absolute* political offence, which is untainted by common crime aspects. The classic definition derives from the French case of *Re Giovanni Gatti*, which is attractive for its pointiness but also deceptively simplistic:

> In brief, what distinguishes the political crime from the common crime is the fact that the former *only* affects the political organization of the State, the proper rights of the State, while the latter *exclusively* affects rights other than those of the State.[21]

The category comprises such 'classics' as treason, sedition and espionage, but it probably includes electoral fraud ('stuffing the ballot box') as well, although one might perhaps counter that this activity is contaminated by common crime elements.[22] Gilbert correctly observes that absolute political offences did not cause many problems in bilateral treaties of older date as they were not incorporated as listed offences under the enumerative method, adding that the recourse to the elimination method has changed the situation.[23] Espionage is a case in point, illustrative of the extreme sensitivity of the political offence exception. Whereas many will consider espionage as a political act *par excellence* – it depends on national legislation whether it also qualifies as a crime – Gilbert points out that general opinion has followed the rather peculiar point of view of a British judge that acts of espionage are not political in character at all.[24] The predicament is obvious. While many states will practice espionage themselves, discovery is likely to ignite great indignation (on the part of the affected state) and cause embarrassment (on

20 In *Schtraks v. Government of Israël*, supra footnote 15, p. 899.

21 *Re Giovanni Gatti*, supra footnote 15, p. 145. Italics added.

22 See on the first three offences, M.R. Garcia Mora, 'Treason, Sedition and Espionage as Political Offences under the Law of Extradition,' 26 *University of Pittsburgh Law Review* (1964/1965), p. 65.

23 Gilbert, supra footnote 9, p. 215.

24 Gilbert, supra footnote 9. The case in question is *R v. Government of Pentonville Prison, ex part Rebott*, [1978] L.S. Gaz. R. 43.

the part of the unmasked state). If the conflict cannot be solved by expelling the spy to his home country, the latter will be reluctant to add insult to injury, by subsequent refusal of extradition.[25] The spy will thus be exposed to a regime that bears a special grudge against him or her and is not likely to treat him (or her) fairly. In these situations, the humanitarian rationale of the exception of the political offence is conspicuous.

A complex political offence (*Délit Complexe*) is in a narrow sense often defined as the *concursus realis* of an absolute political offence and a common crime. The scholarly example is the assault on the life of a head of state, which constitutes, of course, simultaneously murder and an attack on the very embodiment of sovereign power. As we have seen before, this crime is generally excluded in treaties from the purview of the political offence exception. More generally, suspects of complex political offences are rarely exempted from extradition because the common criminal aspects are usually found to outweigh the political dimension, an issue that we will address in the next paragraph. Under a broader definition, complex political offences are understood as being 'directed at both the political order and private rights.'[26] For the sake of terminological purity, that approach should, in our view, not be followed as it collapses complex political offences with relative political offences.

The European Convention on Extradition, like many other extradition treaties, expands the scope of the political offence exception by putting 'offences connected to political offences' on the same par.[27] Such *connected political offences* are by definition common crimes that are committed in the course of or in furtherance of a political offence.[28] The extradition case of Kurt Folkerts, frontman of the German urban guerrilla movement/terrorist cell Rote Armee Fraktion (RAF) provides a good example. The Dutch Supreme Court considered the abduction of the chairman of the German Employers Association Hans Martin Schleyer with the intention to exert pressure on the German government to release their imprisoned comrades as an (absolute/complex) political offence. The killing of his bodyguards which was instrumental if not indispensable, to accomplish the abduction

25 In my view, the psychology component of international relations underlying espionage is a better explanation for its exclusion from the purview of the political offence exception than Gilbert's assumed increased cohesiveness among States within western industrialised society. See on the controversial position of espionage and spies also Asaf Luba, 'Espionage as a Sovereign Right under International Law and its limits,' 24 *LSA Quarterly* (2015–2016), p. 22

26 I.A. Shearer, *Extradition in International Law*, Manchester University Press: Manchester 1971, p. 181.

27 European Convention, supra footnote 1.

28 Compare Supreme Court of Chile, *In the Matter of Hector José Campora and Others,*' 58 *American Journal of International Law* (1957), pp. 690 and 698: 'connected political offences, which are common crimes committed in the course of attempts against the security of the state or related to political offences, it being necessary to examine intent to determine whether the ordinary crime is connected, or not, to a political one.'

was subsequently qualified as a connex political offence for which extradition would, in principle, be equally precluded.[29]

The large category of offences displaying some political aspect is generally known under the tag of *relative political offences*, although sometimes complex and connex political crimes are comprised under this heading as well. The bottom line for a relative political offence is that it concerns a crime that is inspired by the motive to achieve a political purpose and which is, judged by its outside appearance, related to that political objective.[30] Whereas political motive alone does not suffice (see *supra*), we might as well focus on the nature of the political aim and the connection between crime and the political goal. For the time being, we need not bother about the question of whether the offence is, in fact, fit to accomplish the political purpose and whether it is proximate to that goal because these are additional requirements that have been developed in order to assess whether a (relative) political offence justifies the refusal of extradition. To be sure, any attempt to identify the skeleton of (relative) political offences by consulting the case law on the topic is hampered by the fact that courts are inclined to skip such scrutiny of the essence in their search for an answer whether the offence at hand qualifies for refusal. The identification of the parameters of a relative political offence and the requirements that entitle such an offence to be encompassed under the treaty provision thus get easily blurred, the former being engulfed by the latter. Indeed, both the British 'political incidence' theory and the Swiss 'predominance' doctrine refer to the final outcome of the assessment of whether the political offender should be extradited or not.[31] Nonetheless, one can sometimes read 'between the lines' what features the offence should, according to the courts, possess in order to qualify as 'political' in the first place, in particular as to the nature of the aspired goal.

In the *Schtraks* case, the House of Lords ventured to discuss the widest meaning of a political offence. The case itself emerged from a quarrel between the parents and the grandparents of a boy whose religious education constituted the bone of contention. Child abduction and perjury were the charges on the basis of which the Israeli government sought to obtain the extradition of the fugitive, who argued that the offence had clearly political overtones, reflecting a conflict between his religious views and the secular

29 Dutch Supreme Court 8 May 1978, NJ 1978, 314. The decision sparked critical comment, as the Supreme Court had not taken into account whether the harm that had been done to civilians was proportionate to the political objective. See also the conclusion of the Advocate General in Dutch SC 7 May 2004, NJ, 2007, 276; https://uitspraken.rechtspraak.nl/inziendocument?id=ECLI:NL:HR:2004:AF6988.

30 Compare the Swiss court in the *Ktir* case, 34 *International Law Reports* (1961), pp. 143 and 144.

31 It should be emphasised that I am not criticizing this approach as it is functional to the legal decision on the case before the court.

government. The Divisional Court had offered a definition of a political offence, holding that it was 'committed as part of a political movement with the object of influencing the policy of the government of the state.'[32] While the definition was developed in the context of the inquiry whether *Schtraks* should be extradited or not, its contours were so wide as to serve a generic definition of a(relative) political offence. The relator's claim was hopeless, as Amerasinghe has aptly demonstrated:

> Since there was nothing in the case to suggest that the acts of the applicant were done as a part of a movement or struggle rather than as part of a purely religious and domestic dispute within the family, albeit it occurred at a time when there was a political struggle, one of the primary requirements of the definition had not been satisfied and the offence could not be characterized as political.[33]

But more interesting than the outcome of the case itself were the deliberations of the Lords. Lord Reid, in particular, reduced the concept of political offence to its core essence by leaving out all restrictive features:

- It is not necessary that there be an open insurrection. Offences committed by an underground resistance movement attempting to overthrow a government could be political.
- It is not necessary that there be an attempt to overthrow the government. Attempts to compel a government to change its advisers or its policy could give rise to political offences.
- It is not necessary that the offender's party should be trying to achieve power in the state. It would be sufficient if they had been trying to make the government concede some measure of freedom.
- It is not necessary that there be some disturbance of the public order. Thus, for instance, where an offence, perhaps of a non-violent kind, had been committed as part of a campaign to compel or induce an autocratic government to grant a measure of civil or religious liberty, it could not be excluded from the concept of political offence purely on the ground that there had been no public disturbance.
- It is irrelevant whether the offender was engaged in a good or bad cause.
- The motive and purpose of the offender is relevant. Thus the commission of a crime in order to satisfy a grudge would prevent the offence from being political. The purpose must be to promote a political cause.[34]

32 *Schtraks v. Government of Israel* (1962), 2 WLR 976, 977.

33 C.F. Amerasinghe, 'The Schtraks Case: Defining Political Offence and Extradition,' 28 *Modern Law Review* (1965), p. 35

34 *Schtraks case*, supra footnote 32, AC 556, 1025/1026.

This interpretation of the political offence differed from classic British case law on the topic in two important respects. First, it no longer required that the conflict to which the offence was related concerned an all-out struggle for power between the sitting government and a contesting faction.[35] A (far) more modest outcome, like the quest for reforms, would suffice. Second, the political controversies did not need to have reached the level of public disturbances. The acknowledgement that an offence could have a political character if it emerged from a conflict between unequal parties, concerned only modest aspirations and did not result in open violence, dovetailed with the sympathy at the time for those seeking refuge from autocratic regimes, to wit, the Soviet Union and its allies. The *Kolczynski* case concerned the mutiny by the crew of a Polish ship that subsequently headed for an English port seeking political asylum.[36] Poland wanted their extradition for the extraditable offence of revolt on the high seas, but evidence was given that mere defection (*Republikflucht*) would be considered treason. What was relevant in this case was that the British authorities harboured the suspicion that the Polish authorities, while requesting extradition for mutiny, would actually punish the fugitives for the political offence of treason.[37]

The Swiss Federal Tribunal had also demonstrated sensitivity to the changed political climate and had accordingly expanded the scope of the political offence. Yugoslavia had sought extradition of the members of an airplane crew who had diverted a local flight and landed in Switzerland. The Swiss court denied extradition and held, referring to and denouncing the interpretation that political offences had to be directly related to a realisation of a major political objective or were occurring within the context of a fight for political power,

That restrictive interpretation does not meet the intention of the law, nor take account of recent historical developments, such as the growth of totalitarian States. Those who do not wish to submit to the regime have no alternatives but to escape it by flight abroad. This more passive attitude for the purpose of escaping political constraint is no less worthy of asylum than active participation in the fight for political power used to be in what were earlier considered to be normal circumstances. Recent practice has been too restrictive in making the relative political character of an offence dependent on its commission in the framework of a fight for power.[38]

35 That was still required in *Re Castioni* [1981] 1 QB 149 [1886-1890], All E.Rep. 640, 644, and in *Re Meunier* [1894], 2 QB 415, 419.

36 *R v. Governor of Brixton ex parte Kolczynski* [1955], 1 All ER 31, [1955] 1 QB 540.

37 As Stanbrook & Stanbrook, supra footnote 6, p. 107, correctly observe, even formal adherence to the specialty principle would not be a sufficient guarantee because the British authorities would, in view of the icy diplomatic relations at the time, not be able to scrutinise the follow up.

38 *Kavic, Bjelanove and Arsenievl case*, 39 ILR (1951), 37.1.

The interpretation of what constitutes a political offence (for the purposes of (non)-extradition is not cast in stone. By searching for the most liberal interpretation, setting the outer limits of what could still be considered a political offence that warrants the refusal of extradition, one approaches the essence of the concept detached from its extradition context. This serves as a good starting point for evaluating the requirements that have been added in a more restrictive interpretation of the political offence exception.

5.3 The ultimate test: not all political offences are excluded from extradition

Courts of several jurisdictions have fine-tuned the criteria for the assessment of whether political offenders would be immune from extradition, effectively reducing the scope of the exception. While states have endeavoured to develop their own vision and policy, they have inevitably influenced each other, evincing the nature of extradition as a device of reciprocity and exchange. As mentioned earlier, the British political incidence theory and the Swiss predominance doctrine have been leading in the field.[39] Three parameters – proximity, proportionality and subsidiarity – have dominated the discussions. While they are interrelated, for analytical purposes they should be distinguished.

5.3.1 Proximity

Most jurisdictions require the offence not only to have some connection to a political objective, but also to be sufficiently proximate to the realisation of that goal.[40] To be sure, the test is rather vague and mainly serves to exclude those offences that are manifestly not adapted to accomplish any political objective. Beyond those obvious cases, it raises many questions as to the nature of the goal, the offence and the relation between the two.[41] We have noticed in the previous paragraph that a political objective can be more modest, like the pursuit of governmental reforms or greater freedom for minorities. But if the fugitive were to harbour more ambitious plans, like the toppling of a regime, should his offence then, in time, have been quite near the achievement of that goal or have been, potentially, instrumental in accomplishing it? Apart from being counterfactual, such criteria appear to

39 Gilbert, supra footnote 9, dedicates separate paragraphs to the approaches of the United States, France and Ireland as well.

40 See the Swiss case of *Nappi*, supra footnote 17, and the British case of *Cheng v. Pentonville Prison Governor*, [1973] AC 93, inquiring whether the offence was not 'too remote' from the political object.

41 In the case of *Cheng v. Pentonville Prison Governor*, Lord Diplock admitted this implicitly by holding that 'It is unnecessary for the purposes of the present appeal, and would, in my view, be unwise, to attempt to define how remote that object might be.'

be either rather arbitrary or too demanding. A reasonable interpretation of the 'proximity test' would allow the offence to be directed at some intermediate result, as a stepping stone towards the realisation of the ultimate objective.[42] However, as long as it remains unclear whether the ultimate political goal or some intermediate success is the correct point of reference, the application of the proximity test is fraught with difficulties.[43]

5.3.2 Proportionality and subsidiarity

In British cases, the proximity test has been conflated with the question of whether the offence was proportionate to the harm caused to innocent civilians. In the case of *T v Secretary of State for the Home Department*, the applicant, seeking asylum under the 1951 Refugee Convention, had been involved in a bomb attack at an airport killing 10 people. In addressing the question of whether the crime was a political crime, which, for the purposes of the application of Article 1F of the convention, must be answered on the basis of similar criteria as in extradition cases, the House of Lords repeated the well-known mantra that the offence had to be committed for a political purpose and there was a sufficiently close and direct link between the crime and the alleged political purpose. In determining whether such a link existed, the court

> would consider the means used to achieve the political end and, in particular, whether the crime was aimed at a military or governmental target, or a civilian target, and in either event whether it was likely to involve the indiscriminate killing or injuring of members of the public. Although it was clear that the FIS was a political organisation and that T's motive in becoming involved in the airport bombing was to overthrow the government, the crime, as carried out, was almost bound to involve the indiscriminate killing of members of the public; the link between the crime and the political object which T was seeking to achieve was *therefore* too remote.[44]

The reasoning is inconclusive because it confuses proximity and proportionality. The former requires only the assessment of the efficiency of an instrument – the political offence – to attain a goal, whereas the latter introduces a third parameter into the equation, to wit the 'collateral' – or intended

42 Compare the Dutch case of *Folkerts*, mentioned before (supra footnote 29), in which the Supreme Court held that, for an offence to have a political character, it had to be investigated whether it could, in the reasonable perception of the perpetrator, yield *a result that was directly related* to the ultimate goal (italics mine).

43 Gilbert, supra footnote 9, mentions the Dutch case of *McFarlane v. Public Prosecutor,* 100 *Int. Law Rep.* (1986), 414,425, in which the Supreme Court considered the offences too remote from the offender's goal of the unification of Ireland.

44 *T v. Secretary of State for the Home Department*, House of Lords, 22 May 1996 [1996] 2 All ER, 865 (italics added).

– harm to civilians. No one would deny that the 9/11 attack on the Twin Towers was very efficient in accomplishing a political goal, as it changed, beyond the wildest dreams of Osama bin Laden, world public order. Few would, however, agree that the political purpose justified the sacrifice of thousands of innocent lives.

The Swiss predominance doctrine distinguishes between proximity and proportionality and is, in the opinion of Gilbert, therefore the most refined approach.[45] In case of capital political offences, like homicide and murder, the proportionality test amounts to an inquiry whether it was the sole means of safeguarding the political objective.[46] Proportionality and subsidiarity then coincide, as the political offence would be disproportionate if *and because* other means to achieve the outcome would have been available. To be sure, proportionality and subsidiarity do not always overlap. Even if there are no alternative ways to attain a political objective, a crime may be so heinous that it cannot be justified by any conceivable political goal. Reversely, less serious crimes may be considered a proportionate (and therefore legitimate) tool to further a political object, even if there are other non-criminal, but protracted, alternatives.

5.4 Evaluation: is the political offence exception outdated?

While the legal reasoning may not always have been immaculate and logically sound, courts in several jurisdictions have at least succeeded in developing a consistent pattern of criteria, on the basis of which it can be predicted whether a political offender qualifies to be exempted from extradition. Whenever the fugitive has engaged in excessive violence, when the would-be political offender appears to be a daydreamer and when the extradition request derives from an ally, a befriended state, that can pride itself on institutions respecting democracy and the rule of law, the defence is likely to falter.

It sheds a sobering light on the exception. Detached from its 19th-century high-minded ideals, it has become, as might have been expected, an instrument of political use and abuse. None of the criteria of proximity, proportionality and subsidiarity, as such, are unreasonable, but they have accommodated favourable political outcomes. Besides, their combined application has been conducive to a continuous reduction of the exception.

It begs the question whether the political offence exception should be maintained at all because it often has the adverse effect of antagonizing other states and/or shielding perpetrators of heinous crimes against prosecution.

45 Gilbert, supra footnote 9, p. 236. After having observed that the English case of T. incorporates proportionality in the remoteness test, Gilbert notes that 'the difference from the Swiss test is that under the Swiss interpretation, even if the crime is proximate to the ultimate goal of the transnational fugitive offender's organization, the means used might still be disproportionate and, thus, not political in character.'

46 *Ktir v. Ministère Public Fédéral*, 34 *Int. Law Rep.* (1961), pp. 143–144.

Moreover, many have advocated its replacement by a general human rights exception, arguing that other, more politically inspired, rationales are obsolete in a politically, more strongly integrated world order.[47] Although these arguments make some sense, they are particularly appropriate for like-minded states that have a more or less common political culture, including shared perceptions on the state's limitations vis-à-vis individual freedom and respect for political diversity. Beyond that regional context, political consensus cannot be taken for granted. And even between friends, it may sometimes be wise to keep aloof in internal politically sensitive issues, as the recent case of Julian Assange demonstrates. The quibbling over the political nature of his alleged crimes should not be considered as 'only' a convenient tool for his counsels to obstruct the cause of justice; rather, it reflects true differences of opinion on the reprehensibility of his actions, which are at the core of any political dispute.[48] Moreover, replacing the political offence exception by a general human rights exception comes at a serious price. As noticed earlier, states do not have to elaborate on the reasons why they actually refuse extradition in case of a political offence; the mere announcement that the contracting parties do not extradite for political offences suffices. In contrast, any refusal of extradition on the basis that human rights are likely to be violated in the requesting state implies *eo ipso facto* a disapproval of its legal system. When states consider abandoning the political offence exception, they are well advised to think twice about forfeiting such an important asset.

Nothing prevents states from abolishing the political offence exception in their extradition relations any more than that they are under no obligation to include this exception in the first place. The abolition of the political offence may be considered as a legal imprimatur of the shared sense that states are politically approximated sufficiently to do so. However, politically, it would be unsound to reverse the order and get rid of the exception as an incentive to shrug off political disputes.[49]

As has been briefly noted before, the political offence exception has completely vanished within the legal framework of the European Arrest Warrant. This development reflects the high level of political integration within the European Union, which has made the rationales underpinning the exception largely obsolete. It is not likely that states will sympathise with the cause of

47 See, for instance, Christine van den Wyngaert, 'The Political Offence Exception: How to Plug the Terrorist Loophole without Departing from Fundamental Human Rights,' 62 *International Review of Penal Law* (1991), p. 291.

48 See: Politico, 11 April 2019: 'Dispute over Political Crimes Looms over Assange's Extradition'; https://www.politico.com/story/2019/04/11/julian-assange-extradition-1271842.

49 That was the main purport in an earlier contribution on the topic, see Harmen van der Wilt, 'The Political Offence Exception in Extradition Law: An Antidote to Pre-fixed Ideas about Political Integration in Europe?' 4 *Maastricht Journal of European and Comparative Law* (1997), p. 25.

political radicals or separatists who seek to challenge the political institutions of their allies, nor would they wish to keep aloof in case of such serious internal political disturbances. Moreover, any concerns that the fugitive may be exposed to unfair proceedings and discriminatory treatment are difficult to square with the presumed trust in the criminal law systems of the member states, which sustains the principle of mutual recognition of judicial decisions. It does, of course, not imply that surrender proceedings are never affected by political tensions, as the case of former Catalan president Carlos Puigdemont amply demonstrates. Spain has issued three European Arrest Warrants – two to Belgium and one to Germany – to obtain custody over the figurehead of the Catalan separatist movement, causing much embarrassment amongst the requested states. So far, its efforts have not yielded the desired result as courts have refused the surrender by invoking lack of dual criminality.[50] The outcome of the still pending procedures in Belgium is uncertain because the conduct for which the surrender is requested, to wit, sedition and embezzlement of public funds, arguably constitute criminal offences under Belgian law.[51]

It is questionable whether the political offence exception – had it been preserved in the Framework Decision on the European Arrest Warrant – would have provided an easy way out of the conundrum. Whatever decision the Belgian or German courts would have taken by either accepting the defence or rejecting it, they would have been accused of political bias.[52] Perhaps we should submit that such highly sensitive political issues cannot be resolved by relatively straightforward legal devices.

Beyond the regional context of the European Union, the political offence exception will probably survive.[53] It is incorporated in extradition treaties

50 According to the German Oberlandesgericht of Schleswig Holstein, sedition would not constitute a crime under German criminal law. For a very critical comment, see Daniel Sarmiento, Verfassungsblog, 11 April 2018, 'The Strange (German) Case of Mr. Puigdemont's Arrest Warrant'; https://verfassungsblog.de/the-strange-german-case-of-mr-puigdemonts-european-arrest-warrant/.

51 Compare Auke Willems, 23 October 2019, 'Will Spain's Latest Attempt to Extradite Carles Puigdemont Succeed?'; https://blogs.lse.ac.uk/europpblog/2019/10/23/will-spains-latest-attempt-to-extradite-carles-puigdemont-succeed/.

52 Briefly on the political offence exception in the context of the Puigdemont case, Alex Tinsley, who merely observes that the demise of the political offence exception is not remarkable, as it has lost currency; https://www.freemovement.org.uk/european-arrest-warrant-carles-puigdemont/.

53 Even in a regional extradition treaty like the Inter-American Convention on Extradition, OAS, Caracas, 25 February 1981, A 36 Organización de los Estados Americanos, it features as an, albeit optional, ground for refusal in Article 4: 'When, as determined by the requested State, the offense for which the person is sought is a political offense, an offense related thereto, or an ordinary criminal offense prosecuted for political reasons. The requested State may decide that the fact that the victim of the punishable act in question performed political functions does not in itself justify the designation of the offense as political.'

worldwide and regularly invoked and accepted. In reducing the ambit of the exception more systematically, states have opted for piecemeal solutions, first investigating the common ground and then inquiring why they agreed that some crimes should be outside the scope of the exception. In essence, this strategy is no different from the one adopted by the European states, albeit on a more limited scale.

6 Extradition and international crimes

War crimes and crimes against humanity

6.1 Introduction

It is clearly understood that perpetrators of international crimes should be punished.[1] During the period that preceded the establishment of the ad hoc tribunals and the International Criminal Court, no other option was available than that states would engage in such criminal law enforcement and, to that purpose, extradition was considered an indispensable legal instrument. The title of the UN General Assembly resolution on the topic stressed the relevance of extradition within the matrix of international cooperation: 'Principles of international cooperation in the detection, arrest, extradition and punishment of persons guilty of war crimes and crimes against humanity.'[2] Paragraph 5 of this resolution stipulates that

> persons against whom there is evidence that they have committed war crimes and crimes against humanity shall be subject to trial and, if found guilty, to punishment *as a general rule in the country in which they have*

1 This chapter addresses some of the international crimes *stricto sensu,* in other words, the so-called core crimes under the jurisdiction of the International Criminal Court. It will deal with only two categories, to wit war crimes and crimes against humanity and not engage in a discussion of aggression and genocide. Moreover, the focus in this chapter will be on war crimes. Currently, no comprehensive convention on crimes against humanity exists, obliging states parties to extradite (or prosecute) perpetrators of such crimes. A draft convention is under the scrutiny of the International Law Commission. See the special issue of the *Journal of International Criminal Justice*, Volume 16(4), September 2018: Laying the Foundations of a Convention on Crimes against Humanity,' in particular the opening article by Leila Nadya Sadat, 'A Contextual and Historical Analysis of the International Law Commission's Draft Article for a New Global Treaty on Crimes against Humanity,' 16 *Journal of International Criminal Justice* (2018), pp. 683–704. On extradition provisions in the draft convention: Harmen van der Wilt, 'Extradition and Mutual Legal Assistance in the Draft Convention on Crimes against Humanity, 16 *Journal of International Criminal Justice* (2018), pp. 795–814.

2 UN Gen. Ass. Res. A/RES/3074 (XXVIII), 3 December 1973.

DOI: 10.4324/9780429956683-6

> *committed these crimes*. In that connection, States shall cooperate in *questions of extraditing such persons*.[3]

The provision displays a preference for prosecution and trial in the state *loci delicti* whose citizens have primarily been the victims of atrocities and suggests that war criminals are to be surrendered to that state. Simultaneously, other paragraphs allude to potential obstacles to extradition we encountered in previous chapters, sometimes simply noting them, sometimes attempting to remove them. Accordingly, paragraph 2 refers to and even indirectly acknowledges the non-extradition of nationals by recognising every state's right to try its own nationals for war crimes and crimes against humanity. And paragraph 7 makes it quite clear that the political offence exception is not available for those suspected of war crimes or crimes against humanity.[4]

Like most (non-binding) resolutions of the United Nations, the intentions are lofty, but, as the focus is on the end result, the problems and contradictions are clothed in vague language, left to be resolved by the states. The main issue with international crimes is that there is no one, single state that is eligible or has a primary right to take on prosecution and trial because it is inherent to international crimes that their prosecution is the (common) responsibility of all states. The Preamble of the Rome Statute makes this perfectly clear by forging a link between the selection of 'the most serious crimes of concern to the international community as a whole,' the urgency that 'they must not go unpunished' and making this 'the duty of every State to exercise its criminal jurisdiction over those responsible for international crimes.'[5] Yet, the Preamble bears also evidence to the fact that we have not made much progress since 1973 in determining who (which state) has to do what and when. After all, it rather generally, only 'affirms that the effective prosecution must be ensured by taking measures at the national level and by enhancing international cooperation.'

To be sure, the improvement of the horizontal system of international criminal law enforcement, predicated on interstate cooperation, was not the priority of the states at the Rome Conference. It was precisely the awareness that this 'indirect enforcement system', to coin the words of Bassiouni, was fallible that prompted them to establish the International Criminal Court. However, the major problems haunting the entire system of international criminal justice have always loomed in the background. The gist of the paradox is that the state that, under general international law and principles

3 Italics added.

4 'Par. 7: In accordance with Article 1 of the Declaration on Territorial Asylum of 14 December 1967, states shall not grant asylum to any person with respect to whom there are reasons for considering that they have committed a crime against peace, a war crime or a crime against humanity.'

5 Preamble to the Rome Statute of the International Criminal Court, 17 July 2002, A/CONF. 183/9.

of sovereignty, would be most qualified and eligible to engage in criminal investigation and prosecution has either no interest in doing so, because it is involved in the crimes, or is too partisan to mete out fair justice. In other words, it is either unwilling or too willing. The former problem is acknowledged and addressed in the famous complementarity principle that presumes the state to have priority, but it already takes into account that it will fail to live up to its primary obligations. The entire system of shared responsibility to end impunity is therefore not only meant to herald the common concern of the international community, but also construed as a watertight backup in case states bearing prime responsibility fail to comply with their obligations. The Preamble thus sends a double message of urgency, combined with awareness of the inherent complexity of the project of international criminal justice. The second problem of the too zealous state has less prominence in the major texts, architecture and case law of the International Criminal Court, presumably because the major objective is indeed to end impunity.

This work addresses and discusses interstate cooperation in criminal matters and will therefore not further elaborate on the vertical relationship between the International Criminal Court and states parties. The brief excursion to the Rome Statute merely served to identify the paradoxes and problems that are inherent in the prosecution of international crimes. Part 9 of the Rome Statute on international cooperation has borrowed from horizontal systems but has also tried to emulate them by tailoring conditions to the specific mission the International Criminal Court seeks to accomplish. Most exceptions, like double criminality, political offence and non-extradition of nationals, have been abolished because they would only obstruct the fluid surrender of suspects to the court.[6] Earlier academic writings have expressed concern that the ironing out of the wrinkles did not go far enough in making the system work because it would allow states parties still too much leeway to refuse surrender.[7] However, in practice, the greatest problems have emerged from the systemic paradox that states parties are expected to cooperate faithfully, after their criminal law system has been denounced as inadequate.[8]

If we turn now to the horizontal context of interstate cooperation in respect of the prosecution of war crimes and crimes against humanity, we

6 See B. Swart & G. Sluiter, 'The International Criminal Court and Inter Criminal Co-operation,' in: H.A.M. von Hebel. J. G. Lammers & J. Schukking (eds.), *Reflections on the International Criminal Court: Essays in Honour of Adriaan Bos*, T.M.C. Asser Institute: The Hague 1999, pp. 9–128; and B. Swart, 'International Cooperation and Judicial Assistance – General Problems,' in: A. Cassese et al. (eds.), *International Criminal Court: A Commentary*, Oxford University Press: Oxford 2002, pp. 1561–1579.

7 Sunil Kumar Gupta, 'Sanctum for the War Criminal; Extradition and the International Criminal Court,' 3 *California Criminal Law Review* (October 2000), p. 1.

8 Compare Darryl Robinson, 'Inescapable Dyads: Why the International Criminal Court Cannot Win,' 28 *Leiden Journal of International Law* (2015), p. 323.

should start from the natural reluctance of states to prosecute their own state officials, as identified before. Are there any incentives for a state to overcome such restraint? We will try to prove that there are, but that such willingness is predicated on the assumption that the other state will reciprocate in kind by starting criminal proceedings against its own nationals. While this attitude requires a bigger leap of faith in reciprocity than is usual in the run-of-the-mill extradition configuration, it is only the first step. After all, the second step requires the state to forego its primary claims to territoriality or nationality as a basis for criminal prosecution because otherwise extradition will simply not materialise.

We can elucidate this state of affairs by giving some examples. Let us assume that State A and State B have come to peace after a bloody conflict and State A harbours its own nationals and nationals of State B, both allegedly having been involved in war crimes. If State B moves to seek the extradition of both categories, State A can refuse, claiming a stronger territorial interest in respect of the crimes committed by B's nationals and invoking nationality as a ground for refusal in respect of its own people. At first blush, the situation appears to be quite similar to general extradition of common crimes, but there are two important differences. First of all, an extradition request of B in respect of its own nationals is not likely to come forward (unless B fears that its nationals will face unfair treatment) and, second, B will be apprehensive as to A's vigour to bring its own people to trial. In the worst-case scenario – at least from the perspective of B – A will crackdown on B's nationals while leaving its own people untouched. A can at least partially allay the fears of B by starting criminal proceedings against its own nationals, but it is under no obligation to do so unless a treaty provision explicitly holds otherwise.

It is this stalemate of distrust that is obviously aggravated by the preceding conflict that the 1949 Geneva Conventions have sought to thwart. To that purpose, Article 146 of the Fourth Geneva Convention on the protection of civilians in armed conflict introduces a – qualified – obligation for all states' parties to apply its criminal law system in respect of suspects of 'grave breaches' of the Convention:

> Each High Contracting Party shall be under the obligation to search for persons alleged to have committed, or to have ordered to be committed, such grave breaches, and shall bring such persons, regardless of their nationality, before its own courts.[9]

The provision entails a duty to prosecute, irrespective of the nationality of the perpetrator and addresses, at least partially, the concerns of B in the example (the 'first step'). Interestingly, the article continues by holding that

9 Convention (IV) relative to the Protection of Civilian Persons in Time of War, Geneva 12 August 1949, 75 UNTS 287. The same provision in respect of 'grave breaches' features in Articles 49, 50 and 129 of, respectively, the First, Second and Third Geneva Conventions.

> It may also, if it prefers, and in accordance with the provisions of its own legislation, hand such persons over for trial to another High Contracting Party concerned, provided such High Contracting Party has made out a 'prima facie' case.

The article contains therefore an *aut dedere, aut judicare* construction with the emphasis on and preference for *aut judicare*.[10] It is my contention that the specific design of the principle is related to the nature of war crimes. [11]After all, extradition of war criminals requires a next step on the part of the requested state, putting a heavy burden on its confidence. If State A extradites B's nationals, it not only forfeits its stronger territorial claims, but also it throws its faith in the hands of B that it will indeed genuinely prosecute its fellowmen. If State A extradites its own nationals, it must be confident that State B will not treat them too harshly, while State A has no guarantee that State B will return the favour.

In case of war crimes, extradition shifts the balance of benefits entirely to the requesting state (to the detriment of the requested state). Basically, this can be attributed to the fact that the requested state has a greater interest in the conduct of proceedings in the requesting state than in 'normal' extradition cases and has every reason to be apprehensive of the result. One can easily understand that former enemies will not be inclined to engage in extradition and international cooperation in the wake of an armed conflict because of the lingering distrust. The previous analysis provides a slightly more sophisticated explanation for this attitude based on a balancing of reciprocal obligations and benefits.

Additional Protocol I to the Geneva Conventions extols the advantages of criminal prosecution and trial in the state of commission, where it stipulates that

10 Remarkably, the Pictet *Commentary to the 4th Geneva Convention relative to the Protection of Civilian Persons in Time of War*, International Committee of the Red Cross, Geneva 1958, p. 593 reverses the order between *dedere* and *judicare*, giving the precedence to the former: 'Most national laws and international treaties on the subject refuse the extradition of accused who are nationals of the State detaining them. In such cases, Article 146 quite clearly implies that the State detaining the accused person must bring him before its own courts.'

11 See also the acute observations of Raphaël van Steenberghe, who notes that, contrary to 'later generation' treaties on terrorism and transnational crimes that give priority over extradition to prosecution, the Geneva Conventions and Additional Protocol I, reversely, put emphasis on prosecution: 'Rather, the formula "prosequi vel dedere" (referring to the applicable cooperation regime in these instruments, addition HvdW) seems to be more suitable,' R. van Steenberghe, 'The Obligation to Extradite or Prosecute; Clarifying Its Nature,' 9 *Journal of International Criminal Justice* (2011), p. 1114. For other reflections on the 'hierarchical order' between the two options: Miša Zgonec-Rožej & Joanne Foakes, 'International Criminals: Extradite or Prosecute?' Chatham House Briefing Paper, July 2013; https://www.chathamhouse.org/sites/default/files/public/Research/International%20Law/0713bp_prosecute.pdf, especially, pp. 6–8.

> Subject to the rights and obligations established in the Conventions and in Article 85, paragraph 1, of this Protocol, and when circumstances permit, the High Contracting Parties shall co-operate in the matter of extradition. They shall give due consideration to the request of the State in whose territory the alleged offence has occurred.[12]

There is an implicit encouragement to states parties to desist from their right to refuse extradition of their nationals, but in view of the *aut judicare* alternative it remains an open question whether states will indeed oblige.

While extradition of war criminals in the heat of or shortly after an armed conflict, especially after World War II, has been rare for the reasons expounded above, cases have proliferated after a cooling-off period. They involved suspects who had managed to escape, keeping a low profile and remaining 'under the radar' in their new 'homeland.' Detached from the previous political antagonism, they actually resembled the 'normal' extradition case, the requesting state being the territory where the crimes had been committed and/or representing its nationals who had suffered from the crimes. Nevertheless, such prototypical cases displayed a number of features and raised problems that were inherent both to the nature of the crimes and to the lapse of time since they had been committed.

6.2 Extradition of war criminals: problems and prospects

6.2.1 Issues of time lapse/statutes of limitations

One of the practical problems of any criminal prosecution after a lapse of time is that evidence may have become stale. This is bound to affect extradition proceedings as well, especially if the requested state requires prima facie evidence. One of the reasons why the extradition of Andrija Artuković, who acted as minister of interior in the Nazis-controlled Croatian government during World War II and had allegedly ordered in that capacity the killing of more than 30,000 persons, was that the requesting state – Yugoslavia – had not presented sufficient evidence to sustain the charges.[13] In the *Demjanjuk* case, the court was convinced by sworn statements of witnesses, stating that

> Demjanjuk was a guard who herded prisoners into the gas chambers and then actually operated the mechanism which filled the chambers with gas. In addition, several of the witnesses testified that they saw Demjanjuk beat and maim prisoners, some of whom died.

12 Article 88(2) of the Protocol Additional to the Geneva Conventions of 12 August 1949 and Relating to the Protection of Victims of International Armed Conflicts, 8 June 1977, UNTS, vol. 1125, pp. 3–608.

13 On the authority of Geoff Gilbert, *Transnational Fugitive Offenders in International Law: Extradition and Other Mechanisms*, Martinus Nijhoff: The Hague 1998, p. 386: *Artukovic v. Boyle*, 170 F. Supp. 383 (1959) DCSD Cal.

Surely this was enough evidence that warranted the finding that there was reasonable ground to believe that that the accused was guilty.[14] Ironically, Demjanjuk was later acquitted by an Israeli court, finding that he had been mistaken for Ivan the Terrible, who conducted a reign of terror in Treblinka concentration camp.[15]

The more substantial risk of a prosecution after lapse of time is that the crime may have become statute barred. The topic came to the fore and was most thoroughly discussed in the case of Erich Priebke, whose extradition was sought from Argentina by Italy. Priebke was alleged to have ordered as an SS officer the summary execution of captives as a reprisal for an attack by the Italian Resistance. The bloodbath became notorious as the Fosse Ardeatine Massacre. Priebke was charged with war crimes and crimes against humanity. One of the major issues was whether the crimes had not become subject to statutory limitations, as more than 40 years had passed since their commission. The Argentinean Supreme Court first noted that the topic had not been regulated in the Geneva Convention, but that it had been the subject of the 1970 Convention on the Non-Applicability of Statutory Limitations to War Crimes and Crimes against Humanity.[16] To counter any accusations of retroactive application of this convention, the court had to prove that the Convention was merely declaratory and not constitutive of a rule of international law. The court referred to the final sentence of the Convention's Preamble – 'Recognizing that it is necessary and timely to affirm in international law, through this Convention, the principle that there is no period of limitation for war crimes and crimes against humanity, and to secure its universal application' – and continued as follows:

> That, in respect of this final paragraph of the Preamble, it is noteworthy to observe that the word 'to declare' that featured in the Draft of the Convention was substituted by the word 'to affirm', as a result of the general consensus to consecrate the conventional reception of the already existing principle in international law, implying the imprescriptibility in respect of both war crimes and crimes against humanity.[17]

While the court's subsequent contentions that the prohibition of war crimes and crimes against humanity belonged to the realm of *jus cogens* and were

14 *Demjanjuk v. Petrovsky*, 776.F. 2d, 571.

15 Much later he was extradited by the United States to Germany where he stood trial and was ultimately convicted for complicity in war crimes, being a guard in the death camp of Sobibor. He had used that capacity as an alibi to refute the charges of him being Ivan the Terrible.

16 Erich Priebke, Corte Suprema de Justicia de la Nación, 2 November 1995, section 66. The convention was approved by the General Assembly of the United Nations in its Declaration 2391 (XXIII) and entered into force on 11 November 1970.

17 Priebke, footnote 16, section 68.

therefore not subject to statutory limitations were perhaps slightly apodictic, the court's ruling that the extradition was admissible was an important warning that war criminals could not reap the benefits from keeping aloof for quite some time.

6.2.2 *War crimes and political offences*

As might have been expected (and as was briefly mentioned in the previous chapter), relators have often invoked the political offence exception. Initially, Artuković found a willing ear at the District Court and the Appeals Court, holding that his crimes were indeed political offences because they had been committed at the time of a political uprising. The US District Court of California, after the case having been remanded by the Supreme Court, ultimately made short shrift, and rightly so, of such an overly broad reading of the political offence exception, holding that mere coincidence of the impugned offences and a political disturbance would never suffice. Admitting that evidence corroborated that political uprisings and disturbances indeed existed at all pertinent times, the Court continued:

> Nevertheless, respondent cannot avail himself of the defense merely because the alleged crimes occurred at the same time as a political disturbance. A rational nexus between the alleged crimes and the prevailing turmoil must be demonstrated. In searching for such a connection, the focus of inquiry is on the circumstances, and on the status of those harmed, and not on whether the acts merely were committed during the disorder.

And the court, assessing the context in which the murders were committed, concluded:

> The facts and circumstances in evidence show that the murders were not of a 'political character' within the meaning of the Treaty; they were for personal gain, racial or religious hatred, and/or impermissible vengeance upon disarmed enemy soldiers. Ridding a country of some of its population for such reprehensible reasons, as part of some larger political scheme, is not a crime of a 'political character' and is thus not covered by the political offense exception to extradition.[18]

The court correctly emphasised that, at a minimum, there should be a connection between the offence and a political conflict, in the sense that the offence was instrumental in achieving the political objective. And such relationship was blatantly absent in the case at hand.

18 *Artukovic v. Rison (in the matter of the Extradition of Artukovic)*, 628 F. Supp. 1370 (1986).

Another element of the political offence exception – at least within the conceptual framework of the political incidence doctrine – is that the relator is 'at odds' with the powers that be. From the perspective of the humanitarian rationale of the exception, this requirement makes sense, as the underdogs vying for political power have reasons to be apprehensive of the wrath of their mighty opponents. This aspect was emphasised by a French court in the case of *Spiessens*, a Belgian national who was charged with having collaborated with the Nazis both in Belgium and in France and whose extradition was sought by Belgium. In considering whether the offence would qualify as a political one, the court held that

> Collaboration with the enemy is not considered by French legislation or judicial decisions to be a political offence. Moreover, in time of war, in a country occupied by the enemy, collaboration with the later excludes the idea of a criminal action *against the political organization of the State which characterizes the political offence.*[19]

A similar reasoning would seamlessly apply in case of crimes against humanity and many war crimes that are actively pursued or endorsed by state policy.

Swiss courts have faced no problems in arriving at similar conclusions on the basis of the predominance theory. In the case of Kroeger, the Swiss Federal Tribunal took the opportunity to explain why mass executions and other crimes against humanity should be excluded from the scope of the political offence exception. Former SS Sturmbahnführer Kroeger had been part of an Einsatzgruppe and, in that capacity, had been involved in the killing of Jews and communists, one particular notorious incident being the execution of Jews in Dobromyl. In 1966 the *Land* of North Rhine Westphalia sought Kroeger's extradition from Switzerland. Kroeger argued that his offences – if crimes at all, as he considered them to be legitimate reprisals – had been political in character. The Federal Tribunal rejected his claims, holding that, for a crime to qualify as a political offence:

> The offence must have been committed in the course of a struggle for power in the State and must also be in appropriate proportion to the object pursued, in other words suitable to the attainment of that object. The extinction of human life, one of the most reprehensible crimes, can only appear excusable if it constitutes a last resort in the pursuit of a political objective. On the facts, such a situation does not come into question. The accused was acting at a time when the nationalist socialist regime stood at the pinnacle of its power. He acted against helpless

19 *In re Siessens*, Court of Appeal of Nancy, 10 November 1949, 16 *Int. L. Rep.* 276 (1949) (italics added).

women, children and sick persons who could not possibly have threatened German dominion.[20]

The language is moving and the argument is both succinct and compelling, where the Tribunal succeeds in presenting all ingredients of the predominance doctrine in a forceful rebuttal of the claim that crimes against humanity could ever qualify as political offences. Moreover, the Tribunal inserts elements of the political incidence theory (offence must have been committed in the course of a struggle for power and suitable to the attainment of the object) and demonstrates that these are causally related to the proportionality requirement. The butchering of innocent civilians – apart from being appalling – cannot be a political offence *because* it is never instrumental to the achievement of any political objective.[21]

While the end result is therefore deeply satisfactory, it must be observed that mass executions of defenceless persons and other crimes against humanity are easy nuts to crack. The regime that has consolidated its power and can, far away from the battlefield, indulge in mass atrocities against defeated opponents is the very antithesis of the paradigmatic political offender that faces a mighty adversary and often has no other option than to resort to violence in order to enforce (legitimate) concessions. The former configuration fits the definition of crimes against humanity like a glove: a widespread or systematic attack on the civilian population, in furtherance of a state or organisational policy.[22] It bears emphasis that ever since the *Tadić* judgement of the ICTY, it is clear that a crime against humanity does not need to have a nexus with an armed conflict.[23]

None of the rationales sustaining the political offence exception would support the inclusion of crimes against humanity. Such atrocities elicit universal abhorrence and condemnation. They do not feature as some kind of internal disturbance, from which other states might better stay aloof. While not all authorities and states would be prepared to accept the right or even

20 *Kroeger v. The Swiss Federal Prosecutor's Office*, 72 *Int. L. Rep.*, pp. 612–613.

21 In the *Arambasić* case, a US court in South Dakota followed a similar approach. Arambasić's extradition was sought by the Republic of Croatia on account of his alleged commission of 'criminal acts against humanity and international law.' The court found that the 'evidence show[ed] that the alleged victims were policemen who were unarmed and had surrendered while others were unarmed civilians' and concluded that such 'atrocities committed upon these unarmed people were not in furtherance of a political cause.' *Arambasić v. Ashcroft and others*, Judgment on Petition for Writ of Habeas Corpus (403 F. Supp. 2d 951 (D.S.D. 2005)), ILDC 709 (US 2005), 18 November 2005, sections 39–41.

22 See Article 7(1) of the Rome Statute.

23 *Prosecutor v. Tadić*, Decision on the Defence Motion for Interlocutory Appeal, Appeals Chamber, IT-94-1, 2 October 1995, section 78, noting that the reintroduction of the nexus requirement between crimes against humanity and armed conflict was only for the purposes of the jurisdiction of the Tribunal, 'since customary international law no longer requires any nexus between crimes against humanity and armed conflict.'

the obligation of states to use coercive power to relieve people from repression, the competence of the International Criminal Court and single states to prosecute and try perpetrators of crimes against humanity is universally acknowledged.[24] And finally, suspects of crimes against humanity will not be able to submit principled reasons why a criminal court will be biased against them and therefore unable to dispense fair justice. Of course, they will claim that the requesting state is 'at odds' with them, but that is not different from a common crime; it does not derive from and is not aggravated by political antagonism that impairs fair judgment. And even if, in a particular case, there may be reasons that the relator will face a violation of fair trial rights on return, that can be addressed in the context of a human rights exception.

Whereas most cases discussed before concern crimes against humanity or the most egregious war crimes, they present a slightly distorted picture. They are the 'obvious cases.' War crimes, however, are a motley grouping. It is not self-evident that none of them would ever qualify as a political offence.[25] The 1975 Additional Protocol to the European Convention on Extradition is therefore rightly cautious in excluding, next to genocide and crimes against humanity, only *explicitly* the grave breaches of the Geneva Conventions.[26] The final section of this chapter addresses the question of why war crimes cannot categorically be excluded from the purview of political offences.

6.3 War crimes as a challenge to the political offence exception

War crimes can be defined as serious violations of the law of war. They originate therefore in international humanitarian law that seeks to regulate

24 See on the concept of humanitarian intervention, Anne Rijniker, 'The ICRC's Position on Humanitarian Intervention,' 83 *ICRC* (June 2001), p. 527. For an adequate definition, see *Humanitarian Intervention, Legal and Political Aspects*, Danish Institute of International Affairs 1999, p. 11: 'Humanitarian intervention is defined as coercive action by States involving the use of armed force in another State without the consent of its government, with or without authorisation from the United Nations Security Council, for the purpose of preventing or putting to a halt gross and massive violations of human rights or international humanitarian law.'

25 The contention of Gilbert, supra footnote 13, p. 395, that 'there is a developing customary international law to the effect that war crimes and crimes against humanity are not to be regarded as political offences' is therefore too sweeping. A mitigating circumstance is that, at the time Gilbert wrote his book, the law had not fully crystallised into the sophisticated doctrines of today.

26 1975 Additional Protocol to the European Convention on Extradition, Strasbourg, 15 October 195, ETS 86. This cautious approach is, however, largely nullified by the open-ended sub c) that excludes also 'any comparable violations of war having effect at the time when this Protocol enters into force and of customs of war existing at that time, which are not already provided for in the above-mentioned provisions of the Geneva Conventions.'

the conduct of combatants, and they are governed by two principles of paramount importance, the principle of distinction between combatants and persons not actively taking part in hostilities and the principle of proportionality. Attempts to identify war crimes in the Charter of the International Military Tribunal at Nuremberg, in the Geneva Conventions and their Additional Protocols and in the Statutes of the ad hoc Tribunals for the former Yugoslavia, Rwanda and Sierra Leone were never meant to be exhaustive. Article 8 of the Rome Statute offers the most comprehensive codification of war crimes so far, but the Rome Statute does not aim to stifle further development of the concept.[27] The provision is classified along two axes. The first one distinguishes between war crimes committed in international armed conflicts and in non-international armed conflicts (Article 8, section 2 sub a and b, versus Article 8, section 2 sub c and e, respectively). The second one is engrafted upon the distinction between the protection of vulnerable persons (civilians, POW's, soldiers being *hors de combat:* Article 8, section 2 sub a ('grave breaches' of the Geneva Conventions) and serious violations of Common Article 3 of the Geneva Conventions: Article 8 section 2 sub c), on the one hand, and – mainly – prohibited means and methods of warfare (Article 8, sub b and sub e), on the other hand.[28]

Libraries are filled with commentaries on war crimes and it is the topic of an ever-expanding body of case law of domestic and, especially, international criminal tribunals, including the International Criminal Court. This work does not aspire to make a new contribution to this impressive amount of knowledge and wisdom. What concerns us is how war crimes fit into the typology of political offences that has been developed in case law, with the very intent to exclude them from its ambit. We wish to identify four features that challenge conventional wisdom on the topic.

First of all, it bears emphasising that war crimes, in contradistinction to crimes against humanity, require a nexus with an armed conflict. In the *Kunarac* case, the Appeals Chamber of the ICTY has clarified what this nexus requirement actually entails:

> The armed conflict need not have been causal to the commission of the crime, but the existence of an armed conflict must, at a minimum, have played a substantial part in the perpetrator's ability to commit it, his decision to commit it, the manner in which it was committed or the purpose for which it was committed. Hence, if it can be established, as in the present case, that the perpetrator acted *in furtherance* of or under

27 Article 10 of the Rome Statute provides that 'Nothing in this Part shall be interpreted as limiting or prejudicing in any way existing or developing rules of international law for purposes other than this Statute.'

28 The second ax more or less coincides with the difference between 'Hague law' and "Geneva law,' but that terminology is outdated and not entirely accurate.

the guise of the armed conflict, it would be sufficient to conclude that his acts were closely related to the armed conflict.[29]

As we may recall, the wording is strongly reminiscent of the criteria, used by a US district court in the *Artukovic* case to exclude the crimes against humanity that Artukovic allegedly had committed from the scope of the political offence exception. In other words, if the district court, in the hypothetical case that it had to assess Kunarac's claim of a political offence, would have consistently applied the benchmark that the crime had been connected to and instrumental in achieving the political goal, it might have offered Kunarac the protection of the exception.

Our second observation touches upon the assertion, sometimes made in case law, that the prototypical political offender is 'at odds' with the powers that be. The inference, then, is that international crimes that are committed at the instigation of, or at least are condoned by, the state would not qualify. However, war crimes are not a prerogative of the state.[30] They can be – and in practice are – also committed by insurgents and rebel groups that seek to challenge the power of the state.[31] On the basis of the 'at odds' yardstick, such non-state actors should at least be allowed to raise – and maybe sometimes will qualify for entitlement to – the political offence exception.

Third, war crimes are not always perpetrated against civilians, a circumstance that serves as an important benchmark to gauge whether a politically inspired offence is disproportionate. The prohibited means and methods of warfare that feature in Article 8(2), sub b and e serve to protect both

29 *Prosecutor v. Kunarac*, Appeal Judgment, IT-96-23 &IT-96-23/1-A, 12 June 2002, section 58, (italics ours). The holding of the Appeals Chamber was quoted verbatim (and confirmed by the Appeals Chamber in *Prosecutor v. Rutaganda*, Appeals Judgment, ICTR-96-3-A, 26 May 2003, section 569. For more detail on the topic, see Harmen van der Wilt, 'War Crimes and the Requirement of an Armed Conflict,' 10 *Journal of International Criminal Justice* (2012), p. 1113.

30 Whether crimes against humanity always require state involvement has long been a matter of controversy. The disjunctive 'state *or* organizational policy' in Article 7 of the Rome Statute points at a negative answer. The Pre Trial Chamber in the Kenya case has confirmed that powerful organisations can engage in crimes against humanity (Decision of the ICC's Pre Trial Chamber), *Situation in the Republic of Kenya*, Decision Pursuant to Article 15 of the Rome Statute on the Authorization of an Investigation into the Situation of the Republic of Kenya, ICC-01/09, 31 March 2010, sections 115–128. What divided the judges was the issue of which features organisations should possess to qualify as potential perpetrators of crimes against humanity. In his dissenting opinion, Judge Kaul professed a more stringent test than the majority, inquiring whether the organisation had 'state-like features'. See on this topic, Claus Kress, 'On the Outer Limits of Crimes against Humanity: The Concept of Organization within the Policy Requirement: Some Reflections on the March 2010 ICC *Kenya* Decision,' 23 *Leiden Journal of International Law* (2010), pp. 855–873. For the current discussion, however, the more pertinent issue is that crimes against humanity are, by definition, not *directed* at the state.

31 It should be recalled that the Rome Statute has codified the war crimes that are committed in a non- international armed conflict.

combatants and non-combatants. They derive from one of the central principles in international humanitarian law, stipulating that the right of parties to an armed conflict to choose methods and means of warfare is not unlimited.[32] The pursuit of victory must always be balanced against the moral and legal imperative to prevent excessive human suffering, which implies, of course, a proportionality test. On the basis of this principle, Article 8(2), sub b, under xvii–xx prohibits the employment of weapons, projectiles and material that cause superfluous injury or unnecessary suffering.[33] These provisions are rather straightforward. If a person's extradition would be sought on the charge of the individual allegedly having committed such a war crime, the requested state would not have many problems in granting the extradition because the disproportionality of the action is implicit in the very criminal provision. More difficult is the famous provision on 'collateral damage' that prohibits an attack if the incidental loss of life or injury to civilians would be 'clearly excessive' to the anticipated military advantage.[34] It requires drawing a balance between the protection of the legal interests of civilians and military necessity, the outcome of which is often uncertain.[35] Now one might counter that this is the job of the requesting state, to be performed during the full criminal trial, but the problem with that argument is that states may harbour different opinions on these sensitive issues.

Finally, targeting civilians may be an intentional strategy to achieve a political objective. Such a sobering establishment of fact challenges the position of the Swiss court in *Kroeger* and of other case law that the attack on civilians, besides being disproportionate, is not effective in the pursuit of a political outcome. Obviously, surprise attacks on civilians, as a method to ignite fear amongst the population, is the favourite weapon of terrorists. One may argue that terrorism is distinct from war crimes. However, the dividing line is extremely thin. The main difference is that war crimes are

32 Article 35(1) of Additional Protocol (I) to the Geneva Conventions.

33 It is rather disturbing that a corresponding provision is lacking in the section on non-international armed conflict, in view of the proliferation of such conflicts.

34 Article 8(2), sub b, under iv considers as a war crime: 'Intentionally launching an attack in the knowledge that such attack will cause incidental loss of life or injury to civilians or damage to civilian objects or widespread, long-term and severe damage to the natural environment which would be clearly excessive in relation to the concrete and direct overall military advantage anticipated.' Again, a corresponding article is lacking in the case of non-international armed conflicts. See, critically, Harmen van der Wilt, 'Towards a Better Understanding of the Concept of "Indiscriminate Attack" – How International Criminal Law Can Be of Assistance,' in; Terry Gill et al. (eds.), *Yearbook of International Humanitarian Law 2019*, Asser Press/Springer: The Hague 2021, pp. 40–41.

35 Compare Jeroen van den Boomgaard, *Proportionality in International Humanitarian Law: Principle, Rule and Practice*, PhD, Amsterdam, 2019, pp. 345–347, who points out that the balancing act in (international) criminal law is easier than in international humanitarian law, as the former requires the degree of excess to be 'clearly,' while in international humanitarian law 'excessive' suffices.

committed during and in connection with an armed conflict (as expounded above) and that war crimes often have a systematic character.[36] That acts of terrorism qualify as war crimes whenever they are committed during a (non-international) armed conflict is explicitly acknowledged in the Statutes for the International Criminal Tribunal for Rwanda and for the Special Court for Sierra Leone.[37] Moreover, the Trial Chamber of the ICTY in the *Galić* case carefully inquired whether Article 51(2) of Additional Protocol ('Acts or threats of violence, the primary purpose of which is to spread terror among the civilian population are prohibited') would qualify as a violation of the laws or customs of war under Article 3 of the ICTY Statute and answered the question in the affirmative.[38] In short, agreement is widespread that terrorism is a war crime whenever it is committed during an armed conflict. The borderline between 'political or religious' terrorism, understood in the colloquial sense, and terrorism as a war crime is thin and somewhat arbitrary, as it depends on whether the conflict has reached the threshold of intensity and protractedness (and the level of organisation of the warring parties) to trigger the applicability of international humanitarian law.[39]

We will separately address the crime of terrorism in the next chapter, so it need not detain us here. Suffice to conclude that war crimes are a multifaceted and complex concept that defies many attempts to exclude these crimes categorically from the purview of the political offence exception. We are not in doubt that most – if not all – war crimes can and should be

36 Although the latter is not a definitional requirement. Article 8, section 1 of the Rome Statute, providing that 'the Court shall have jurisdiction in respect of war crimes, *in particular* when committed as part of a plan or policy or as part of a large scale commission of such crimes,' is indicative of the ICC's jurisdictional priorities and already implies that war crimes need not be systematic.

37 Statute for the ICTR, UNSC Res. 955 (1994), 8 November 1994, Article 4, sub c; Statute for the Special Court of Sierra Leone, UNSC 1315 (2000), 16 August 2000, Article 3 sub d. In both Statutes under the heading of 'Violations of Article 3 Common to the Geneva Conventions and of Additional Protocol II.'

38 *Prosecutor v. Galić*, Judgement, IT-98-29-T, 5 December 2003. The Trial Chamber identified the following elements in the crime of terror as a violation of the law and customs of war (section 133): '1. Acts of violence directed against the civilian population or individual civilians not taking direct part in hostilities causing death or serious injury to body or health within the civilian population. 2. The offender willfully made the civilian population or individual civilians not taking direct part in hostilities the object of those acts of violence. 3. The above offence was committed with the primary purpose of spreading terror among the civilian population.'

39 In an earlier publication, we have advanced this rather arbitrary division between terrorism as a war crime and terrorism 'in peace' as an argument to incorporate terrorism within the jurisdiction of the International Criminal Court; see Harmen G. van der Wilt & Inez Braber, 'The Case for Inclusion of Terrorism in the Jurisdiction of the International Criminal Court,' in: T. Mariniello (ed.), *The First Ten Years of the International Criminal Court: Achievements and Challenges*, Routledge: London 2015.

kept outside the realm of political offences, but such a definite conclusion requires a more profound analysis of the nature of the crime. The arguments sustaining that final conclusion largely coincide with the reasons why terrorism is to be excluded from the political offence exception, so we will revisit the topic at the end of the next chapter.

7 Extradition and terrorism

7.1 Introduction

Terrorism sets the political offence exception in extradition law on edge. The paradox is obvious. Whereas terrorism is the prototypical political offence, every effort has been made to exclude the crime from its ambit, as this would nurture impunity. Such attempts have been thwarted by the fact that there is no generally accepted definition of terrorism, which, of course, illustrates the lack of (political) consensus on the topic. Indeed, terrorism is a notoriously elusive concept. Fletcher has identified a number of characteristics and demonstrates how the concept always succeeds in slipping away from endeavours to get a firmer grip on it.[1]

A helpful working definition has been provided by Bassiouni, who qualifies terrorism as a 'strategy of violence in order to intimidate a population, to achieve a power outcome (for political purposes).'[2]

Bassiouni rightly makes no distinction between state actors and 'private' perpetrators, pointing out that both can be guilty of terrorism, but as the former would, from a semantic point of view, better qualify as perpetrators of war crimes or crimes against humanity – a topic with which we dealt in the previous chapter – the focus will be on the latter.

During the final decennia of the previous century, it seemed nearly impossible to establish a comprehensive convention, taking a generic definition of terrorism as a point of reference. Instead, states focused on the suppression of concrete manifestations of terrorism that captured their attention and the array of so-called sectorial conventions, therefore to a certain extent, mirrors the sequence of favourite strategies of terrorists.[3] A very important break-

1 Compare George Fletcher, 'The Indefinable Concept of Terrorism,' 4 *Journal of International Criminal Justice* (2006), pp. 894–911.

2 M. Ch. Bassiouni, *Legal Responses to International Terrorism*, M. Nijhoff: Dordrecht 1988, p. 87.

3 See, for instance, the Convention for the Suppression of the Unlawful Seizure of Aircraft, The Hague, 16 December 1970, 10 *Int. Legal Materials*, 133 (1971); the UN Convention on the Prevention and Punishment of Crimes against Internationally Protected Persons includ-

DOI: 10.4324/9780429956683-7

through was offered by the International Convention for the Suppression of the Financing of Terrorism.[4] As this convention served to address the financial assistance of all forms of terrorism, the state's parties could simply not evade the troublesome task of agreeing on a generic definition. Article 2 of the convention, therefore, makes the bold step of, finally, grasping the hot potato, when it ventures to qualify as a terrorist offence

> (b) Any other act intended to cause death or serious bodily injury to a civilian, or to any other person not taking an active part in the hostilities in a situation of armed conflict, when the purpose of such act, by its nature or context, is to intimidate a population, or to compel a government or an international organization to do or to abstain from doing any act.[5]

One might have expected that this definition would serve as a model for the convention on penalisation of and international cooperation in respect of the principal crime. It is puzzling why states parties would reverse the natural and logical order by starting with the auxiliary act instead of the main crime, but they could still have easily copied and pasted the definition of the Suppression of Finance Convention into the Comprehensive Convention. However, until today the latter has not materialised.[6] In the latest draft, dating from 2005, the definition of an act of terrorism is included in Article 2:

> 1. Any person commits an offence within the meaning of the present Convention if that person, by any means, unlawfully and intentionally, causes: (a) Death or serious bodily injury to any person; or (b) Serious damage to public or private property, including a place of public use, a State or government facility, a public transportation system, an infrastructure facility or to the environment; or (c) Damage to property, places, facilities or systems referred to in paragraph 1 (b) of the present article resulting or likely to result in major economic loss; when the purpose of the conduct, by its nature or context, is to intimidate a

ing Diplomatic Agents, New York 1973, 13 *Int. Legal Materials* (1974), p. 42; the UN Convention against the Taking of Hostages, New York 1979, 18 *Int. Legal Materials* (1979), p. 1456; and the UN Convention on the Suppression of Terrorist Bombings, 15 December 1997, UNTS, vol. 2149, p. 256.

4 New York, 9 December 1999, UNTS, vol. 2178, p. 197.

5 This section follows (a): 'An act which constitutes an offence within the scope of and as defined in one of the treaties listed in the annex; (The treaties listed in the annex are the sectorial conventions). Both (a) and (b) are the predicate offences that the financer intends to facilitate.'

6 See the UN News Bulletin of 3 October 2018: 'Fight against International Terrorism impeded by Stalemate on Comprehensive Convention'; https://www.un.org/press/en/2018/gal3566.doc.htm.

> population, or to compel a Government or an international organization to do or to abstain from doing any act.[7]

Compared to the corresponding provision in the Suppression of Financing of Terrorism Convention, the *actus reus* has expanded considerably. It comprises not only lethal force, but also damage to property. The focus seems to have shifted to harm to public interests, in view of the explicit concern for government facilities, public transportation systems and economic losses. Moreover, the prudent limitation to the 'civilian or any other person not taking part in hostilities during an armed conflict' has been replaced by 'any person,' obliterating the meaningful differentiation between combatants and non-combatants.

The current drafting of the definition of terrorism in the Comprehensive Convention is deeply troublesome. The gist of the problem is that the concept suffers from obesity. It has become an overloaded monster injected by the worst fears of governments. The downward spiraling probably started with the dissection of the terrorist's motive. Whereas Bassiouni still postulated a graduated intent, in that the intimidation of the population should be instrumental in putting pressure on the government (to achieve a political objective), the current definition(s) have severed the two components. An act of terrorism can thus encompass both an indiscriminate attack on schoolchildren, like the Columbine massacre, that may lack any specific political purpose and a surgical operation on a police office where political prisoners in *garde à vue* are systematically maltreated.

In its careful inquiry into the question whether terrorism had gradually obtained the status of an international crime under customary international law, the Special Tribunal for Lebanon corroborated this 'bifurcated intent.'[8] On the basis of a comprehensive investigation of national legislation, international instruments and case law, the Appeals Chamber acknowledged that such a rule had indeed emerged, at least as far as terrorism in time of peace was concerned, and it identified the following key elements:

> (i) the perpetration of a criminal act (such as murder, kidnapping, hostage-taking, arson, and so on), or threatening such an act; (ii) the intent to spread fear among the population (which would generally entail the creation of public danger) *or* directly or indirectly coerce a national or

7 Draft Comprehensive Convention against International Tterrorism, A/59/894/ Appendix II.

8 The adjective *bifurcated* intent - is an inspired invention of Manuel J. Ventura, 'Terrorism According to the Special Tribunal for Lebanon's Interlocutory Decision on the Applicable Law: A Defining Moment or a Moment of Definition?' 9 *Journal of International Criminal Justice* (2011), pp. 1021–1042.

international authority to take some action, or to refrain from taking it; (iii) when the act involves a transnational element.[9]

The problem with this overly broad definition of terrorism is that its bifurcated intent completely ignores the complicated relationship of terrorism and political offences. Both conventions stipulate in exactly similar words that the political offence exception shall not apply to terrorism:

> None of the offences set forth in article 2 shall be regarded for the purposes of extradition or mutual legal assistance as a political offence or as an offence connected with a political offence or as an offence inspired by political motives. Accordingly, a request for extradition or for mutual legal assistance based on such an offence may not be refused on the sole ground that it concerns a political offence or an offence connected with a political offence or an offence inspired by political motives.[10]

One is inclined to wonder what the purport of this provision actually is. In case of mere intimidation of the population (the massacre variant), it is redundant because any political motive will probably be lacking. But in the case of a criminal offence that is directed at official authority, without the intermediate terrorising of the population as a lever to coerce a government to take some action (or abstain from doing so), it is far too rigorous and it effectively means the death knell for the entire political offence exception. What is worse is that the disjunctive construction dilutes the notion of terrorism and distracts attention from the paradigmatic case in which political offenders indeed target civilians in order to compel governments to give in to their demands. It is clear that such a scenario is *a fortiori* excluded from the purview of the political offence exception – and rightly so – but now that it is buried between the fringes of terrorism that hardly deserve that label, the reason why such exclusion is imperative has become completely obfuscated.

To be sure, Article 2 of the 1999 Convention for the Suppression of Terrorism was still on the right track. While it allowed for the 'bifurcated intent,' thus expanding the concept of terrorism, there was compensation in the *actus reus* that focused on civilians being sacrificed and instrumentalised in order to ignite fear in the population or to obtain political benefits. The degeneration of terrorism gathered momentum in the definition, proposed

9 *Prosecutor v. Ayyash et al.* Interlocutory Decision on the Applicable Law: Terrorism, Conspiracy, Homicide, Perpetration, Cumulative Charging, STL-11-01/I, 16 February 2001, section 85 (italics added). The Special Tribunal added that an incipient rule of customary law would cover terrorism as an international crime during armed conflict and that a broadening of the scope of terrorism might therefore be imminent (section 109).

10 Article 14 of the Convention for the Suppression of the Financing of Terrorism and Article 15 of the Draft Comprehensive Convention on Terrorism.

in the Comprehensive Convention that mirrored in the *actus reus* all the sly attempts of governments to stigmatise their opponents as terrorists. The efforts to come to a common understanding of terrorism have therefore fallen prey to political consumption and it is wry to conclude – although perhaps not more than a commonplace – that 9/11 has been of decisive importance in this process of deterioration.[11]

Regrettably, the Special Tribunal for Lebanon has not been able to stem the tide, although it can hardly be blamed for this, as the tribunal's task was to inquire what the law was rather than to further develop it. The indication of the *actus reus* as 'the perpetration of a criminal act (such as murder, kidnapping, hostage-taking, arson *and so on* (sic))' refers to any violent act and has hardly any restrictive value. A half-hearted attempt is made to delimit the scope of the crime by adding the contextual element that terrorism 'is a threat to the stability of society or the State.'[12] However, as any state would be allowed to indicate that its stability is at risk, this qualification adds little value.

It is to be hoped (and to be expected) that the comprehensive convention will never be accepted, as it is both overinclusive and underinclusive and leads astray from all earnest attempts to grasp the essence of terrorism (and to do something about it). In the rest of this chapter we will try to uncover why the deliberate targeting of civilians as an instrument to obtain political goals – the prototypical terrorist act – is to be excluded from the scope of political offences. To that purpose, we will analyse both case law and academic (political-philosophical and legal) writings on the topic.

7.2 The exclusion of terrorist crimes from the political offence exception: in search of the bottom line

Any examination of the hypothesis that an indiscriminate attack on civilians, as a strategy to obtain political objectives, is outside the realm of the political offence exception must in our view start with the inquiry whether case law indeed acknowledges such an attack as a relevant reason for denying the application of the exception. The next step will be to investigate whether moral and legal arguments sustain that premise.

It is illustrative in this context to contrast two cases that, respectively, dealt with an ambush by a radical offshoot of the Irish Republican Army (IRA) on a British military convoy and an attack on a passenger bus on its way to Tel Aviv by the Palestinian Abu Nidal Organisation. In the first case, the relator, Mr. Doherty, was charged with being involved in the murder

11 Compare Antonio Cassese, 'Terrorism Is also Disrupting Some Crucial Legal Categories of International Law,' 12 *European Journal of International Law* (2001), p. 993.

12 Interlocutory Decision, supra footnote 9, section 97. The phrasing is probably inspired by the European Union Council Framework Decision on Combatting Terrorism, 13 June 2002, OJ EU 164 (2002), p. 3, that reserves the label of terrorism to acts that, given their nature or context, may seriously damage a country or international organisation.

of a British captain, which resulted from the exchange of fire between the two groups.[13] The New York district court accepted Doherty's claim to the political offence exception and refused extradition on that basis. More interesting, however, were its deliberations on the factors that limited the exception's scope. The court started by pointing out that

> no act (should) be regarded as political where the nature of the act is such as to be violative of international law, and inconsistent with international standards of civilized conduct.

It drew an interesting parallel between war crimes and terrorism, as propounded earlier:

> Surely an act which would be properly punishable even in the context of a declared war or in the heat of open military conflict cannot and should not receive recognition under the political exception to the Treaty.[14]

Next, the court contrasted the case under scrutiny with examples of indiscriminate violence that would not qualify as political offences:

> We are not faced here with a situation in which a bomb was detonated in a department store, public tavern, or a resort hotel, causing indiscriminate personal injury, death, and property damage. Such conduct would clearly be well beyond the parameters of what and should properly be regarded as encompassed by the political offense exception to the Treaty.[15]

And it concluded its findings by clarifying that the killing of the British captain was the scholarly example of a political offence:

> Instead, the facts of this case present the assertion of the political offense exception in its most classic form. The death of Captain Westmacott, while a most tragic event, occurred in the context of an attempted ambush of a British army patrol. It was the British Army's response to that action that gave rise to Captain Westmacott's death.[16]

In the *Matter of the Extradition of Atta*, the relator who was allegedly involved in the attack on a passenger bus on its way to Tel Aviv, after some wanderings ended up before a US district court that had to decide on

13 United States District Court, S.D. New York, *Matter of Doherty,* 599 F. Sup, 270.
14 *Matter of Doherty*, supra footnote 13, p. 274.
15 *Matter of Doherty*, supra footnote 13, p. 275
16 *Matter of Doherty*, supra footnote 13, p. 276.

an extradition request of the Israeli government.[17] In rejecting the 'broad approach' to the political offence exception, implying that 'any atrocity, if politically motivated, would constitute a political act,' the court drew heavily on the findings in the *Doherty* case. The court applied the rules of engagement that served as a neutral standard in order to determine what acts are justifiable in an armed conflict by analogy.[18] And on the basis of that standard it concluded that the attack on the bus, not being a military target and its passengers not being part of the Israeli military, would not qualify as a political offence.[19]

In the case of *Eain v. Wilkes,* a US court of appeals reached a similar conclusion, while following a slightly different route.[20] Petitioner, whose extradition was sought by Israel on the charges of him having detonated a bomb in a marketplace in Tiberias that had killed two boys and the maiming of more than 30 other people, had openly avowed that the act had been incidental to the PLO's efforts to expel the (Israeli) civilian population from Palestine. It was therefore directed at (part of) the civilian population. The court countered the petitioner's claim by holding that

> The definition of 'political disturbance,' with its focus on organized forms of aggression such as war, rebellion and revolution, is aimed at acts that disrupt the political structure of a State, and not the social structure that established the government. The exception does not make a random bombing intended to result in the cold-blood murder of civilians incidental to a purpose of toppling a government, absent a direct link between the perpetrator, a political organization's political goals, and the specific act. Rather, the indiscriminate bombing of a civilian populace is not recognized as a protected political act even when the larger 'political' objective of the person who sets off the bomb may be to eliminate the civilian population of a country.[21]

It is quite important to highlight the exact purport of the court's considerations at this point. In our view, the issue is not – at least not primarily – whether the acts would be effective to accomplish the political objective. Nor did the court engage in any evaluation of whether the final political goal was legitimate, by balancing it against the state's repressive policy.[22]

17 *In the Matter of the Extradition of Atta*, 706 F. Supp. 1032 (1981). For a case comment, see Nancy M. Green, 'In the Matter of the Extradition of Atta: Limiting the Scope of the Political Offence Exception,' 17 *Brooklyn Journal of International Law*, 447 (1991).

18 *In the Matter of the Extradition of Atta*, supra footnote 17, pp. 1044–1045.

19 *In the Matter of the Extradition of Atta*, supra footnote 17, pp. 1042–1047.

20 *Eain v. Wilkes*, US Court of Appeals, 7th Cir., 641 F 2d. 504 (1981).

21 *Eain v. Wilkes*, supra footnote 20, p. 520–521.

22 We disagree with Nancy Green's criticising the predominance test, as applied by the Court in *Eain v. Wilkes*, supra footnote 20, p. 463: 'While the predominance test is more flexible

The crux of the matter was that the court made a principled distinction between the political realm, represented by a government in power, and the social fabric underlying the political structures. It noted a certain correspondence between anarchists and terrorists in this respect, observing that 'The anarchist's efforts were not directed at the government, but instead were "directed primarily against the separate body of citizens."'[23]

The separation between the social sphere and the political power that is the actual opponent has a parallel in and is derived from the distinction between civilians and combatants in armed conflict. The principled adherence to keeping these realms apart may be the key to cleansing the political offence exception from terrorism and war crimes alike.

7.3 Reflections on the separation between the social and the political

The distinction between civilians/non-combatants and political power/enemy combatants as a normative basis for denying the political offence exception to terrorists and war criminals hinges on the assumption that such a separation is at all possible. In classic discourses on the law of war this premise was by no means self-evident. Vattel, for instance, contends that:

> When the sovereign or ruler of the state declares war against another sovereign, it is understood that the whole nation declares war against another nation: for the sovereign represents the nation, and acts in the name of the whole society.

And he continues by holding that: 'Hence, these two nations are enemies, and all the subjects of the one are enemies to all the subjects of the other.'[24] He even ranks women and children amongst the enemies, admitting though that they should not be treated like men bearing arms.[25] Later on, he explains why women, children, feeble old men and sick persons are to be spared:

---

than the incidence test, it is open for abuse because it gives the judiciary the task of determining if a given political objective is legitimate. It hardly seems appropriate for a court to pass judgment on either the political structure of a foreign government, or the legitimacy of a political movement to change an existing form of government.' There is no evidence at all that the Eain-court made such value judgments.

23 *Eain v. Wilkes*, supra footnote 20, p. 521. The quotation is from the classic British case of *In re Meunier*, 2 QB 415, 419, in which the British court discounted Meunier's claim that his activities aimed at terrorising an entire population in order to subvert a government through social disorder fell within the political offence exception.

24 Vattel, *Book III Of War*, Chapter V, section 70, available at: constitution.org/2.Authors/vattel/vattel_03.htm.

25 Vattel, supra footnote 24, section 72.

> But these are enemies who make no resistance; and consequently we have no right to maltreat their persons, or use any violence against them, much less to take away their lives.[26]

The rationale has an unmistakably utilitarian lure: because these innocuous beings pose no threat, we can afford ourselves to be merciful and leave them unharmed.

A stronger impetus for the principled separation of the individual and the state/public body is offered in the teachings of Rousseau, who, well known for advocating the subordination of individual liberty to the common good, adamantly insisted that the identification between the individual person and the state/sovereign could never be absolute:

> But we must also consider the private persons who make up the public, apart from the public personified, who each have a life and liberty independent of it. It is very necessary for us to distinguish between the respective rights of the citizens and the sovereign and between the duties which men must fulfill in their role as subjects from the natural rights they should enjoy in their role as men. It is agreed that everything which each individual gives up of his power, his goods, and his liberty under the social contract is only that part of all those things which is of use to the community, but it is also necessary to agree that the sovereign alone is the judge of what that useful part is.[27]

The final part of the quotation opens the abyss to the tensions and contradictions that pervade Rousseau's work in general and his *Social Contract* in particular. After all, what if the state demands total commitment from its citizens, a quest that especially is likely to be made in case of war when the existence of the public community is at stake? Then, the community and the individual will coalesce and any distinction between them is illusory.[28] Rousseau himself is aware of the paradox when he asserts that

> Once the public interest has ceased to be the principal concern of citizens, once they prefer to serve State with money rather than with their

26 Vattel, supra footnote 24, section 145 (emphasis added).

27 Jean-Jacques Rousseau, *The Social Contract*, translated with introduction by G.D.H. Cole, J.M. Dent: London 1993, p. 2; https://oll-resources.s3.us-east-2.amazonaws.com/oll3/store/titles/638/0132_Bk.pdf. Originally published in 1768.

28 See on this merger of the individual and the nation in modern warfare, Geoffrey Best, *War and Law since 1945*, Oxford University Press: Oxford 1994, pp. 33/34.

persons, the State will be approaching ruin. Is it necessary to march into combat? They will pay some troops and stay at home.[29]

Armed conflict in the modern age has corroborated the quandaries, presaged by Rousseau, in particular in the guise of the 'total war' (*Totaler Krieg*), which pits one nation against another. Legal texts that aspired to alleviate the horrors of warfare expressed reluctance in making a radical distinction between combatants and civilians. For example, Article 37 of the famous Lieber Code, which served as a model for the Hague Conventions on the law of war, pledged in somewhat vague terms respect for the persons of inhabitants of hostile countries occupied by the United States and mentioned women in particular.[30]

However, the catastrophic consequences of the total merger between state and individual, characteristic of the totalitarian state,[31] have given the impulse to the post–World War II initiatives to, first, render protection of individuals against their own state and, next, the establishment of the principle of distinction in international humanitarian law. The four Geneva Conventions of 1949 are predicated on the idea that non-combatants, including civilians, are to be protected against attack. And while modern guerrilla warfare has hampered the quest for strict distinction, the principle is now firmly rooted in both international and non-international armed conflicts.[32]

While the principle has emerged in the context of armed conflict, it *a fortiori* applies in peacetime because then relations between the state and its citizens become more relaxed, leaving the latter space to arrange and lead their own lives. Any political offender must observe and respect this distinction, not because an onslaught on civilians is not effective in reaching

29 Rousseau, supra footnote 27.

30 Instructions for the Government of Armies of the United States in the Field; Prepared by Francis Lieber, promulgated as General Orders No. 100 by President Lincoln, 24 April 1863, Article 37: 'The United States acknowledge and protect, in hostile countries occupied by them, religion and morality; strictly private property; the persons of the inhabitants, especially those of women: and the sacredness of domestic relations.'

31 See Hannah Arendt, *The Origins of Totalitarianism*, Penguin: London 1988. Originally published in 1950.

32 Additional Protocol I (1977), Article 48: 'In order to ensure respect for and protection of the civilian population and civilian objects, the Parties to the conflict shall at all times distinguish between the civilian population and combatants and between civilian objects and military objectives and accordingly shall direct their operations only against military objectives.' Additional Protocol II (1977), Article 13: '1. The civilian population and individual civilians shall enjoy general protection against the dangers arising from military operations. To give effect to this protection, the following rules shall be observed in all circumstances. 2. The civilian population as such, as well as individual civilians, shall not be the object of attack. Acts or threats of violence the primary purpose of which is to spread terror among the civilian population are prohibited. 3. Civilians shall enjoy the protection afforded by this Part, unless and for such time as they take a direct part in hostilities.'

the political objective, nor because civilians pose no threat. The principal reason is that an attack on civilians subverts the axiomatic rule that there is never a full amalgamation between political power and individual human beings, which implies that the latter cannot be considered as the political offender's foe.

The principle of strict distinction, both in armed conflict and in peace, obviously does not resolve all the intricacies of the political offence exception. It does not address the problem of conscription, nor does it provide ready-made answers to hard cases in which civilians presumably lose their protected status by taking up arms. However, it offers a solid normative argument for the exclusion of terrorists and the vast majority of war criminals from the ambit of the exception. Moreover, it saves courts from engaging in fatal assessments of the legitimacy or justification of the political offender's cause. There is a dubious tendency to gauge the reprehensibility of terrorist attacks, depending on whether they are committed in democratic or authoritarian states, on the basis of the rationale that the former leaves more room for political opposition. The argument is deeply flawed, as it mistakes the primary target for the ultimate power the terrorist seeks to challenge. The kidnapping of Chibok schoolgirls by Boko Haram is no less objectionable than the assaults on the Bataclan concert hall in Paris in November 2015. The preservation of the political offence exception in extradition law requires sanitising it from any apology for terrorism.

8 Irregular rendition

8.1 Introduction

All the fuss surrounding the increase of transnational crime makes one easily forget that the phenomenon is a product of global capitalism itself. Indeed, unconscionable drug cartels govern the market, linking farmers in Colombia who have exchanged their subsistence crops for more profitable staples to the financial tycoons of Wall Street or the City of London, seeking temporal relief from their stressful existence. Even more disconcerting are the arms traders, reaping handsome benefits from selling their sophisticated merchandise to terrorist zealots from whose religious convictions they could not be further apart.

Leaving all the world's hypocrisy and inconsistency behind, we might soberly ascertain that the improvement of mass communication, travel and economic opportunities have boosted transnational crime. Extradition, a cranky, old-fashioned and protracted device, fails to keep pace with these flashy developments. Law enforcement officials are therefore constantly tempted to resort to more flexible methods. Irregular forms of rendition have from time immemorial been waiting in the wings, challenging the monopoly of extradition as the only (lawful) means to regain custody over a fugitive from justice. In discussing such alternatives to extradition, the ultimate question is always whether any irregularities in obtaining custody over a fugitive impede criminal proceedings against him or her. The rather straightforward and negative answer to that question has gained currency as the *male captus, bene detentus* (or *judicatus*) doctrine.[1] However, the

1 The doctrine has been assessed, predominantly negatively, in a score of books and articles. One of the most searching and comprehensive works is Christophe Paulussen, *Male captus bene detentus? Surrendering Suspects to the International Criminal Court*, Intersentia: Cambridge 2010. See also T. Poort, '*Male captus, bene judicatus*: Disguised Extradition and Other Practices,' 1 *Leiden Journal of International Law* (1988), pp. 65–77; D. Radosavljevic, 'Mala Captus Bene Detentus and the Right to Challenge the Legality of Arrests under the ICC Statute,' 29 *Liverpool Law Review* (2008), pp. 269–285; J.A. Frowein, 'Male Captus Male Detentus – A Human Right,' in: R. Lawson and M. de Blois (eds.), *The Dynamics of*

DOI: 10.4324/9780429956683-8

doctrine has increasingly come under siege and rightly so. After all, what is the sense of entering into international conventions that seek to regulate the legal rights of both states and the individual fugitive if one can easily circumvent them?

Any discussion of the case law on irregular rendition will benefit from and, therefore, is to be preceded by a systemic analysis of the legal interests that may be impaired by such devices. Fundamental to the understanding of the legal issues in this context is the distinction between the position of the state that offers temporary refuge to the fugitive and the predicament of the criminal suspect. Different configurations may give rise to shifting alliances.

Abduction by physical force, exercised by law enforcement officials of a foreign state, obviously constitutes the most flagrant violation of both the territorial sovereignty of a state and the fundamental right to personal freedom of the fugitive. In this case, their legal interests coincide and the fugitive will usually have a powerful ally when he attempts to claim his rights in a court of law. *Luring*, id est using subterfuge to cajole the fugitive to return to the state that intends to prosecute him is a more subtle device, but it still implies the application of investigatory measures on the territory of a foreign state.

At the other end of the spectrum, we find the state of refuge having itself an interest in getting rid of a person who allegedly has committed a crime in another state. The former state may decide to refuse entrance at the border, expel the immigrant forthwith or even resort to deportation. Whenever two states conspire to transfer the fugitive for the purpose of putting him or her on trial, without resorting to formal extradition proceedings, we are entering the realm of *disguised extradition*. The problem is, of course, that shared premeditation is often difficult to prove, as the expelling state will have sufficient reasons of its own to remove the unwelcome guest.

Somewhere in between these extremes is the situation in which a state allows law enforcement officials of another state to pursue and arrest fugitives from justice on its own territory. Such extraterritorial criminal law enforcement can be arranged on an ad hoc basis or regulated by means of a treaty, such as the Schengen Convention within the context of the European Union, which, however, restricts executive powers of foreign police officials to situations of hot pursuit and explicitly prohibits those police officials from apprehending suspects.[2] The exercise of investigative powers on foreign territory is confined to serious offences for which extradition is possible. Beyond these legally restrictive contexts, criminal law enforcement by foreign authorities amounts to a severe infringement of a state's sovereignty.

---

the Protection of Human Rights in Europe: Essays in Honour of Henry G. Schermers, Vol. 3, Nijhoff: Dordrecht 1994, pp. 175–185.

2 Article 41 of the Convention from 19 June 1990, Applying the Schengen Agreement of 14 June 1985 between the Governments of the States of the Benelux Economic Union, the Federal Republic of Germany and the French Republic on the Gradual Abolition of Checks at their Common Borders, OJ L 239, 22 September 2000.

There is obviously a tangible difference in two states acting in unison, colluding to accomplish a result that benefits both of them, when compared to the blunt behaviour of a state that infringes the territorial sovereignty of its neighbour in pursuit of its own criminal law interests. While in the latter situation the offended state is likely to lodge formal diplomatic protests, in the former case the fugitive is basically left on his or her own, unsheltered and bereaved of any assistance. From this perspective, it is indispensable to draw a sharp distinction between these situations, inquiring each time whose legal interests are at stake and whether the individual fugitive has any standing of his own to assert infringement of his rights before the court or whether he needs the support of an aggrieved state.

While this brief exposition serves to clarify the playing field of converging and diverging legal interests, it is matched in the international law context by the inquiry into the relevance of extradition treaties. If one starts from the premise that an extradition treaty is the embodiment of a careful balancing of the legal interests of both the requesting and the requested state and the fugitive, one will be inclined to consider the treaty as the sole lawful framework that enables the physical transfer of suspects for criminal law purposes. By implication, any of the devices, mentioned before, would be strictly prohibited. If, on the other hand, one would be prepared to understand the treaty as a convenient arrangement between states that still leaves them leeway to exchange fugitives from justice by other means, its legal relevance is obviously considerably reduced. Implicit in the latter representation is the view that individuals cannot derive rights from extradition treaties. Depending on the opinion one harbours on the issue, the existence of an extradition treaty is therefore relevant. However, overly formal adherence to the principle that any transfer of fugitives beyond the framework of extradition treaties is anathema is an incentive for states to engage in extradition relations as little as possible because they only make life complicated. In fact, it is a truism of the iron rule that the more restrictive and demanding formal extradition is, the more law enforcement officers will be tempted to resort to easy devices.[3]

A final aspect that is important, especially if the legal interests of other states are involved, concerns the question of whether state officials are directly involved in the venture, whether they condone the operation, acting behind the screens, or whether they merely reap the benefits from irregular action. In international law such issues translate into the question whether the state will incur responsibility and will therefore be bound to remedy the unlawful situation which may amount to the repatriation of the fugitive.

All these aspects will feature in the subsequent discussion of case law. The analysis will be followed by several reflections on the approach of

3 See, on this oxymoron, the perceptive observations of A.H.J. Swart, 'Het eeuwige leven van de verkapte uitlevering' ("The eternal life of disguised extradition"), *Recht en Kritiek* 1981, pp. 334–356.

international criminal tribunals, in which the tensions between effective law enforcement in respect of heinous crimes, procedural rights of the relator and state sovereignty ultimately come to the fore. The chapter will be structured on the basis of the specific 'methods' of criminal law enforcement identified before.

8.2 Abduction

The subsequent survey and analysis of case law initially focus predominantly on judgments of US courts. Such one-sided attention may appear lopsided and even biased but it stands to reason. After all, US law enforcement has the power to engage in extraterritorial 'catch and snatch' operations, and the Ker-Frisbie doctrine has set the standard for legal condoning of these practices. Moreover, the analysis serves to demonstrate that courts have ventured rule of law approaches, a development that has regrettably been reversed in the *Alvarez Machain* case.

8.2.1 The Ker-Frisbie doctrine

In the United States, the Ker-Frisbie rule actually reflects the *male captus, bene judicatus* rule. In the *Ker* case, the relator was living in Peru and charged with embezzlement. A Pinkerton agent was commissioned to serve the request for extradition to the Peruvian government, show the warrant of arrest to Peruvian officials and take the fugitive after the approval of the local authorities back to the United States, where he was to stand trial before an Illinois court. As Peru had been entangled, in the meantime, in an armed conflict with Chile, the formal road was blocked and the Pinkerton agent, acting on his own accord, forcibly kidnapped the suspect. Before the Supreme Court, Ker claimed that his due process rights had been infringed, that there was a violation of the US-Peruvian extradition treaty and that his right of asylum (in Peru) had been violated. Ker found a willing ear on none of these points. The Supreme Court confined the applicability of the due process clause of the Fourteenth Amendment essentially to the criminal proceedings themselves, holding that

> The 'due process of law' here guaranteed is complied with when the party is regularly indicted by the proper grand jury in the state court, has a trial according to the forms and modes prescribed for such trials, and when, in that trial and proceedings, he is deprived of no rights to which he is lawfully entitled.[4]

The Supreme Court admitted that due process rights might 'in some manner' be at stake due to irregularities preceding the trial, but suggested that subsequent appropriate proceedings could 'whitewash' the former irregularities:

4 *Ker v. Illinois*, 119 US 436, 440 (1886).

> He may be arrested for a very heinous offense by persons without any warrant, or without any previous complaint, and brought before a proper officer, and this may be in some sense said to be 'without due process of law.' But it would hardly be claimed that, after the case had been investigated and the defendant held by the proper authorities to answer for the crime, he could plead that he was first arrested 'without due process of law.'[5]

Ker's claim that he had obtained a right of asylum in Peru that was violated by the abduction was derided by the Supreme Court, as it seemed to imply that the extradition treaty would provide for such a right:

> There is no language in this treaty or in any other treaty made by this country on the subject of extradition of which we are aware which says in terms that a party fleeing from the United States to escape punishment for crime becomes thereby entitled to an asylum in the country to which he has fled. Indeed, the absurdity of such a proposition would at once prevent the making of a treaty of that kind.[6]

As the extradition treaty had not been used, this obviated any investigation of whether that convention had been violated. And because neither the US Constitution nor the laws and treaties of the United States offered the abducted person any right to resist a trial on account of him being abducted, the Supreme Court did not feel called upon to decide the issue, leaving it to the discretion of the state courts.[7]

In the case of *Frisbie v. Collins*, which concerned a kidnapping in Chicago and a subsequent forcible transfer to Michigan, the dictum in Ker was merely confirmed, the Supreme Court holding that

> This Court has never departed from the rule announced in *Ker v. Illinois* that the power of a court to try a person for crime is not impaired by the fact that he had been brought within the courts' jurisdiction by reason of a forcible abduction.[8]

The *Ker* case was quite particular and probably not emblematic of the most blatant infringements of international law and the relator's rights. After all, the Pinkerton detective had acted on his own account, the United States had attempted to arrange the transfer via the extradition treaty and the Peruvian

5 *Ker v. Illinois*, supra footnote 4, p. 440.
6 *Ker v. Illinois*, supra footnote 4, p. 442.
7 *Ker v. Illinois*, supra footnote 4, p. 444.
8 *Frisbie v. Collins*, 342 US 519, 522 (1952).

government had not lodged any formal complaints against the infringement of its territorial sovereignty.[9]

Ker clarified, however, that if the state itself was not (directly) involved in the abduction and the aggrieved state made no objections, the fugitive stood no chance of challenging any infringement of his rights by claiming that his prosecution should be canceled. Would the situation be different if government officials *were* active in the kidnapping operation or if the state whose territorial sovereignty was infringed *did* lodge complaints? The two parameters should be assessed separately, as the former would reinforce the position of the fugitive, independent of any violation of international law, while the latter would represent forcible abductions basically as an interstate affair.

8.2.2 Rise and fall of the attention for the rights of the fugitive

In the case of *Jaffe v. Smith* the 11th Circuit Court of Appeals insinuated that the fugitive stood a better chance of vindication of his rights if the government itself would be involved in the abduction. Jaffe, being charged with unlawful land sale practices by the state of Florida, had returned to his home in Toronto and had subsequently been forcibly taken by two bounty hunters and transported to the US-Canadian border from whence he was brought to the Florida court. He had filed a habeas corpus writ, arguing that the court lacked jurisdiction to try, convict and incarcerate him because he was abducted from Canada in violation of the treaty of extradition.[10]

The Appeals Court generally followed the Ker-Frisbie line but made an important qualification:

> Absent governmental action, either through a direct violation of a treaty or through circumvention of the treaty, a fugitive has no basis upon which to challenge his/her return to the prosecuting jurisdiction.

The Court clarified that the involvement of the government implied a violation of the treaty:

> Unless a defendant can prove that she or he was removed from the asylum state by governmental action, *and therefore establish a treaty violation*, she or he may not object to trial in the United States.[11]

Deliberate governmental action would imply a violation of the treaty that the fugitive could invoke in court, apparently irrespective of whether the

9 Although Geoff Gilbert, *Transnational Fugitive Offenders in International Law: Extradition and Other Mechanisms*, Martinus Nijhoff: The Hague 1998, p. 343, somewhat tongue-in-cheek observes that the Peruvian government had more serious business on its mind, alluding to the war with Chile.

10 *Jaffe v. Smith*, 825 F.2d 304.

11 *Jaffe v. Smith*, supra footnote 10, p. 14 and 17 (italics added).

state whose territorial sovereignty had been infringed would have made any formal protests.

In the case of *Toscanino*, an Italian citizen who had been charged with conspiracy to import narcotics into the United States, the Court of Appeal in the Second Circuit focused even more strongly on the rights of the accused.[12] Toscanino alleged that he had been kidnapped from his home in Montevideo and brought into the Eastern District Court of New York, only after having been detained for three weeks for the purpose of interrogation accompanied by physical torture in Brazil. He claimed that the US attorney for the Eastern District had been aware of the interrogations and had actually received the reports on its progress.

The court of appeal extensively discussed the Ker-Frisbie rule and observed that

> under the so-called '*Ker-Frisbie*' rule, due process was limited to the guarantee of a constitutionally fair trial, regardless of the method by which jurisdiction was obtained over the defendant. Jurisdiction gained through an indisputably illegal act might still be exercised, even though the effect could be to reward police brutality and lawlessness in some cases.[13]

However, since *Frisbie* the Supreme Court had expanded the interpretation of due process, as the appeals court explained. Pointing to the 'constitutional revolution' and referring to the landmark cases of *Mapp v. Ohio* and *Miranda v. Arizona*, the Supreme Court elucidated that

> No longer is it limited to the guarantee of ' fair trial' procedures at trial. In an effort to deter police misconduct, the term has been extended to bar the government from realizing directly the fruits of its own deliberate and unnecessary lawlessness.[14]

Assuredly, this liberal development had repercussions in the field of the irregular transfer of fugitives from abroad, as the court was quick to note:

> Faced with a conflict between the two concepts of due process, the one being the restricted version found in Ker-Frisbie and the other the expanded and enlightened interpretation expressed in more recent decisions of the Supreme Court, we are persuaded that to the extent that the two are in conflict, the Ker-Frisbie version must yield. Accordingly we view due process as now requiring a court to divest itself of jurisdiction

12 *US v. Toscanino*, 500 F.2d, 267 (1974).
13 *Toscanino*, supra footnote 12, p. 272.
14 *Toscanino*, supra footnote 12, p. 273.

> over the person of a defendant where it has been acquired as the result of the government's deliberate, unnecessary and unreasonable invasion of the accused's constitutional rights.[15]

Distinguishing the case under scrutiny from both Ker and Frisbie, which did not imply the violation of international law, the court held that the United States had pledged to respect the territorial sovereignty of Uruguay both under the OAS Charter and the UN Charter. The court emphasised – and reiterated the previous holding of the Supreme Court – that an infringement of the extradition treaty was not at issue. Again – and echoing the findings of the court in the *Jaffe* case – this violation could have materialised only in case of substantive involvement of the US authorities and the district court was therefore instructed to investigate whether this had been the case.

Despite its progressive approach, the court of appeals did not move far beyond the framework as laid down in *Jaffe v. Smith*. Both for the violation of due process and the infringement of the territorial sovereignty of another state, substantive involvement of the US authorities was decisive, but the two issues had to be neatly separated. Judge Robert Anderson, concurring as to the result, made it abundantly clear that international treaties were not intended to benefit the individual, at least not directly:

> Violation of the standards laid down by these treaties is again indicative of the denial of due process, but not a defense in and of itself. By and large treaties are to be enforced by governments, rather than by their individual citizens, and neither the United States, Uruguay nor Brazil contemplated that, under these circumstances, a defendant could personally seek to invoke these treaties.[16]

In the case of *Lujan v. Gengler*, the Second Circuit Appeals Court corroborated that international treaties served the interests of states, adding that 'individual rights are only derivative through the state.'[17] The court, however, inferred from this interpretation of international law the conclusion that silence on the part of the aggrieved state would vitiate the individual's claim to redress:

> Lujan fails to allege that either Argentina or Brazil in any way protested or even objected to his abduction. This omission is fatal to his reliance upon the charters. The provisions in question are designed to protect the sovereignty of states and it is plainly the offended state which

15 *Toscanino*, supra footnote 12, p. 275.
16 *Toscanino*, supra footnote 12, p. 281.
17 *United States, ex rel. Lujan v. Gelner*, 510 F.2d 62 (1975).

must in the first instance determine whether a violation of sovereignty occurred or required redress.[18]

While the defendant was thus precluded from indirectly benefiting from a violation of international law if the state did not complain, Toscanino implied that he could still invoke severe impairment of his due process rights, which might ultimately lead to the court's divesting itself from jurisdiction. But the liberal honeymoon for the individual petitioner faced with brutal government action was not long to last. First, the Second Circuit Appeals Court held that 'Toscanino only applied when the defendant could prove torture, brutality or similar outrageous conduct' on the part of the government, thus narrowing down the exception to a considerable extent.[19] But the fatal blow was administered by the Seventh Circuit Appeals Court in the case of *Matta-Ballesteros v. Henman*.[20] 'Squarely facing the Toscanino-exception,' the appeals court started by pointing out the exception's constitutional ambiguity. While the *Toscanino* court invoked the Fifth Amendment 'due process clause' that offers protection against excessive force amounting to punishment during pre-trial detention, it actually relied on the Fourth Amendment exclusionary rule that provides a remedy against abuse during arrest. Turning to the case at hand, the appeals court held that

> The fourth amendment covers claims for excessive force such as Matta's under a reasonableness standard by balancing 'the nature and quality of the intrusion on the individual's fourth amendment interests' against the governmental interests at stake.[21]

But the Fourth Amendment exclusionary rule did not sustain Matta's claim. In essence, the court reasoned that any excessive force inflicted on the body of Matta did not affect the credibility of the evidence against him, which implied that the exclusionary rule would not serve the remedial function for which it was invented. Obviously, this finding has a far wider purport, affecting the roots of the exclusionary rule as such, which the court acknowledged by quoting the Supreme Court's holding in *United States v. Crews:*

> The exclusionary principle of Wong-Sun and Silvershore Lumber Co delimits what proof the Government may offer against the accused at trial, closing the courtroom door to evidence secured by official lawlessness. Respondent is not himself a suppressible 'fruit', and the illegality of his detention cannot deprive the Government of the opportunity to

18 *Lujan v. Gelner,* supra footnote 17, p. 63.
19 *Lujan v. Gelner*, supra footnote 17, p. 65.
20 *Matta Ballesteros v. Henman*, 896 F.2d 255 (7th Cir. 1990).
21 *Matta Ballesteros*, supra footnote 20, p. 262.

prove guilt through the introduction of evidence wholly untainted by the police conduct.[22]

In the particular context of abducting fugitives from justice as an 'informal' alternative to extradition, the findings of the court of appeal in Matta Balleteros were quite disastrous for the legal position of the fugitive. First, the court had effectively shut the door to the relator's free-riding on the back of the foreign government (at least as long as that government did not squeak). And, second, it deprived him of an independent recourse to constitutional protection which had been provided in the *Toscanino* case.

8.2.3 Alvarez Machain*: Vindication of* Male captus, bene detentus

The complete erosion of the legal interests of both the fugitive and the foreign state – and the parallel condoning of wild west practices by US law enforcement acting abroad – reached a climax in the infamous *Alvarez Machain* case.[23] At first blush, all the ingredients were in place for predicting a favourable outcome for the defendant who had been forcibly abducted from Mexico in order to stand trial before a US district court on charges of having participated in the kidnapping and murder of Drug Enforcement Administration (DEA) special agent Enrique Calmera. The DEA had orchestrated the abduction, and the operation was officially endorsed by US authorities. An extradition treaty between the United States and Mexico had apparently been flouted by the United States. And the Mexican authorities had vigorously protested the self-indulging activities of the US government. The court of appeals had initially dismissed and had ordered the repatriation of respondent, relying on its decision in the case of *Verdugo Urquidez*. In *Verdugo,* the court of appeals held that the forcible abduction of a Mexican national with the authorisation or participation of the United States violated the extradition treaty between the United States and Mexico, which, along with a formal protest by the offended nation, would give a defendant the right to invoke the treaty violation to defeat the jurisdiction of the district court to try him.[24] The court, in other words, pooled the parameters, identified before, propounding that their mutual reinforcement supported the defendant's claim.

The Supreme Court systematically rebutted all the elements that sustained the *Verdugo* outcome. That an extradition treaty, in the opinion of the Supreme Court, would not impair a forcible abduction and that the violation of such a treaty was not at stake, need not surprise us, as this

22 *United States v. Crews*, 445 U.S. 463, 474 (1981).
23 *United States v. Alvarez Machain,* 504 US 655 (1992).
24 *US v. Verdugo Urquidez*, 939 F.2d 1341 (CA9, 1991).

was stable legal opinion ever since Ker and Frisby. We had the occasion to discuss this point of view earlier in the context of the specialty doctrine. [25]

Quite astounding, however, was the Supreme Court's turning on its head the argument, advanced in *Matta Ballesteros* and *Verdugo*, that any claim of the defendant required the support of the foreign state's protest. Leaving in abeyance the question of whether the defendant could invoke the extradition treaty independently from the foreign state's objections, the Supreme Court merely reminded the defendant of inconsistent reasoning:

> The Extradition Treaty has the force of law, and if, as respondent asserts, it is self-executing, it would appear that a court must enforce it on behalf of an individual regardless of the offensiveness of the practice of one nation to the other nation.[26]

The Supreme Court separated the legal interests involved and isolated the defendant from a powerful ally, thus shattering the fortification that had hitherto constituted his strongest defence. As the Court had already made short shrift of the claim that the extradition treaty was infringed, it could easily refute the defendant's invoking that instrument. The Court was prepared to accept respondent's argument that his abduction was in violation of general principles of law vis-à-vis the Mexican government, but preferred to deal separately with that issue, advocating a 'diplomatic approach to the resolution of difficulties between two sovereign nations, as opposed to unilateral action by the courts of one nation.'[27]

In his sanguine dissenting opinion, Justice Stevens addressed the issue, largely ignored by the majority, that the abduction had been officially approved by US authorities, and he considered this aspect crucial to the question of whether the extradition treaty had been violated:

> A critical flaw pervades the Court's entire Opinion. It fails to differentiate between the conduct of private citizens, which does not violate any treaty obligation, and conduct expressly authorized by the Executive Branch of the Government, which unquestionably constitutes a flagrant violation of international law, and in my opinion, also constitutes a breach of our treaty obligations.[28]

To buttress the relevance of this distinction, Justice Stevens referred to the findings of Justice Brandeis in the case of *US v. Cook*, in which the latter explained that any agreements on the extraterritorial exercise of governmental power that would trespass on another state's sovereign prerogatives

25 See Chapter 4.
26 *United States v. Alvarez Machain*, supra footnote 23, p. 668.
27 *United States v. Alvarez Machain*, supra footnote 23, p. 669.
28 *United States v. Alvarez Machain*, supra footnote 23, p. 682.

were intended to delimit the scope of such power. The encroachment of these limitations would void any subsequent legal action that was predicated on that power in the first place:

> The objection is that the Government itself lacked power to seize, since by the Treaty it had imposed a territorial limitation upon its own authority. The Treaty fixes the conditions under which a 'vessel may be seized and taken into a port of the United States, its territories or possessions for adjudication in accordance with' the applicable laws. Thereby, Great Britain agreed that adjudication may follow a rightful seizure. Our Government, lacking power to seize, lacked power, because of the Treaty, to subject the vessel to our laws. To hold that adjudication may follow a wrongful seizure would go far to nullify the purpose and effect of the Treaty.[29]

Translated to the context of forcible abduction, Brandeis's reasoning would imply that the government would have no right to put the fugitive on trial because it had no power to obtain physical custody over him beyond the confinements expressly indicated in the extradition treaty.

8.2.4 Rising opposition against male captus, bene detentus

Alvarez Machain has been widely commented upon, mostly in negative terms.[30] Nonetheless, it has never been officially revoked by the Supreme Court. Other jurisdictions, however, have, after initial hesitance, gradually become more critical of the *male captus, bene judicat*us doctrine.

In the French case *In re Jolis, t*he defendant, a French citizen, had been captured by French agents in Belgium and had been transferred to France. The court released the defendant, considering the abduction a violation of international law.[31] However, the embrace of the *male captus bene judicatus* doctrine came to the fore in the case of Argoud, an ex-colonel of the French army, who was indicted – and condemned to death in absentia – for his involvement in an attempted assault on the life of General Charles De Gaulle. Arnoud had escaped to Germany, where he had been captured by

29 *Cook v. United States*, 288 US, 102,122 (1933).

30 Compare, for instance, Abraham Abramovsky, 'Extraterritorial Abductions: America's "Catch and Snatch" Policy Run Amock,' 31 *Virginia Journal of International Law* (1991), p. 151; Jonathan A. Bush, 'How Did We Get Here? Forcible Abduction after *Alvarez Machain*,' 4594) *Stanford Law Review* (1993), pp. 939–983; Ruth Wedgwood, 'The Argument against International Abduction of Criminal Defendants, Amicus Curiae Brief Filed by the Lawyers Committee for Human Rights in *United States v. Humberto Alvarez-Machain*,' 6(4) *American University International Law Review* (1991), pp. 537–569. For a 'rare' defence, see Andrew J. Calica, 'Self-Help Is the Best Kind: The Efficient Breach Justification for Forcible Abduction of Terrorists,' 37(2) *Cornell International Law Review* (2004), pp. 389–429.

31 *In Re Jolis*, Tribunal Correctionel d'Avesnes, 7 *Annual Digest* 191 (1933–1934).

private individuals and brought back to France. During his subsequent trial, the French court held:

> [l]a capture à l'étranger d'un citoyen ne priverait pas les tribunaux de son pays du droit et de la compétence de le juger.[32]

In the United Kingdom and its former dominions whose criminal law systems are modeled after the common law, courts made an interesting turn. Initially, they adhered to the *male captus* rule by holding that they lacked the power to inquire into the circumstances under which the defendant had been brought before the court. Whether officials of the forum state had been involved in the operation or not made no difference: the court had no competence to adjudicate the behaviour of law enforcement actions abroad.[33]

However, more or less simultaneously, courts of common law systems started to invoke the abuse of process doctrine as a vehicle to dismiss trials that had been tainted by preceding irregularities in the capture and arrest of fugitives from justice. In the United Kingdom, the first overture to this novel approach was made in *R v. Bow Street Magistrates ex parte Mackeson*.[34] As this concerned a case of deportation – disguised extradition, we will address it later on. But it was New Zealand that deserved the credit for first breaking with the *male captus* rule. In *Regina v. Hartly*, the defendant, charged with murder, had fled to Australia and had subsequently been put on a plane by Australian police officials at the instigation of New Zealand authorities. While an extradition treaty was in force between the two countries, it had been ignored. Judge Woodhouse, speaking for the majority, commented:

> in our opinion there can be no possible question here of the Court turning a blind eye to action of the New Zealand police which has deliberately ignored those imperative requirements of the statute. ... But this must never become an area where it will be sufficient to consider that the end has justified the means. The issues raised by this affair are basic to the whole concept of freedom in society.[35]

Apparently, the court attached importance to the fact that a legal and available route – formal extradition – had been disgarded. Australian courts followed the example of that of their smaller neighbour in the case of *Levinge*, which concerned a coordinated operation by Mexican and US agents in an abduction of an Australian citizen from Mexican territory, his forcible transfer to the United States and his subsequent extradition to Australia.

32 *In Re Argoud,* Cour de Cassation, 4 June 1964, 45 ILR 90 (Cass Crim. 1964).
33 *In Re Scott*, 10 Eng. Rep., at 167; *Ex parte Eliott*, 1 All E.R. 373 (K.B.) 1949, at 376–377.
34 *R v. Bow Street Magistrates, ex p. Mackeson*, 75 Cr. App. R 24 (1981).
35 *R v. Hartley*, 2 NYLR 199 (1978).

The Australian court made the important proviso, however, that it would stay proceedings only if it became clear that the Australian executive branch had been a direct or indirect party to the venture. As such involvement was not proven, the court decided not to stay the proceedings.[36]

Two cases were especially relevant for the vindication of a more rule of law–oriented approach towards irregular renditions, one South African case (*Ebrahim*) because the court neatly expounded the legal interests that were affected by the abduction, the other an English case (*Ex parte Bennett*) because the court clarified under what conditions and why it had to stay proceedings.

In the case of *Ebrahim*, two South African police officers had seized a South African member of the militant wing of the African National Congress in Swaziland. Ebrahim was bound, gagged, blindfolded and brought before a court in Pretoria on charges of treason. The court invoked Dutch-Roman common law and concluded that it lacked jurisdiction to try a person brought before it from another state by means of forcible abduction. It was noteworthy that Swaziland had not objected against the infringement of its territorial sovereignty. The Supreme Court, seized to assess the legality of the arrest, held that

> [t]he individual must be protected against illegal detention and abduction, the bounds of jurisdiction must not be exceeded, sovereignty must be respected, the legal process must be fair to those affected and abuse of law must be avoided in order to protect and promote the integrity of the administration of justice. This applies equally to a state. When the state is a party to a dispute, as for example in criminal cases, it must come to court with "clean hands". When the state itself is involved in an abduction across international borders, as in the present case, its hands are not clean.[37]

Interestingly, the Supreme Court enumerated the legal interests affected, lumping together the sovereignty of the state and the fairness of the procedure that would benefit the defendant, without indicating whether and, if so, how these were interrelated. It begs the question whether the fair trial rights of the defendant had been impaired by the very violation of the foreign state's sovereignty. The better view seems to be that the exceeding of jurisdiction by the forum state is the lynchpin connecting the two interests, but that the stakes of the state and the defendant must be separated. The issue is of utmost importance for a proper understanding of the phenomenon of *male captus*, and we will shortly return to this in the discussion of the case law of the international criminal tribunals.

36 *Levinge v. Director of Custodial Services*, 23 July 1987, 9 *N.S.W.L.R.*, 456.
37 *State v. Ibrahim*, 1991 (2) SALR, 553.

In the case of *Bennett*, which involved a rather complicated scheme in which the South African and British police colluded to forcibly transfer a citizen of New Zealand from South Africa to the United Kingdom where he was charged with fraudulent activities related to the purchase of a helicopter, the House of Lords did not shed new light on the precise connection of the legal interests affected. However, the case is of major importance, as it heralded the renouncing of the *male captus* rule. The House of Lords held that

> [t]he maintenance of the rule of law prevailed over the public interest in the prosecution and punishment of crime where the prosecuting authority had secured the prisoner's presence within the territorial jurisdiction of the court by forcibly abducting him or having him abducted from within the jurisdiction of some other state in violation of international law, the law of the state from which he had been abducted and his rights under the laws of that state and in disregard of available procedures to secure his lawful extradition to the jurisdiction of the court from the state where he was residing. It was an abuse of process for a person to be forcibly brought within the jurisdiction in disregard of extradition procedures available for the return of an accused person to the United Kingdom.[38]

We can easily identify some of the features we encountered in other case law. Crucial is the involvement of the authorities of the forum state ('the prosecuting authority had secured the presence by abducting him or having him abducted'). Moreover, the available extradition procedures should have been flouted ('in disregard of available procedures to secure his lawful extradition'). Interestingly, an official protest of the state whose sovereignty has been infringed is not required, which obviously would be an inapposite demand, as the states had colluded.

It has been observed that the approach taken by the House of Lords in *Bennett* is now generally considered to be the ruling principle for cases where representatives of a state have been involved in the violation of international law and which amount to a violation of the rule of law. Maybe this contention is a bit too optimistic and sweeping. One might make a more cautious observation that the approach is indicative of a burgeoning rule that applies at least in the most flagrant cases of abduction. Whenever either the infringement on territorial sovereignty or impairment of the fugitives' rights is less obvious or apparent, the outcome may still be different. It is to these situations that we now turn.

38 *Re Bennett*, House of Lords, 24 June 1993, All E. Rep. (1993), 3, at 138–139.

8.3 Luring

In case of abduction, both the violation of the territorial sovereignty of another state and the infringement of the fugitive's rights to physical liberty are usually quite obvious. When suspects are lured by subterfuge or ruses, such impairments are often less apparent. How should such unilateral operations be assessed from a legal point of view? Both aspects – the potential violation of territorial sovereignty and the infringement of constitutional rights – came to the fore in the *Yunis* case that came before US courts.

The FBI arrested Yunis in international waters off the coast of Cyprus for having allegedly led the 1982 high jacking of a Royal Jordanian Airlines jet in Beirut. As American citizens were amongst the passengers on board the airplane, the United States had jurisdiction on the basis of the passive nationality principle. 'Operation Goldenrod' was launched to lure Yunis into international waters. The plan succeeded when Yunis, allegedly drawn by the promise of a profitable drug transaction, boarded a yacht manned by FBI agents. Yunis was not treated softly. During the firm 'take down' he was grabbed by the arms, his feet were kicked out from under him and he was shackled and handcuffed to the deck. As a consequence, he sustained two broken wrists. Yunis claimed that, under the pressure of the circumstances, he had involuntarily waived his right not to incriminate himself during interrogations. The preliminary issue that the court had to decide was whether Yunis as an alien enjoyed constitutional protection against abusive action by US officials beyond the territorial borders of the United States. The district court had confirmed that he did.[39] The court of appeals was prepared to acknowledge that the interrogation of Yunis did not qualify as a model of law enforcement behaviour. However, the proper standard was whether 'he was involuntarily impelled to make a statement, when but for the improper influences he would have remained silent.'[40] Mere discomfort and surprise would never suffice to render a waiver involuntary, provided that the police officials had properly warned the suspect and had not resorted to 'intimidation, coercion and deception.'[41] The initial suppression of the confession by the district court on the basis of the exclusionary rule was therefore unwarranted.

In essence, the *Yunis* dictum is no different from the *Toscanino* approach discussed above. The courts admit that US officials, acting abroad, are bound to observe the constitutional rights of suspects, but they find that the behaviour does not reach the threshold of outrageousness that would warrant exclusion of the evidence, let alone the dismissal of the trial. By holding that US law enforcement is under an obligation to abide by the

39 *United States v. Yunis*, 681 F. Supp. 896, 917 (DDC 1988).
40 *United States v. Yunis*, 859 F 2d. 953, 87 (referring to *Miranda v. Arizona*, 384 US at 462).
41 *United States v. Yunis*, supra footnote 40.

Constitution to a similar extent as if it acted at home, the courts effectively strip the operation of its international dimension. The question of whether US officials are authorised to engage in criminal law enforcement beyond the national borders in the first place and whether any violation of international law might indirectly benefit the suspect is completely discarded. While Operation Goldenrod triggered protests from the Lebanese minister of justice, who labeled it 'an act close to piracy' and an 'aggression against the dignity of Lebanon,'[42] the courts did not consider the question whether the territorial sovereignty of a foreign state was impaired. Legal authority is divided on the issue. Some hold that the infringement of the sovereignty, in contradistinction to abduction, is too slight or even absent.[43] Others have more critically recognised that veiled measures can equally amount to an incursion of another state's sovereignty. Frederick Mann observes in this context that

> an international law violation occurs where the State or its agents induces a person by fraud or other illegal means to leave the country of refuge and proceed to some other country where he is apprehended . In such circumstances, the wrong is committed in the foreign state [the host], because the illegal means are used or have their effect there. A State, being sovereign, is not expected to tolerate acts that involve generally recognized illegality, though they are not performed by force. It is not necessarily the use of force, but the illegality, that constitutes the wrong done to the sovereignty of the State.[44]

Mann's analysis is perceptive, where he suggests that the more sophisticated method of luring conceals the heart of the matter, inducing courts to focus on the treatment of the fugitive, while losing sight of the broader issue that foreign law enforcement officials act without authority in another country. It is at this point that the interests of the fugitive and the aggrieved state converge, although, for analytical purposes, they are still to be considered separately. At the end of the day, it is not the brutality applied during arrest or detention, nor the flagrancy of the incursion on territorial sovereignty that counts, but the mere fact that law enforcement officials, in principle, do not act under the cover of law in another country. The question then arises if any transfer of suspects for the purpose of prosecution beyond the framework of extradition would be prohibited if the forum

42 See David A. Sadoff, *Bringing International Fugitives to Justice: Extradition and Its Alternatives*, Cambridge University Press: Cambridge 2016, p. 503.

43 Ethan Nadelmann, *Cops across Borders: The Internationalization of US Criminal Law Enforcement,* University Park: Pennsylvania State University Press 1994, p. 454.

44 Fredrick A. Mann, 'Reflections on the Prosecution of Persons Abducted in Breach of International Law,' in: Yoram Dinstein (ed.), *International Law at a Time of Perplexity: Essays in Honour of Shabtai Rosenne*, Kluwer Academic: Deventer 1989, pp. 408–409.

state is not trespassing on the territory of the 'requested' state. That takes us to the next topic.

8.4 Disguised extradition

One of the prerogatives of a state is that it has the power to allow or to refuse aliens the right to reside on its territory. This discretionary power has its limitations, however, as states are prohibited to return refugees to a state in the event that such individuals have a 'well-founded fear' of persecution in that state (the so-called rule of non-refoulement).[45] Moreover, as we will demonstrate in the next chapter, states are inhibited from expelling, deporting or extraditing persons to a state where they face a substantial risk of being tortured or being exposed to other flagrant violations of basic human rights.

In this section, we are primarily interested in the question whether there are any limitations to a state's right to expel or deport persons to another state that has expressed interest in his or her criminal prosecution (or the execution of a sanction) without making use of formal extradition proceedings. This practice has, in common with abduction and luring, discussed in the previous sections, that it challenges extradition as the singular mode of transfer of suspects and prisoners. It is different from these devices in that the territorial integrity of the state of refuge is not affected; on the contrary, expulsion or deportation is executed by that state itself. The illegitimacy of the practice is even more contested than abduction and luring. To explore this delicate area, fraught with difficulties, it is mandatory to clarify some terminological issues. Sadoff makes a distinction between de facto and disguised extradition.[46] The former, broader term does not necessarily imply a value judgment as to its legality; rather, it simply refers to a state's exercise of 'non-extradition-related laws, authorities, or administrative procedures that yields the delivery of a fugitive directly or indirectly to a State with a law enforcement interest in him.' He defines disguised extradition as a 'subset of *de facto* extradition that entails a purposeful circumvention of extradition laws or treaties by the host State to deliver a fugitive directly or indirectly to a State with a law enforcement interest in him, most commonly via immigration laws.'[47] The distinction is helpful to the extent that the latter definition connotes 'bad faith,' the intent to use procedures for another purpose than for which they have been created (*détournement de pouvoir*).

45 Article 33 of the Refugees Convention, Geneva 1951. The 'non-refoulement' principle is considered to have the status of customary international law. See T. Rodenhaüser, The Principle of Non-refoulement in the Migration Context: 5 Key Points, 30 March 2018, *International Review of the Red Cross*; https://blogs.icrc.org/law-and-policy/2018/03/30/principle-of-non-refoulement-migration-context-5-key-points/.

46 Sadoff, supra footnote 42, pp. 50–52.

47 Sadoff, supra footnote 42.

However, it is slightly confusing and therefore somewhat unfortunate as well because Sadoff seems to suggest that, in the absence of extradition relations, states have more or less carte blanche. We have pointed out this paradox before. The sources that Sadoff invokes to sustain his distinction seem to avoid this restriction. In his searching analysis of the *Soblen* case, Paul O'Higgins, defines disguised extradition as 'cases in which by the use of a power, with which it has been vested for another and different purpose, the state may give effect to a request for the surrender of a fugitive criminal which it is not lawfully authorized to do so.'[48] No mention is made that the request for surrender must (initially) have been predicated on an extradition treaty and has run astray because of some impediment. To be sure, Sadoff's rather narrow understanding of disguised extradition is reflected in case law, where, for instance, the French Cour de Cassation in the *Barbie* case did not bother to investigate whether Barbie's 'informal' removal to France was the result of a setup between colluding Bolivian and French authorities. In the absence of an extradition treaty, there was no other way to obtain custody over the suspect, so in such a case any potential scheming is conveniently glossed over.[49]

In our view, the emphasis in the assessment of disguised extradition should be on the deliberate (ab)use of immigration law for criminal law purposes rather than on the circumvention of existing extradition instruments. The latter may serve as evidence of the intent to accomplish the former. That disguised extradition does not require the existence of an extradition treaty that is subsequently circumvented transpired in a Dutch case in which a Dutch citizen, suspected of sexual abuse of a minor in Thailand, was expelled by the Thai authorities to the Netherlands.[50] As there was no extradition treaty in force between the Netherlands and Thailand, the court held that disguised extradition – as counsel for the defence had claimed – would be at stake only if Thailand had surrendered the suspect on the request of the Netherlands. There was no proof for such an assertion. The Thai authorities had acted on their own. While the Supreme Court thus rejected applicant's claim, it implicitly confirmed that a disguised extradition could occur in the absence of any framework of extradition relations.

Proof of the intent to accomplish extradition by means of immigration law is the gist and the complicating feature of disguised extradition. As the device serves as a substitute to extradition, it usually has the nature of a transaction. The Dutch Supreme Court therefore correctly emphasised that contact between authorities presents a strong presumption of a shared

48 Paul O'Higgins, 'Disguised Extradition: The Soblen case,' 27 *Modern Law Review* (September 1964), pp. 521, 522.

49 *Fédération Nationale des Déportés et Internes, Résistants et Patriotes and Others v. Barbie*, Cour de Cassation, 6 October 1983, 78 ILR 125 (1988).

50 Dutch Supreme Court, 12 September 2017, ECLI:NL:HR:2017:2321.

intent to surreptitiously transfer suspects, evading the formal and legal channels. If, for instance, the state of refuge informs another state of the time and modus of expulsion, one may readily assume that the states conspire to achieve the unlawful result. On the other hand, in the absence of contact between the states, one would expect the state that expels or deports an undesired alien to act out of its own interests. After all, it would not be reasonable to inhibit a state from expelling or deporting persons posing a threat to public security on the basis of the consideration that the fugitive is subject to criminal investigations in his home state. Mere knowledge of an impending criminal prosecution in the other state, therefore, does not suffice. In the *Wallace* case the Dutch Supreme Court held that 'the mere circumstance that an expulsion may have the consequence that an alien, after having been removed from the territory of the state of residence, ends up in the power of a state in which he runs the risk of being exposed to criminal prosecution or the execution of a criminal sentence, as such does not warrant the conclusion that in such a case the expulsion must be equated with a (disguised) extradition.'[51] Decisive is whether the state was inspired by other motives than the desire to remove relator from its territory.[52] A strong indication for an affirmative answer is prior contact between the states involved, whereas the fact that the state would have no other option than to expel the fugitive to his home state, which has incidentally an interest in his criminal prosecution, would generally clear the state from suspicion.

The unmasking of deportation as (unlawful) disguised extradition is therefore a question of casuistry, boiling down to the proof of *mala fides* and complicated by state-specific and technical immigration law. The fact that disguised extradition is often contemplated as a joint venture between two states implies that the fugitive can, in principle, challenge the unlawfulness of the practice both in the state of deportation and in the state of reception where he stands trial. As the alleged violation of the law is primarily committed by the state of deportation, the former avenue tackles the issue head on. The paradigmatic *Soblen* case illustrates the quasi insurmountable burden on the part of applicant to prove 'bad faith' of the authorities.[53] Soblen was convicted of espionage in the United States and sentenced to life imprisonment. After he had been released on bail, he left by air for Israel. He was removed from Tel Aviv and flown to Athens, where he was transshipped to an aircraft for carriage back to the United States via London. During the journey, he inflicted severe wounds on himself with a knife with the sole object of ensuring that he would be landed in the United Kingdom. Soblen was removed to a hospital and was served with notice containing

51 Dutch Supreme Court, 13 September 1963 , NJ 1963, 509 (*Wallace*).

52 Dutch Supreme Court, 18 November 1994, NJ 1996, 579.

53 R *v. Secretary of State for the Home Department, Ex Parte Soblen*, 26 July 1962 [1962] 3 All ER 373.

a refusal of leave to land. In his writ of habeas corpus, he challenged the deportation order, arguing, amongst others, that it had been 'issued for an *ultra vires* object by the Home Secretary, in that Soblen was being returned to the United States to serve a prison sentence for an offence for which extradition could not be granted, namely espionage.' The standard is remarkably similar to the one advanced by the Dutch Supreme Court in the case of *Wallace*. In his highly critical discussion of the case, Geoff Gilbert points out that the Home Secretary claimed crown privilege in respect of correspondence between himself and the United States, enabling him to conceal all the evidence the deportee required to raise a prima facie case or 'sow such substantial and disquieting doubts in the mind of the court about the *bona fides* of the order he is challenging, that the court will consider that some answer is called for.'[54] The House of Lords found that Soblen had failed to discharge the burden of proof, but Gilbert acidly comments that on the basis of the evidence available it was crystal clear that the Home Secretary was determined to assist the US criminal law enforcement, 'whether Soblen's presence in the United Kingdom was conducive of the public good or not.'[55] Therefore, *Soblen* is to be considered as a notorious and very tragic example of disguised extradition.[56]

In the *Bozano* case, the European Court of Human Rights was charged with assessing the arrest and removal of an Italian citizen to Switzerland, in execution of a deportation order, in light of the right to be protected against arbitrary deprivation of liberty.[57] The entire case originated in a verdict in absentia by the Genoa Assize Court of Appeal, sentencing Bozano to life imprisonment in being found guilty of the abduction and subsequent murder of a 13-year-old girl. Bozano succeeded in escaping to France. After being arrested by the French gendarmerie during a routine control check he was brought before the Court of Limoges, which refused his extradition, considering the Italian trial in the absence of the accused incompatible with French public order.[58] At the end of October 1979, Bozano was seized by three French plainclothes policemen, who served him with a makeshift deportation order and quickly transported him to the Swiss border. It transpired that Interpol Rome had shortly before telexed several states, including Switzerland, that deportation of Bozano was imminent. As soon as Bozano had arrived in Switzerland, Italy indeed submitted an extradition request, which was granted in 1980. Bozano's lawyers attempted to have the deportation order quashed. The judgment of the Administrative Court of Limoges was highly critical of the action and held that

54 Gilbert, supra footnote 9, pp. 367 and 371.
55 Gilbert, supra footnote 9, p. 371.
56 On the morning of his intended deportation, Soblen committed suicide.
57 EctHR, 18 December 1986 Appl. no. 99900-82 (*Bozano v. France*).
58 *Bozano*, supra footnote 57, par. 18.

> the Minister of the Interior had committed 'a manifest error of judgment' and the administrative authorities an 'abuse of powers.'

In clarifying the abuse of powers, the French court unabashedly depicted the deportation as a disguised extradition:

> Whereas the haste with which the impugned decision was enforced, when the individual concerned had not even indicated his refusal to comply, and the choice of the Swiss border which was imposed on the individual clearly show the real reason behind the decision: in reality the executive sought, not to expel the applicant from French territory, but to hand him over to the Italian authorities via the Swiss authorities, with whom Italy had an extradition agreement; the executive was therefore seeking to circumvent the competent judicial authority's negative ruling which was binding on the French Government; ... the impugned decision was [therefore] an abuse of powers.[59]

For the European Court of Human Rights, the legal question at issue was whether Bozano's arrest had been lawful and in accordance with a procedure prescribed by law. To that purpose, the court had to inquire whether the arrest and subsequent detention had been performed with a view to deportation, as Article 5(1), sub f acknowledges that objective as an exception to the prohibition of deprivation of liberty.[60] The court carefully assessed the circumstances and the sequence of events. It noted that the operation had been performed in great haste, apparently to prevent Bozano from making use of legal remedies. All preparations had been concealed and he had not been expelled across the nearest border, that of Spain, but – quite contrived – had been brought to Switzerland. It recalled the prior contacts between Italy and Switzerland and pointed out that all these aspects taken together revealed a premeditated sham:

> Viewing the circumstances of the case as a whole and having regard to the volume of material pointing in the same direction, the Court consequently concludes that the applicant's deprivation of liberty in the night of 26 to 27 October 1979 was neither 'lawful,' within the meaning of Article 5 § 1 (f) (art. 5-1-f), nor compatible with the 'right to security of person.' Depriving Mr. Bozano of his liberty in this way amounted in fact to a *disguised form of extradition* designed to circumvent the negative ruling of 15 May 1979 by the Indictment Division of the Limoges

59 *Bozano*, supra footnote 57, par. 35.

60 Article 5(1), f also mentions extradition, but it was obvious that formal extradition proceedings were not followed.

> Court of Appeal, and not to 'detention' necessary in the ordinary course of 'action ... taken with a view to deportation.'[61]

The Bozano case is a principled appeal, directed towards states parties, to abide by the rule of law whenever they engage in international cooperation in criminal matters and demonstrates that disguised extradition can be exposed when a court is willing and able to recognise the signs.

In the *Ocalan* case, the European Court seemingly retreated from its principled course.[62] The (in)famous leader of the Kurdistan Workers' Party (PKK) had been removed from Kenyan territory, allegedly with the connivance of Kenyan authorities, and had been arrested on board a Turkish airplane by Turkish police officials to stand trial in Turkey on charges of terrorism and sedition. In the absence of an extradition treaty between Turkey and Kenya, no formal extradition procedures had been used. The court observed that it was bound to strike a fair balance between the general interest of the community in (criminal) law enforcement and the protection of the individual's fundamental rights, and it noted that nothing in the Convention precluded states from cooperating, even if this amounted to engaging in an 'atypical' extradition.'[63] The court confined its analysis to an inquiry whether the applicant's interception immediately before he was handed over to Turkish officials had violated Kenyan sovereignty and found that this was not the case, pointing at the absence of any protest on the part of Kenya.[64] Distinguishing the situation under scrutiny on the facts of the *Bozano* case, the court pointed out that Kenya was not a party to the Convention, which implied that the court was not called to examine whether the arrest would amount to a violation of Kenyan law.[65] Consequently, the entire legal issue was reduced to a potential infraction of state sovereignty, from which the applicant could only indirectly reap the benefits. One might object that the court's approach was overly cautious, as the custody over Ocalan had been obtained by means of measures that were arguably in contravention of the Convention. It reflects the Court's reluctance to pronounce on irregularities that occur outside the remit of its jurisdiction.

On closer inspection, the *Ocalan* judgment did not overrule the findings of the court in the *Bozano* case. It confined its critical assessment of disguised extradition only to situations in which both states are party to the Convention. We will therefore return to the *Bozano* case in our final analysis because the European Court offers a general normative framework to gauge all irregular forms of rendition.

61 *Bozano*, supra footnote 57, par. 60 (italics mine).

62 ECtHR (Grand Chamber), 12 May 2005, Appl. No. 46221/99 (*Ocalan v. Turkey*).

63 *Ocalan* case, supra footnote 62 , section 88.

64 *Ocalan* case, supra footnote 62 , sections 93–95.

65 *Ocalan* case, supra footnote 62, section 90.

8.5 International criminal tribunals and irregular rendition

It is no coincidence that international criminal tribunals have often been confronted with irregular renditions and have been compelled to consider the question of what legal remedies they should offer. After all, these tribunals have no law enforcement organisation at their disposal. They must often operate in the context of national law systems in disarray as the consequence of armed conflict, often hostile to their involvement and at least reluctant to surrender their people. Any assistance is most welcome, especially in view of the urgent need to bring the perpetrators of the most heinous crimes to justice.[66] Precisely because the interests are enormous – and given the predicament of international tribunals, as just indicated – dismissal of the indictment is generally considered as too high a price. In the case of Jean-Bosco Barayagwiza, who had been kept in pre-trial detention in Cameroon for more than three years while his being properly informed of the nature of his charges had sustained considerable delay, the appeals chamber had initially ordered direct release. The chamber held that the accumulation of procedural violations for which the prosecutor was at least partially to blame had moved the court to take such radical measures as continuing of the trial would amount to an abuse of process.[67] However, when new information came to light that alleviated the responsibility of the prosecutor, the appeals chamber reviewed its former decision, repealed the release, qualifying it as disproportionate, and ordered the more moderate remedy of reduction of sentence (provided the defendant would be found guilty).[68]

The *Dokmanović* case before the International Tribunal for the former Yugoslavia (ICTY) concerned an instance of luring. Dokmanović, charged with complicity in a hospital massacre in eastern Croatia, was tricked into leaving Serbia for UN-controlled Croatian territory on the pretext that he would receive compensation for abandoned property. He was apprehended and transported to The Hague to stand trial before the ICTY. Defence counsel sought his release on the grounds that his arrest had been illegal, violating the Statute and Rules of the Tribunal, the sovereignty of the Federal Republic of Yugoslavia (FRY) and international law. The Trial Chamber, however, rejected the claim, finding that the means used to accomplish the

66 As is eloquently put by the Appeals Chamber of the International Criminal Tribunal for Rwanda in the case of *Prosecutor v. Barayagwiza*, Decision, ICTR-97-19AR72, 3 November 1997, par. 42: 'Unlike national systems which have police forces to effectuate the arrest of suspects, the Tribunal lacks any such enforcement agency. Consequently, in the absence of the suspect's voluntary surrender, the Tribunal must rely on the international community for the arrest and provisional detention of suspects.'

67 *Prosecutor v. Barayagwiza*, supra footnote 66 , par. 102–112.

68 *Prosecutor v. Barayagwiza,* Decision on the Prosecutor's request for Review or Reconsideration, ICTR-97-19-AR72, 31 March 2000, paras. 74–75.

arrest had neither violated principles of international law nor the sovereignty of the FRY.[69]

The most sophisticated analysis of the *male captus, bene detentus* doctrine in a vertical context was performed by a Trial Chamber of the ICTY in the case of *Nikolić*. Nikolić had been abducted from Serbian territory by unknown individuals who had allegedly acted in collusion with the peacekeeping forces of the Stabilisation Force in Bosnia and Herzegovina (SFOR) and the Prosecutor.[70] The Trial Chamber began with a comprehensive analysis of national law cases, distilling from these judgments the already familiar parameters: whether the forum state itself was involved in any irregularities, protests by the aggrieved state, the existence of an extradition instrument that had potentially been circumvented and the treatment of the accused during arrest and detention. From the outset, the Trial Chamber emphasised that these core elements had been developed in the context of horizontal relationships between sovereign states, suggesting that the outcome of the analysis might be different in the particular vertical context in which the ICTY operates.[71] The difference between the two configurations came especially to the fore in the sharp distinction made by the Trial Chamber, separating the violation of state sovereignty from infringement of human rights and due process of law.[72] In its assessment of whether state sovereignty had been violated, the Trial Chamber admitted that involvement of executive authorities of the forum state was a factor of paramount importance that might, in principle, impair jurisdiction. However, the Chamber did not find evidence of collusion, noting that there had not been contact between the unknown individuals and SFOR or Prosecutor prior to the crossing of the border between the FRY and Bosnia and Herzegovina and that the abductors had not been offered any incentives.[73] Moreover, no extradition arrangement had been flouted for the simple reason that extradition treaties did not apply between the ICTY and national states. The latter were supposed to comply with the de jure arrest warrants of the ICTY in accordance with the terms of the ICTY Statute (Article 29). But the knock-out argument for the Chamber's finding that violation of state sovereignty was not at issue in this case was that the value of state sovereignty diminishes when states are interacting with an international tribunal. While recognising that 'it is of the utmost importance that national jurisdictions, being equal, respect each other's sovereignty,' the Chamber attributed a higher hierarchical position

69 *Prosecutor v. Dokmanović* Decision on the Motion for Release by the Accused, Case No. IT-95-13a-PT, Tr. Ch. II, 22 October 1997.

70 *Prosecutor v. Nikolić,* Decision on Defence Motion Challenging the Exercise of Jurisdiction by the Tribunal, Case No. IT-94-2-PT, 9 October 2002.

71 *Nikolić*, supra footnote 70, par. 27.

72 See also, on this separation, H. van der Wilt, 'Het Joegoslavië Tribunaal en het beginsel *male captus, bene judicatus*,' 34 *Delikt en Delinkwent* (2004), pp. 274–300.

73 *Nikolić*, supra footnote 70, par. 33.

to the ICTY, as the fruit of an enforcement measure under Chapter VII of the UN Charter.[74]

At first blush, this position may seem a bit presumptuous and the disparaging of state sovereignty may offer tribunals full leeway to reap the benefits of brutal activities of irresponsible vigilantes. However, an *obiter dictim* of the Chamber sheds a slightly different light on its intentions. Even if a violation of state sovereignty had occurred, so the Chamber asserts, the appropriate remedy would have been to return the accused to the FRY, which would have had no other option than to surrender him again on the basis of Article 29 of the Statute.[75] In other words, the outcome would not be different and the suppression of jurisdiction would amount to a redundant formality. This presentation shifts the emphasis from the hierarchical superiority of the ICTY to the obligations of states in respect of the prosecution of international crimes. The change in perspective is more poignant in the Interlocutory Decision of the Appeals Chamber, which balances the requirement to observe the territorial sovereignty of states against the need to bring perpetrators of international crime to justice. Clearly, in the opinion of the Appeals Chamber, the latter should outweigh the former:

> the damage caused to international justice by not apprehending fugitives accused of serious violations of international humanitarian law is comparatively higher than the injury, if any, caused to the sovereignty of a State by a limited intrusion of its territory, *particularly when the intrusion occurred in default of the State' s cooperation.*[76]

The final part of the sentence suggests that the state has itself more or less to blame for an incursion of its sovereignty, as it is rooted in a prior flouting of its obligations. One wonders why this reasoning would apply only to international criminal tribunals. After all, if the condoning of (slight) incursions on the sovereignty of the state hinges on the nature of the crimes and the concomitant non-fulfillment of obligations, one might argue that the interest of bringing war criminals to justice equally trumps territorial sovereignty in interstate relations. Such a line of reasoning finds support in the *Eichmann* case, in which the forcible abduction of the infamous Nazi bureaucrat (*Schreibtischtäter*) from Argentina to Israel did not preclude the Israeli court from exercising jurisdiction.[77] Argentina had lodged a feeble

74 *Nikolić*, supra footnote 70, par. 32.

75 *Nikolić*, supra footnote 70, par. 36.

76 *Prosecutor v. Nikolić*, Decision on Interlocutory Appeal Concerning Legality of Arrest, Case No. IT-94-2-AR73, par. 26 (italics mine).

77 District Court of Jerusalem, 11 December 1961, Criminal case No. 40-61. Initially, it was assumed that the abduction was performed by private individuals, but President Ben Gurion later admitted that the operation had been operated by agents of the Mossad. See for comments, amongst others, F.E.S. Fawcett, 'The Eichmann Case,' 27 *British Yearbook*

protest in the UN General Assembly, but it was quickly assuaged by Israeli apologies. The court, supported by legal commentaries, opined that the urgency of bringing the perpetrator of such heinous crimes to justice warranted the unorthodox methods.

It is not entirely clear if the Trial Chamber in the *Nikolić* case endorsed the view that sovereignty concerns equally dwindle in the horizontal context when international crimes are at stake. The Trial Chamber identifies the nature of the crimes for which the accused is sought as one of the core elements in the assessment of whether a forcible abduction affects the jurisdiction in a subsequent criminal trial.[78] Apparently, the Chamber makes no distinction between the horizontal and the vertical context, but this interpretation is refuted by its pompous elevation of the ICTY, as observed before. The Appeals Chamber appears to consider the ICTY and states on the same par, where it holds that

> in cases of Universally Condemned Offences, jurisdiction should not be set aside on the ground that there was a violation of the sovereignty of a State, when the violation is brought about by the apprehension of fugitives from justice whatever the consequences for the international responsibility *of the State* or the organisation involved.[79]

The Appeals Chamber goes a step further than the Trial Chamber in contending that 'even if the abduction could have been attributed to SFOR (or the Prosecutor),' the courts should not decline from exercising jurisdiction. The sovereign interests of the state being slighted, all the attention is drawn to the predicament of the accused. The Chamber perfectly explains the strict distinction between the two legal dimensions. In exploring whether the violation of the fugitive's human rights and due process of law would affect the jurisdiction of the Tribunal, the Trial Chamber starts by observing that the two components are closely related. Respect for due process of law entails not only that the court should guarantee the suspect a fair trial, but it must also take into consideration prior conduct of law enforcement during arrest and detention. At this point, the Chamber concurs with earlier findings in national case law (see the *Ebrahim* and *Toscanino* cases above). Simultaneously, the Chamber sets the bar high by holding that only egregious violations of the rights of the accused would prompt the court to apply the abuse of process doctrine.[80] In this context it would make a difference if SFOR or the Prosecution had orchestrated the abduction, in the sense

of International Law (1962), p. 181; William Schabas, 'The Contribution of the Eichmann Trial to International Law,' 26 *Leiden Journal of International Law* (2013), pp. 667–699.

78 *Nikolić*, supra footnote 70, par. 27.

79 *Nikolić*, Appeals Chamber, supra footnote 76, par. 26 (italics mine).

80 *Nikolić*, supra footnote 70, par. 43.

that such involvement would yield an even stronger incentive to decline jurisdiction. But in case of the most serious violations, like inhuman, cruel, degrading treatment or torture, it would be immaterial who was responsible, which implied that the court would suppress the trial if private individuals had engaged in serious mistreatment of the accused during the abduction.[81] The approach is commendable because it sends the message that no criminal prosecution should reap the benefits from 'law enforcement' that is inherently criminal itself. At the end of the day, the Trial Chamber found that the treatment of the accused did not reach the level of seriousness as envisaged and the Appeals Chamber agreed with that conclusion.[82]

The attitude of international criminal tribunals towards irregular renditions reveals a somewhat twisted approach. Whereas in respect of the evaluation of infringements on territorial sovereignty it resembles the tough position of the US Supreme Court in *Alvarez Machain*, the greater concern for the rights of the accused reminds us of the *Ebrahim* and *Toscanino* cases. There is a certain intuitive appeal in depicting international crimes as a special category and in the argument that bringing the perpetrators of such crimes to justice should take priority over concerns for sovereignty, especially as states themselves are often involved in those crimes and accountable for their impunity. Consistency would require that states would equally be absolved from meticulous respect for the sovereignty of other states, but, at this point, international relations and Realpolitik are likely to supersede both logics and legal idealism. An international criminal tribunal, backed by the Security Council, can afford to be less circumspect than states. The focus of international criminal tribunals has been on the potential infringement of the rights of the accused. At this point, they have embraced the rule of law–oriented approach displayed by national courts, which could have been expected because international tribunals, as role models, are supposed to observe fair trial rights. However, in balancing the primordial goal of holding perpetrators of international crimes accountable with the human rights of the accused, international tribunals and courts have, until now, never given precedence to the latter.

8.6 Final reflections

The phenomenon of irregular renditions has produced a patchwork of judicial findings. The reasoning of the most staunch supporters of the *male captus* doctrine is shockingly simple. The criminal court is bound to offer the

81 *Nikolić*, supra footnote 70, par. 46. The Trial Chamber concurred with the Appeals Chamber in the *Barayagwiza* case on this point, which had held that in cases of egregious violations of the rights of the accused it is 'irrelevant which entity or entities were responsible for the alleged violations of the Appellant's rights.'

82 *Nikolić*, supra footnote 70, par. 42.

defendant and all other participants in the process a fair trial, but it must confine its due process efforts to the courtroom. It is incapable of assessing irregularities in the apprehension and provisional detention of the accused and any involvement of the state's law enforcement officials therein, especially if they occurred on distant shores beyond its jurisdiction. Violation of extradition treaties is in order only if the convention itself explicitly precludes alternative methods of obtaining custody over the fugitive – a purely hypothetical proposition as no instrument contains such clauses. If the aggrieved state is not happy about the conduct of foreign police officials on their territory, they should submit a complaint to that state's executive and try to solve the conflict by diplomatic means.[83]

Some amendments have been made to alleviate the dire results of this rigid position. In connection with the incursion of territorial sovereignty, it has been argued that involvement of state officials in irregular renditions should prompt the court to negate jurisdiction because such behaviour would constitute an international wrongful act.[84] The fugitive's fundamental rights in respect of bodily integrity, security and liberty have been heeded in the *Toscanino* case, which postulated the need for a court to divest itself from jurisdiction if the forcible abduction was so egregious as to shock the judges' sense of decency. Courts in other jurisdictions have followed suit.[85] However, the threshold of seriousness is sufficiently high as to spare the courts from having to take such drastic measures. No domestic court has, to our knowledge, bothered to indicate whether and, if so, how the incursion on territorial sovereignty and violation of fugitive's rights are connected. They suffice by lumping them together, contending that international law and fundamental rights of territorial sovereignty and due process of law have been impaired. The international criminal tribunals have even deliberately severed the links between the legal dimensions by addressing them separately.

The most perceptive approach to the problem of irregular renditions *in toto* has, in my opinion, been offered by the European Court of Human Rights in the *Bozano* case. In only a couple of paragraphs, the European Court has provided a comprehensive framework for the analysis of all its modalities and the key to understanding the relationship between the legal interests that are at stake. What all forms of irregular rendition have in common is that the person who arrests and subsequently detains the fugitive for the purpose of surrendering him to another state that has a criminal enforcement interest in him acts without proper legal title. The requirement that deprivation of liberty should be 'lawful' and 'in accordance with a procedure prescribed by law' contains a twofold restriction. First, powers

83 This is, in a nutshell, the core of the *Alvarez Machain* judgment, compare section 8.2.3.
84 *Vide* Justice Stevens in his dissenting opinion in re *Alvarez Machain*.
85 See the cases of *Bennett* and *South Africa v. Ebrahim*, section 8.2.4.

of arrest and detention are, in principle, bestowed only on the state's law enforcement officers, which excludes private individuals and foreign police officials. And, second, these powers are granted for a certain purpose, which is reflected in the court's emphasising that 'lawfulness in any event implies absence of any arbitrariness.'[86] Any deprivation of liberty that is not 'lawful' because it is performed either by a person lacking the authority to do so or by a person who has such authority but acts beyond the provenance for which it is granted *eo ipso facto* infringes on a fundamental right of the fugitive. Abduction (and arguably luring) by a foreign police official or a private individual equally intrudes on the territorial sovereignty of a state. The interests of the fugitive and the state converge at this point because the state wields a monopoly of sword power within its territory. In case of disguised extradition, the impairments of the powers of the state of refuge are far less apparent, but they are nonetheless present in that the forum state induces the former to transgress its own law. It is for this reason that complicity of the forum state is an indispensable element of disguised extradition.

Obviously, there are degrees in seriousness of the infringement of sovereignty – as there are shades in egregiousness in the treatment of individual suspects. Government-sponsored abductions are clearly the most offensive to foreign jurisdictions, while deportations, serving as disguised extradition, only scratch the surface of international inequities and may even be mutually beneficial. But from a normative perspective, it is important to emphasise they have more in common than meets the eye.

At the beginning of this chapter, it was observed that law enforcement officials are tempted to resort to 'unorthodox measures' because they feel straight-jacked by the formalities of extradition proceedings. The predicament can be solved only by the introduction of more flexible instruments that expedite procedures and remove time-worn obstacles. Alternatively, neighbouring states can make arrangements enabling their police officials to engage in law enforcement on each other's territory. The European Arrest Warrant and the Schengen Convention provide for such devices and they may deserve imitation. On the other hand, such arrangements are feasible only if they are grounded on solid mutual trust. The lack of such trust takes us to the topic of the next chapter.

86 *Bozano* case, supra footnote 57, par. 59.

9 Extradition and human rights

9.1 Introduction to the problem

In the previous chapter we discussed impairments of the fugitive's rights during arrest and detention that precede the criminal trial. In this chapter we will address the mirror image of that situation: there may sometimes be credible indications that the requested person runs the risk of being exposed to maltreatment or an unfair trial in the requesting state after having been extradited. The recurring question is whether extradition should in such cases be reconsidered or even refused.

In terms of international law, the situation just expounded may give rise to a conflict of treaty obligations. This configuration, apart from causing much embarrassment, may at first blush appear to be rather paradoxical. After all, states would normally be expected to establish extradition relations only with those states whose administration of criminal justice displays a minimum level of quality and therefore yields sufficient confidence. There are several reasons, however, why the existence of an extradition treaty can be only a rough and ready yardstick for mutual trust. First of all, many treaties that are established with a view to the suppression of specific international crimes contain a provision stipulating that states parties may, at their option, consider the treaty an appropriate basis for extradition. As such treaties are, in principle, open to all, states parties cannot be picky in selecting those countries with whom they wish to cooperate or not. However, as these treaty provisions are not drafted in mandatory terms, the requested state is always at liberty to refuse extradition, concomitantly assuming the alternative obligation to start criminal investigations and prosecution itself.

A true conflict of treaty obligations emerges whenever the extradition treaty compels states parties to oblige, without making amendments for exceptions in case of impendent human rights violations. Such human rights exceptions are extremely rare because they call into question the trust on which the very extradition treaty is predicated. However, the observance of the rule of law may have declined ever since the extradition treaty was established. Some fugitives may have good reasons to fear discriminatory treatment on the basis of their belonging to a political, ethnic or religious

DOI: 10.4324/9780429956683-9

group. Or the requesting state may simply lack the resources to maintain prison facilities meeting minimum standards of decent treatment.

While states would naturally be inclined to avoid a conflict of treaty obligations, the question arises whether human rights considerations would prevail over extradition obligations whenever they cannot be reconciled. There is no straightforward answer, apart from those human rights that belong to the sacred realm of *jus cogens*, which obviously begs the question which rights would qualify as such. There are two typical features inherent to the entire configuration that complicate a proper assessment of the issue. For one, the requested state is usually not directly engaging in infringements of human rights itself, by, for instance, depriving the requested person of a fair trial or maltreating him/her. The fugitive is exposed to rights violations in a state that may be bound by a human rights instrument or not as a consequence of the act of surrender to which the requested state is perfectly entitled (if not obliged). Second, the human rights violation in the requesting state has, by definition, not materialized; it is the mere risk of its occurrence that impels the requested state to be apprehensive. The assessment, therefore, boils down to balancing a definite violation of the obligation of an extradition treaty against an uncertain event that may engage the (co-) responsibility of the requested state, bound by its being a party to a human rights instrument.

In its landmark decision in the *Soering* case, the European Court of Human Rights acknowledged and addressed both elements.[1] It started by emphasizing that Article 5(1), sub f of the Convention explicitly allowed for deprivation of liberty with a view to extradition, which implied that no right not to be extradited could be derived from the Convention. The court admitted, however, that extradition could, in principle, attract the responsibility of the requested state, party to the Convention, 'in so far as a measure of extradition has consequences adversely affecting the enjoyment of a Convention right.'[2] The court identified the issue at stake therefore as

> whether Article 3 (entailing the right to be free from torture, and other forms of cruel, inhuman or degrading treatment, addition HvdW) can be applicable when the adverse consequences of extradition are, or may be, suffered outside the jurisdiction of the extraditing State as a result of treatment or punishment administered in the receiving State.[3]

The court reasoned with much circumspection. It emphasised that the provisions of the Convention in no way governed the activities of a (requesting) state not a party to the Convention, which was relevant in the case at hand

1 EctHR, 7 July 1989, Appl. no. 14038/88 (*Soering v. United Kingdom*).
2 *Soering* case, supra footnote 1, par. 85.
3 *Soering* case, supra footnote 1, par. 85.

as the extradition was sought by the state of Virginia, USA. Nor would the Convention impede the contracting state from surrendering an individual unless it was satisfied that the conditions awaiting him in the country of destination were in full accord with each of the safeguards of the Convention. However, recalling that the object and purpose of the Convention required its safeguards to be practical and effective, the court held that a contracting state could incur responsibility for foreseeable consequences of extradition suffered outside its jurisdiction.

While the court acknowledged that 'the establishment of such responsibility inevitably involves an assessment of conditions in the requesting country against the standards of Article 3 of the Convention,' it reiterated that 'there is no question of adjudicating on or establishing the responsibility of the receiving country, whether under general international law, under the Convention or otherwise.'

What was at stake was 'the liability incurred by the extraditing Contracting State by reason of its having taken action which has as a direct consequence the exposure of an individual to proscribed ill-treatment.'[4]

The issue of responsibility of a contracting state for certain violations that occurred beyond its jurisdiction having been settled, the question remained whether that state could incur responsibility for prospective violations. The court also affirmed this by holding that the serious and irreparable nature of a violation of Article 3 required the Court to depart from its general habit not to pronounce on the existence or otherwise of any potential violations of the Convention.[5]

In actual practice, the court found that the so-called death row phenomenon to which the applicant would probably be exposed in the requesting state would constitute 'torture or cruel, inhuman or degrading treatment,' in the sense of Article 3 of the Convention and held the United Kingdom responsible for exposing him to that risk. Many domestic courts and human rights organs have followed suit by addressing the question of human rights in the context of extradition. The topic has received worldwide media attention for the massive popular protest in Hong Kong against the proposed bill of the government allowing extradition of its citizens to China.[6] A comprehensive discussion of even only the most conspicuous case law and legal issues would exceed the scope of this monography.[7] The focus in this chap-

4 *Soering* case, supra footnote 1, par. 91.

5 *Soering* case, supra footnote 1, par. 90.

6 https://www.cnbc.com/2019/06/15/hong-kong-government-reportedly-will-suspend-china-extradition-bill.html.

7 See, for interesting analyses, Michael P. Shea, 'Expanding Judicial Scrutiny of Human Rights in Extradition Cases after *Soering*,' 17 *Yale Journal of International Law* (1992), pp. 86–138; J. Dugard & Chr. van den Wyngaert, 'Reconciling Extradition and Human Rights,' 92 *American Journal of International Law* (1998), pp. 187–212; Alette Smeulers, *In Staat van Uitlevering*,' Intersentia: Antwerp 2003; Miguel Joao Costa, *Extradition Law: Review-*

ter is on the question to what extent states – sometimes prompted by human rights organs – are prepared to refuse extradition out of a concern that the human rights of the fugitive are likely to be infringed in the requesting state. Such a decision would entail that the state considers the observation of human rights to take precedence over extradition and raises the issue of the hierarchy between obligations stemming from conventions respectively governing these legal constructs (par. 9.2). The emphasis will be on the violations of those human rights that are most closely connected to the criminal trial and subsequent punishment, to wit, capital punishment, torture and other cruel, inhumane or degrading treatment, (arbitrary) deprivation of liberty and infringements of fair trial rights. These topics will be addressed separately in subsequent paragraphs (9.3–9.5). As will transpire in these sections, the balancing of a duty to extradite and concern for human rights can indeed be conducive to a real conflict of obligations. As states are naturally inclined to evade such a predicament, they have endeavoured to 'ease their conscience' by speculating either that the violation of human rights will not occur or that the infringement will be less serious than asserted by the fugitive. Such 'techniques' to avoid conflicts of treaty obligations include asking for assurances from the requesting state that the fundamental rights of the fugitive will be observed (par. 9.6), the guarantee that the requested person will have access to a legal remedy whenever his rights have nonetheless been violated (par. 9.7) and the raising of the evidential standard imposed on the fugitive to prove that his rights will be impaired (par. 9.8). The main question in these sections will be whether such devices have found favour in the eyes of the European Court of Human Rights and other international or regional human rights bodies.

The obligation to extradite or surrender a fugitive from justice need not necessarily collide with the duty of a state to protect this person against a prospective violation of his fundamental rights. After all, an extradition treaty may allow for an exception whenever human rights may be jeopardized in the requesting state. Although such exceptions have traditionally been scarce, international instruments on international cooperation in criminal matters have increasingly acknowledged the relevance of due process rights in particular by permitting the requested state to refuse surrender or extradition when such rights are at risk. In this context, the Framework Decision on the European Arrest Warrant deserves special attention, as it provides for a mandatory ground for refusal in case of double jeopardy (*non bis in idem*) and comprises a comprehensive regulation to secure the presence of the accused during his trial. These topics will be discussed in

ing Grounds for Reprisal from the Classic Paradigm to Mutual Recognition and Beyond, Brill/ Nijhoff: Leiden 2019; and Harmen van der Wilt, 'On the Hierarchy between Extradition and Human Rights,' in Erika de Wet & Jure Vidmar (eds.), *Hierarchy in International Law: The Place of Human Rights,* Oxford University Press: Oxford 2012, pp. 148–175.

paragraph 9.9 and par. 9.10, respectively. The chapter rounds off with concluding observations (par. 9.11).

9.2 On the hierarchy between extradition and respect for human rights

Within the context of extradition, conflicts between a treaty-based obligation to extradite and an obligation to observe human rights of the fugitive, stemming from human rights conventions, are likely to arise. As indicated in the previous section, the reasons for this embarrassing situation are not difficult to understand. States are inclined to enter into extradition relations if they have confidence in each other's administration of justice. The incorporation of a clause that questions this mutual trust would appear to be self-contradictory.

Nonetheless, some (extradition) treaties prescribe that extradition should be refused in case of a prospective violation of the human rights in the requesting state, suggesting that respect for human rights should prevail over extradition. An early example is Article 3(2) of the European Convention on Extradition, which contains the 'discrimination' or *non-refoulement* clause, stipulating that extradition must be refused if the requested state

> has substantial grounds for believing that a request for extradition for an ordinary offence has been made for the purpose of prosecuting or punishing a person on account of his race, religion, nationality or political opinion, or that that person's position may be prejudiced for any of these reasons.[8]

The Model Treaty on Extradition, which has been adopted by the United Nations General Assembly, also includes this discrimination clause, but it has extended it with the provision that the extradition is to be refused if the requested person 'has not received or would not receive the minimum guarantees in criminal proceedings, as contained in the International Covenant on Civil and Political Rights, Article 14.'[9]

An even more comprehensive espousal of human rights is exhibited in the Preamble of the Framework Decision on the European Arrest Warrant, paragraph 12 of which declares that 'this Framework Decision respects fundamental rights and observes the principles recognized by Article 6 of the Treaty of the European Union and reflected in the Charter of Fundamental Rights of the European Union.' The subsequent paragraph 13 confirms that

8 European Convention on Extradition, Paris, 13 December 1957, European Treaties Series No. 024.

9 GA Res. 45/116, annex, UN Doc, A/45/49 (1990), 30 ILM 1407 (1991). Compare Dugard & van den Wyngaert, supra footnote 7, pp. 192–193.

'No person shall be removed, expelled or extradited to a State where there is a serious risk that he or she would be subjected to the death penalty, torture or other inhuman or degrading treatment or punishment.'[10]

The legal relevance of this rather sweeping, but implicit, allegiance to human rights is not entirely clear. Mark Mackarel correctly observes that 'the text of the Framework Decision does not include any express provision preventing surrender where the rights of the accused have been or may be infringed' adding that 'the FD does not explicitly allow a refusal to execute an EAW where the relevant law or procedure of the issuing State does not meet its obligations under the ECHR.'[11] More specific guarantees, like protection against double jeopardy and trials in absentia, remain indispensable. We will have an opportunity to revisit these issues in later paragraphs.

The treaty provisions, just mentioned, exemplify Article 30(2) of the Vienna Convention on the Law of Treaties, which indicates that, in case of potential conflict, treaties may regulate their mutual hierarchical relationship themselves.[12]

In the absence of clear priority rules, states are confronted with a conflict of obligations, stemming from treaties that require contrary decisions. If a state decides to refuse an extradition request out of concern for the prospective fate of the requested person, it will flout its obligations, whenever the treaty does not expressly permit the state to do so. If, on the other hand, the requested state decides to take the risk and surrenders the fugitive, that state may turn out to be co-responsible for a violation of human rights, not only vis-à-vis the victimized individual, but also towards its contracting partners of a human rights convention.[13] Some authors have attempted to resolve this quandary by postulating the wholesale supremacy of human rights on the basis of Article 30(1) of the Vienna Convention.[14] This provision refers to Article 103 of the UN Charter that stipulates that all Charter obligations prevail over obligations stemming from other treaties. Article 55 of the UN Charter qualifies the promotion of universal respect for, and protection of human rights as one of the major purposes of the United Nations and

10 Council Framework Decision of 13 June 2002 on the European Arrest Warrant and the Surrender Proceedings between Member States, (2002/584/JHA), OJ L 190, 18 July 2002, p. 1.

11 Mark Mackarel, 'Human Rights as a Barrier to Extradition,' in: Nico Keijzer & Elies van Sliedregt (eds.), *The European Arrest Warrant in Practice*, TMC Asser Press: The Hague 2009, p. 143.

12 Vienna Convention on the Law of Treaties, Vienna, 23 May 1969, 1155 UNTS 331. The provision stipulates that 'when a treaty specifies that it is subject to, or that it is not to be considered as incompatible with, an earlier or later treaty, the provisions of that other treaty prevail.'

13 Van der Wilt, supra footnote 7, p. 148.

14 See, in particular. W. Kälin, *Das Prinzip des Non-Refoulement*, Peter Lang: Bern 1982, p. 166.

could therefore be considered as such an obligation.[15] It is questionable, however, whether such a general reference could sustain the hierarchical superiority of all human rights as it fails to mention which human rights should prevail and what level of infringement is required.[16] From this perspective, it is imperative to distinguish between those 'robust' rights that are unassailable under all circumstances and those human rights that are less absolute, a distinction that the European Court of Human Rights has corroborated. In the *Soering* case, the court has qualified the prohibition against torture and inhuman or degrading treatment as 'absolute.'[17] And in a more general sense, the court has held that Article 3 of the Convention makes no provision for exceptions and no derogations from it permissible under Article 15 even in the event of a public emergency threatening the life of the nation.[18] Although the European Court does not explicitly refer to *jus cogens,* it seems fair to assume that the non-derogable and absolute character of the prohibition of torture and inhuman treatment coincides with its status of peremptory norm under international law.[19] Swart has observed that, should the compliance with an extradition request be incompatible with a *jus cogens* norm, the extradition treaty must, in accordance with Article 31(3) sub c of the Vienna Convention, be interpreted in such a way as to avoid a conflict with that norm. After all, *jus cogens* norms belong to the category of 'any relevant rules of international law applicable in the relations between parties.'[20] In actual practice, this implies that the compliance with the request should yield to the concern that the fugitive might face torture or inhuman treatment.

We can therefore conclude that the norms provided for in international conventions on human rights do not, as a matter of principle, prevail over obligations to extradite based on preexisting extradition treaties. Such supremacy is reserved only for those absolute human rights that belong to the realm of *jus cogens*, which include the prohibition against torture or inhuman treatment and the *nullum crimen* principle, as far as the conduct for which the extradition is requested does not constitute a criminal offence in the requesting state.

15 Kälin, supra footnote 14.
16 Van der Wilt, supra footnote 7, p. 151.
17 *Soering* case, supra footnote 1, section 88.
18 ECtHR, *Ireland v. United Kingdom*, App. No. 5310/71 (1978), Series A no. 25, section 163.
19 The International Criminal Tribunal for the former Yugoslavia has explicitly held that the obligation to forestall the occurrence of torture, cruel, inhuman or degrading treatment and the concomitant prohibition of exposing someone to such treatment is part of *jus cogens,* ICTY, *Prosecutor v. Furundžija,* No. IT-95-17/1-T, Judgment, 10 December 1998, section 147.
20 A.H.J.Swart, Nederlands Uitleveringsrecht, Tjeenk Willink: Zwolle 1986, p. 95.

9.3 Capital punishment versus the right to life

Although the abolitionist movement against capital punishment is winning ground, one must admit that the assertion of Dugard and van den Wyngaert that 'it is difficult to argue that customary law contains a rule prohibiting the death penalty' still holds true 20 years later.[21] The lingering controversy over the moral and legal acceptability of capital punishment is reflected in the Model Treaty on Extradition, which qualifies the death penalty only as an optional ground for refusal.[22] Regional instruments on extradition often exhibit a bolder approach by categorically excluding extradition in case of impending capital punishment.[23]

Usually, the legal position of the requested state is taken as a point of reference, allowing this state to refuse extradition whenever it would be precluded from imposing capital punishment, either by its own national law or by its being party to a human rights instrument that prohibits the death penalty. Accordingly, Article 11 of the European Convention on Extradition allows the refusal of extradition:

> If the offence for which extradition is requested is punishable by death under the law of the requesting Party, *and if in respect of such offence the death-penalty is not provided for by the law of the requested Party or is not normally carried out*, ... unless the requesting Party gives such assurance as the requested Party considers sufficient that the death-penalty will not be carried out.[24]

The European Convention thus saves contracting states from the predicament of having to observe contrary obligations. On the other hand, if the extradition treaty does not contain such a safety valve, the requested state has no other option than to cajole the requesting state to offer assurances that capital punishment will not be imposed. The case of *Short v. the*

21 Dugard & van den Wyngaert, supra footnote 7, p. 196.

22 Model Treaty on Extradition, supra footnote 9, Article 4, sub d: '(Extradition *may* be refused) If the offence for which extradition is requested carries the death penalty under the law of the requesting State, unless that State gives such assurance as the requested State considers sufficient that the death penalty will not be imposed or if imposed will not be carried out' (italics mine).

23 Compare paragraph 13 of the Preamble to the European Arrest Warrant (supra footnote 10) and Article 9 of the Inter-American Convention on Extradition, Caracas, 25 February 1981: 'The States Parties shall not grant extradition when the offence is punishable in the requesting State by the death penalty ..., unless the requested state has previously obtained from the requesting State ... sufficient assurances that this penalty will not be imposed on the person sought or that, if this penalty is imposed, it will not be enforced.' This progressive position is surprising given that capital punishment is not abolished regionwide.

24 European Convention on Extradition, supra footnote 8, italics added.

Netherlands provides an interesting example.[25] The Dutch Supreme Court held that the surrender of an American serviceman to the American NATO forces under the Strategic Forces Agreement (SOFA) would amount to a tort towards the fugitive if the requesting party would not offer guarantees that the death penalty would not be imposed. As the SOFA did not contain an exception clause allowing the refusal of the surrender in case of imminent capital punishment, the Netherlands was confronted with a conflict of obligations, because it was duty bound, by the Sixth Protocol to the European Convention on Human Rights, to refrain from any action that would result in capital punishment. The Netherlands eventually succeeded in obtaining sufficient guarantees from the United States.[26]

While the imposition of capital punishment as such does not per se preclude extradition, the way the penalty is executed may well amount to cruel or inhuman treatment. In the case of *Ng v. Canada*, the UN Human Rights Committee found that 'execution by gas asphyxiation may cause prolonged suffering and agony and does not result in death as swiftly as possible, as asphyxiation by cyanide gas may take over 10 minutes.' As the method of execution did not meet the requirement that capital punishment 'must be carried out in such a way as to cause the least possible physical and mental suffering,' the committee censured Canada's extradition of the fugitive to California, which practiced this method.[27] The decision was in line with the preceding *Soering* judgment of the European Court and exhibited the roundabout strategy of human rights bodies to oppose extradition that might result in capital punishment in the requesting state. The European Court reiterated and even subtly expanded its position in the case of *Al Saadon & Mufdhi v. the United Kingdom*, which involved the transfer of two Iraqi soldiers who had been accused of the murder of British soldiers to Iraq. The applicants claimed that they would run a real risk of being sentenced to death by hanging on return. The court found that the procrastination by the British courts had caused the applicants' psychological suffering, amounting to inhuman treatment under Article 3 of the European Convention.[28] In other words, the court moved the agony of the death row phenomenon to the languishing proceedings in the requested state (-party to the European Convention) and construed an even more direct responsibility for its violation of the Convention. However, as the court ultimately classified the course of events under the heading of Article 3, rather than under Article 2 and the 13th Protocol, one is tempted to ask whether a more

25 Dutch Supreme Court, 30 March 1990, NJ 1991, 249.

26 Van der Wilt, supra footnote 7, p. 165.

27 *Ng v. Canada*, Communication No. 469/1991, U.N. Doc. CCPR/C/49/D/469/1991 (1994).

28 ECtHR, 2 March 2010, Appl. No. 61498/08, *Al Saadon & Mufdhi v. United Kingdom*, section 144.

'sterile' or ' humane' execution would still be acceptable to the European Court.[29]

9.4 Torture and cruel, inhuman or degrading treatment or punishment

9.4.1 Introduction

If there is any human right that would be eligible for trumping extradition obligations, it is assuredly the prohibition of torture. While human rights treaties usually group torture with cruel, inhuman or degrading treatment, the status under customary international law of the latter is less certain because its contours are vague.[30] But even in case of the prospect that the fugitive might be tortured after being surrendered, refusal of extradition is not self-evident. The recurring question is what evidence the requested person is expected to adduce that (s)he will indeed run a real risk of being tortured. We will address the issue in more detail in Section 9.8. Second, torture in the broader sense of the word may be committed not solely by public officials but may be inflicted by non-state actors. In view of the positive obligations that are inherent in the prohibition of torture, extradition (or expulsion) may be refused if it is demonstrated that 'the risk is real and that the authorities of the receiving State are not able to obviate the risk by providing appropriate protection.'[31] The threshold is rather high and will not be easily met.[32]

Balancing extradition and the risk of exposing the fugitive to 'cruel, inhuman or degrading treatment or punishment' is compounded by the nebulous character of that concept. As indicated above, the European Court of Human Rights has acknowledged that the death row phenomenon qualifies as inhuman or degrading treatment. More recently, both the ECtHR and the European Court of Justice have charted new waters by inquiring whether life-long imprisonment and deplorable prison conditions in the requesting state may qualify as 'inhuman or degrading treatment' and may accordingly preclude extradition or surrender.

9.4.2 Life sentences

The findings of the European Court of Human Rights on the question of whether a prospect of life-long imprisonment in the requesting state may preclude extradition must be considered against the backdrop of its general assessment of the (in)compatibility of life imprisonment with Article 3. In the leading

29 In a similar vein, Costa, supra footnote 7, p. 76.

30 Dugard & van den Wyngaert, supra footnote 7, p. 198.

31 ECtHR (Grand Chamber), 22 April 1997, App. No. 11/1996/813, *HLR v. France*, 26 E.H.H.R 29.

32 See also Costa, supra footnote 7, p. 72.

case of *Kafkaris v. Cyprus*, the European Court held that an irreducible life sentence might amount to a violation of Article 3, but only if that sentence was 'grossly disproportionate' to the acts allegedly committed.[33] In *Vinter and others v. the United Kingdom* the court further elaborated its position in holding that, even in the absence of such gross disproportionality,

> a mandatory sentence of life imprisonment without the possibility of parole could give rise to an issue under Article 3, if it could be shown that i) the applicant's continued imprisonment can no longer be justified on any legitimate penological grounds (retribution, deterrence, special prevention); and ii) that the sentence is irreducible *de facto* and *de jure*.[34]

The fact that the court presented these aspects as cumulative conditions demonstrates that the court would apparently find life imprisonment acceptable, provided that such incarceration continued to serve a penological purpose. What is of decisive importance is that revision procedures are in force and applied that enable judicial authorities to reassess continued imprisonment in light of penological objectives.[35]

The execution of life sentences is shrouded in uncertainty and this explains why fugitives face nearly insurmountable hurdles in proving that their extradition should be refused in view of the dismal fate of their never being set free. After all, it involves a matter of (much) speculation on future events. Accordingly, the European Court was not convinced that the applicant, Harkins, whose extradition was sought by the United States on charges of murder and attempted robbery in Florida, would face an inhuman and degrading punishment in the sense of Article 3 because he would be exposed to a mandatory life sentence without parole. The court started by finding that '[Mr. Harkins] has not yet been convicted, still less begun serving his sentence.' It followed by holding that

> Mr. Harkins had not shown that, upon extradition, his incarceration in the United States would not serve any legitimate penological purpose. Indeed, if he is convicted and given a mandatory life sentence, it may well be that, as the Government has submitted, the point at which his continued incarceration would no longer serve any purpose may never arise.

33 ECtHr (Grand Chamber), 12 February 2008 App. No. 21906/04), *Kafkaris v. Cyprus*, sections 97/98.

34 EctHR, 17 January 2012, App. Nos. 66069/09, 130/10, 3896/10), *Vinter and Others v. United Kingdom*, section 93.

35 Such review procedures must at least accommodate the virtual possibility of release, as the Grand Chamber explained in the *Vinter* case: EctHR (GC), 9 July 2013, App. Nos. 66069, 130/10 and 3896/10, sections 109/110.

And the court completed by contending that

> it is still less certain that, if that point were ever reached, the Governor of Florida and the Board of Executive Clemency would refuse to avail themselves of their power to commute the applicant's sentence.[36]

The judgment reveals all the intricacies of assessing prospective violations of human rights in extradition cases, a situation that is aggravated if the potential violation is even further remote in time.

In view of the above, it may come as a surprise that the European Court has found that the extradition of a fugitive to a state where he faced the risk of being sentenced to life imprisonment might affect his right to be protected against inhuman and degrading treatment.[37] Borrowing from the Grand Chamber's findings in the *Vinter* case, the court subjected the review mechanism in force to some quality standards. The gist of the matter was that the convict, at the time of the imposition of the initial sentence, should have a clear idea at what time intervals and on the basis of which standards his continued detention would be reviewed, so that he could adapt his behavior in order to qualify for release.[38] In the absence of mechanisms meeting this standards at the domestic level, 'the incompatibility with Article 3 on this ground already arose at the moment of the imposition of the whole-life sentence and not at a later stage of incarceration.'[39] In assessing the possibilities of reduction of sentences and presidential pardons in the requesting state, to wit, the United States, the Court concluded that

> none of the procedures provided for amounts to a review mechanism requiring the national authorities to ascertain, on the basis of objective, pre-established criteria of which the prisoner had precise cognizance at the time of imposition of the life sentence, whether, while serving his sentence, the prisoner has changed and progressed to such an extent that continued detention can no longer be justified on legitimate penological grounds.[40]

On the basis of the findings of the court in the case of *Trabelsi v. Belgium*, in which the court held that the applicant should be able to ascertain and

36 EctHR, 17 January 2012, Appl. Nos. 9156/07 and 32650/07, *Harkins & Edwards v. United Kingdom*, section 140.

37 EctHr, 4 September 2014, App. No. 440/10, *Trabelsi v. Belgium*.

38 Referring to the *Vinter* case (Grand Chamber) the Court held that 'a whole-life prisoner was entitled to know, at the outset of his sentence, what he must do to be considered for release and under what conditions, including when a review of his sentence would take place or could be sought,' *Trabelsi v. Belgium*, supra footnote 37, section 315.

39 *Trabelsi v. Belgium*, supra footnote 37, referring to paragraph 122 of the *Vinter* judgment.

40 *Trabelsi v. Belgium*, supra footnote 37, section 137.

predict in advance whether and under which conditions he would be eligible for release, one would indeed expect that life imprisonment without parole might be found in contravention of Article 3 and would hence preclude extradition. After all, national systems that fell short of the *Vinter* criteria and in which the fugitive would only be at the mercy of the executive's decision would be found wanting in observing the requirements of Article 3.

However, the subsequent outcome in the case of *Hutchinson v. United Kingdom* casts doubt on this hopeful conclusion.[41] In this case, the European Court suddenly found favour in the British review system that had not fundamentally changed and was largely predicated on the Secretary of State's power of release. Submitting to the British court's conclusion that the Home Secretary must consider all exceptional circumstances that would warrant a sentence reduction, the court confirmed that the UK's system of reviewing whole life sentences complied with Article 3. The European Court thus appears to recant its former principled position that the convicted person should at the sentencing trial have some perspective that he might at some point be released. Such a retreat may easily backfire on the extradition context, as the Court may find peace with an extradition that exposes the requested person to lifelong imprisonment, speculating that there is always an opportunity to obtain a pardon from the executive. This takes us effectively back to the *Harkins* and *Edwards* era. However, one should not forget that the *Hutchinson* outcome was situation specific, representing a truce after a protracted conflict between the European Court and the United Kingdom over the compatibility of the British review system with Article 3 of the Convention.[42] Moreover, I agree with Costa that the *Trabelsi* case constitutes an important precedent that cannot be simply set aside by a more 'lenient' approach that is unrelated to the extradition configuration.[43] We will have to wait whether the court, in an extradition case, will stick to its *Trabelsi* judgment or will apply its view as expressed in *Hutchinson*.

In the meantime, Article 5(2) of the Framework Decision on the European Arrest Warrant allows member states to make execution of an EAW conditional on a guarantee that, if the offence for which the EAW has been issued is punishable by a life sentence, the requesting state provides for a review of that sentence. The provision reads as follows:

41 ECtHr, 3 February 2015, App. No. 57592/08, *Hutchinson v. United Kingdom*.

42 The *Hutchinson* outcome has been fiercely criticized in English legal literature; see, for instance, Naomi Hart, 'Case Comment: Whole Life Sentences in the United Kingdom: Volte-face for the European Court of Human Rights?' 74 *Common Law Journal* (2015), p. 215; and Mark Pettigrew, 'A Vinter Retreat in Europe: Returning to the Issue of Whole Life Sentences in Strasbourg,' 8 *New Journal of English Criminal Law* (2017), p. 132.

43 Costa, supra footnote 7, p. 82.

Article 5 The execution of the European Arrest Warrant by the executing judicial authority may, by the law of the executing Member State, be subject to the following conditions

...

2. If the offence on the basis of which the European arrest warrant has been issued is punishable by custodial life sentence or life-time detention order, the execution of the said arrest warrant may be subject to the condition that the issuing Member State has provisions in its legal system for a review of the penalty or measure imposed, on request or at the latest after 20 years, or for the application of measures of clemency to which the applicant is entitled to apply for under the law or practice of the issuing Member State, aiming at a non-execution of such penalty or measure.

In an early commentary on the European Arrest Warrant, Judge Rob Blekxtoon has censured the arrangement for putting clemency measures, which are by definition not enforceable, on the same par with an obligatory reassessment of the sentence.[44] The discussion reminds us of the easy conflation of rights and favours by the European Court of Human Rights, as expounded above.

9.4.3 Prison conditions

While the provision on (guarantees in case of) life sentences in the EAW Framework Decision appears to be rather disappointing, the European Court of Justice (ECJ) has made considerable progress in addressing poor prison conditions within the European Union and considering such conditions as a potential ground for refusing the execution of an EAW. In 1998, Dugard and van den Wyngaert could still contend that 'there is judicial support for the view that poor prison conditions, including gross overcrowding, qualify as inhuman and degrading punishment.'[45] Nowadays, such assertion seems rather demure, at least within the legal context of the European Arrest Warrant. In a landmark decision, the ECJ held that mutual trust on which the entire EAW system is predicated could be rebutted if the execution of a European Arrest Warrant would result in a real risk of torture or degrading treatment of the requested person if he were to be transferred to the issuing state.[46] So far, the European Court of Justice obviously did not transcend the well-known *Soering* dictum of its colleague in Strasbourg,

44 Judge Rob Blekxtoon, 'Commentary on an Article by Article Basis,' in: Judge Rob Blekxtoon & Wouter van Ballegooij, *Handbook on the European Arrest Warrant*, TMC Asser Press: The Hague, 2005, p. 241: ' This subparagraph juxtaposes ... both ways of adapting of a life sentence as if they are more or less equivalent. This is not realistic.'

45 Dugard & van den Wyngaert, supra footnote 7, p. 200.

46 ECJ, 5 April 2016, C-404/15 and C-659/15 PPU, *Aranyosi and Căldăraru*.

but the court explicitly tied the concept of 'degrading treatment' to prison conditions. It proceeded by holding that

> If the judicial authority of the executing Member State is in possession of evidence of a real risk of inhuman or degrading treatment of individuals detained in the issuing Member State, this judicial authority is bound to assess the existence of that risk.[47]

The assessment involved a two-step procedure. It should start with an inquiry of a general nature that should be based

> on information that is objective, reliable, specific and properly updated on the detention conditions prevailing in the issuing Member State and that demonstrates that there are deficiencies, which may be systemic or generalised, or which may affect certain groups of people, or which may affect certain places of detention.[48]

But such a general assessment would not suffice and justify the refusal of the execution of the EAW. The executing judicial authority must also investigate 'specifically and precisely' whether 'the person concerned will actually be subjected to this risk in the particular circumstances of the case.'[49] To that purpose, the executing judicial authority should attempt to obtain additional information, setting a time limit on the procurement of such information. The approach of the ECJ is reminiscent of the position of the ECtHR that is never satisfied with loose claims as to the general lack of human rights protection in the requesting state, but requires that the defence enters into detail, explaining why the fugitive would be particularly at risk.

The ECJ is less clear, however, on how the executing state should proceed if such information is not forthcoming or if the risk of degrading or inhuman treatment, due to dismal detention conditions, cannot be discounted. It indicates that in such a case the surrender must be suspended and that Eurojust and the Council of the EU should be informed. However, an outright refusal seems to be taboo. In the meantime, however, the fugitive remains in detention, awaiting a possible surrender, and, as such a detention cannot be perpetuated indefinitely, the executing judicial authority must decide whether the surrender procedure must be brought to an end.[50] The meanderings of the court illustrate its utter reluctance to ques-

47 *Aranyosi and Căldăraru,* supra footnote 46, section 88.

48 *Aranyosi and Căldăraru,* supra footnote 46, section 89

49 *Aranyosi and Căldăraru,* supra footnote 46, section 94.

50 *Aranyosi and Căldăraru,* supra footnote 46, section 104. In the case of *Lanigan v. Minister for Justice and Equality* (ECJ, 16 July 2015, Case C-237) the ECJ held that, in case of surrender proceedings, the requested state may still be required to prolong detention if time limits have been exceeded, but only 'provided that that duration is not excessive in the light

tion the principle of mutual recognition and its aversion to thwart the 'free movement of suspects and convicts' beyond the scope that the Framework Decision provides. Nonetheless, the *Aranyosi and Căldăraru* judgment has been welcomed with relief by executing judicial authorities in the EU member states because it alleviated growing concerns and confirmed the practice of making surrender conditional on guarantees that the fugitive would be properly treated during detention.[51]

The European Court of Human Rights, on its part, has provided a very useful normative framework by indicating in much detail whether overcrowded prisons, in particular, would amount to inhuman and degrading treatment in the sense of Article 3. In its pilot judgment *Ananyev and others v. Russia* the court set the standard by holding that each inmate should be afforded sufficient 'personal space,' This implied that

> (1) each detainee must have an individual sleeping place in the cell; (2) each detainee must dispose of at least 3 sq. m of floor space; and (3) the overall surface of the cell must be such as to allow detainees to move freely between furniture. The absence of any of these elements created a strong presumption that the conditions of an applicant's detention were inadequate.[52]

In *Muršič v. Croatia*, the Grand Chamber of the ECtHR confirmed this minimum standard but elaborated on it by holding that this presumption of a violation of Article 3 could be rebutted if the extremely limited personal space was compensated by short periods of restriction to such detention, adequate out-of-cell facilities, freedom of movement and general (decent) detention conditions.[53] Moreover, the court found that general prison conditions, like access to air and light and compliance with basic sanitary and hygienic requirements, would still have to be taken into account, even if the 'personal space' was not at issue.[54] Executing judicial authorities have followed suit by applying the Muršič standards. A detailed discussion of the case law would exceed the limits of a general introduction to the problem.[55]

---

of the characteristics of the procedure followed in the case in the main proceedings, which is a matter to be ascertained by the national court' (section 63).

51 See also T.P. Marguery, 'Towards the End of Mutual Trust? Prison Conditions in the Context of the European Arrest Warrant and the Transfer of Prisoner Framework Decisions,' 25(6) *Maastricht Journal of European and Comparative Law* (2019), pp. 704–717; https://journals.sagepub.com/doi/full/10.1177/1023263X18818662.

52 ECtHR, 10 January 2012, App. Nos. 42525/07 & 60800/08, *Ananyev v. Russia*, section 148.

53 ECtHR (Grand Chamber), 20 October 2016, App. No. 7334/13, *Muršič v. Croatia*, section 135.

54 ECtHR (Grand Chamber), supra footnote 53, section 139.

55 Compare Marguery, supra footnote 51, who specifically mentions Italy – courts tend to ask the name of the prison, the expected minimum individual space, hygiene conditions, clean-

Suffice to observe that the growing concern for prison conditions in Europe illustrates more generally that human rights of the fugitive are to be taken seriously and that such attention should counterbalance a lopsided emphasis on efficient crime repression by means of international cooperation. This development is of course made possible by the incorporation of a general human rights clause in the legislation of the member states, but spurred by the European Court of Justice and the ECtHR which offer normative guidance in their case law.

9.5 Fair trial rights

Before we turn to the question if and to what extent (prospective) violations of fair trial rights in the *requesting* state should impede extradition, it bears emphasis that – at least theoretically – the compatibility with Article 6 of the European Convention and Article 14 of the ICCPR could arise in respect of extradition proceedings themselves. It begs the question whether such a procedure involves the 'determination of a criminal charge,' as indicated in Article 6. On several occasions, the ECtHR has answered this question in the negative:

> The words 'determination … of a criminal charge' in Article 6(1) of the Convention relate to the full process of examining an individual's guilt or innocence in respect of a criminal offence, and not merely, *as in the case of extradition proceedings,* to the process of determining whether or not a person may be extradited to a foreign country.[56]

One may be tempted to wonder whether such a bold assertion would be tenable in respect of surrender proceedings under the European Arrest Warrant scheme. After all, one could argue that such proceedings, also in view of the reduced number of grounds for refusal, are an integrated part of the criminal process in the executing state. Pointing at the different character of extradition and surrender, Paul Garlick has indeed contended that

> The importance of this distinction is that the EAW is actually one of the steps in the criminal proceedings in the issuing state, and therefore it is plainly arguable that not only the fundamental human rights enshrined

liness of cells and inquire if mechanisms are available to control effective detention conditions – and the Netherlands – requesting the issuing authority to ensure that the requested person is not detained in a specific prison. Marguery expresses his concern, however, that such laudable standards are not taken into consideration in case of transfer of prisoners.

56 ECtHR, 4 February 2005, Appl. Nos. 46827/99 and 4695/99, *Mamatkulov and Askarov v. Turkey*, section 82; ECtHR 20 February 2007, App. No. 35865/03, *Al-Moayad v. Germany*, section 93 (italics added).

in Articles 3 and 5 of the ECHR are engaged in the process of executing the EAW, but so are the fair trial rights enshrined in Article 6.[57]

It remains to be seen whether the ECJ will share Garlick's point of view. Until now, no judgment on the specific legal issue has been rendered.

In line with the configuration as expounded above, concerns about the fairness of the criminal trial in the requesting state may hamper the decision to grant extradition. In the *Soering* case, the European Court of Human Rights acknowledged the possibility, but its language was extremely cautious: 'it *cannot be ruled* out that an issue might *exceptionally* arise under Article 6 of the Convention by an extradition in circumstances where the fugitive has suffered or risks suffering a *flagrant* denial of a fair trial in the requesting country.'[58] Whereas the court apparently does not differentiate between past and prospective violations ('suffered or risks suffering'), Dugard and van den Wyngaert rightly avow that it makes sense to make such a distinction.[59] From an evidentiary point of view, it is obviously much easier to determine the seriousness of an impairment of due process that already occurred, for instance, if procedures have sustained undue delay or if extradition is requested in order to enforce an *in absentia* judgment, which did not allow a retrial on the facts. The point is that, apart from the infringement being obvious, the damage can sometimes not be repaired. We will address these aspects in subsequent sections. Nonetheless, the ECtHR has been reluctant to acknowledge that a contracting party might be duty-bound to refuse international cooperation if its counterpart had already violated due process rights, reasoning that states parties were not expected to impose their standards on third states. Moreover, such a review of fair trial standards would also thwart international cooperation from which the persons concerned might benefit.[60] This observation requires some clarification. Different from extradition in which the requested person is exposed to foreign justice with all its concomitant uncertainties, in case of the transfer of the execution of a foreign sentence the convicted person has the advantage that (s)he is allowed to serve her/his sentence in her/his native country. The device of transfer of execution of sentences can from this perspective be considered as the mirror image of extradition. If the courts of the executing state were to tie their approval of taking over the execution of the foreign sentence to stringent conditions as to the quality of the preceding trial, a negative outcome would deprive the person from a clear advantage.

57 Paul Garlick, 'The European Arrest Warrant and the ECHR', in: Blekxtoon & Van Ballegooij, footnote 44, pp. 167–168.

58 *Soering* case, supra footnote 1, section 319 (italics added).

59 Dugard & van den Wyngaert, supra footnote 7, p. 203. They point out that the 1990 UN Model Treaty on Extradition does not differentiate either.

60 ECtHR, 26 June 1992, App. No. 56176 (1992), *Drozd and Janousek v. France and Spain*, section 110.

The predicament came to the fore in the case of *Drozd and Janousek v. France and Spain* that indeed concerned a transfer of the execution of a judgment by a court of Andorra. As that country lacked proper prison facilities, the convicts were left the choice to serve their sentences in either France or Spain. The applicants, however, claimed that the Andorran court did not qualify as an independent and impartial court in the sense of Article 6, par. 1 of the Convention and that their right of a fair trial was therefore compromised. For all practical intents and purposes, the court applied the rigid standard of the *Soering* case, holding that a state would be obliged to refuse cooperation 'if it emerges that the conviction is the result of a *flagrant denial* of justice.'[61] While the court thus condoned the infringement of fair trial rights and thereby removed an obstacle for international cooperation that might indeed be in the interest of the convicted person, it aggravated the principle problem. After all, the court's finding implied that contracting states would be under an obligation to refuse the execution of a foreign judgment that flouted the most basic due process rights, thus preventing their nationals from serving a prison sentence in their home country. It is a quandary that cannot easily be resolved.[62]

While the *Drozd and Janousek* case involved the assessment of a preceding procedure that could at least be tested against the prerequisites of Article 6 ECHR, the situation is more complicated if the fugitive claims that (s)he will face a risk of being exposed to violation of her fair trial rights after being extradited. Between national jurisdictions, there is no common understanding on what exactly constitutes a 'fair trial' and civil and common law systems differ to a considerable extent as to the requirements this concept entails in the realm of disclosure obligations, regulation of cross-examination and prohibition of double jeopardy.[63] Any refusal of extradition on that basis will soon invite the criticism that the requested state engages in legal imperialism, while a prediction is notoriously difficult to make because the assessment of the fairness of a trial can usually occur only in retrospect.

Such considerations explain why the European Court and other human rights bodies are inclined to apply a high threshold, requiring the requesting contracting party to refuse extradition only in case of blatant violations of fundamental fair trial rights, which emanate from previous infringements. Accordingly, the ECtHR elaborated in the *Al Moayad* case on the content of the *Soering* standard, holding that

61 *Drozd and Janousek v. France and Spain*, supra footnote 60.

62 Compare for these problems in the Dutch legal context, H.G. van der Wilt, 'De WOTS jubileert: Maar valt er eigenlijk wel wat te vieren?' 28 *Delikt en Delinkwent* (1998), p. 236.

63 Dugard & van den Wyngaert, supra footnote 7, p. 204. For a different, slightly more nuanced view, see Chr. Brants, S.A. Field, N. Jörg, 'Are adversarial and inquisitorial systems converging?' in: Chr. Harding, P.W.H. Fenell, N. Jörg and B. Swart, *Criminal Justice in Europe; A Comparative Study*, Clarendon Press: Oxford, 1995, pp. 41–56.

> A flagrant denial of a fair trial, and thereby a denial of justice, undoubtedly occurs where a person is detained because of suspicions that he has been planning or has committed a criminal offence without having any access to an independent and impartial tribunal to have the legality of his or her detention reviewed and, if the suspicions do not prove to be well-founded, to obtain release... Likewise, a deliberate and systematic refusal of access to a lawyer to defend oneself, especially when the person is detained in a foreign country, must be considered to amount to a flagrant denial of a fair trial within the meaning of Article 6 of §§ 1 and 3c.[64]

Again, the court alluded only to a theoretical possibility because in the case under scrutiny the court denied that the applicant would be exposed to such an ordeal.[65]

In actual practice, the court has concluded only that the deportation of a fugitive to another country would amount to a violation of Article 6 if there was a real risk that evidence obtained by torture of third persons would be admitted at the applicant's retrial. In the case at issue, *Othman v. United Kingdom*, which concerned an expulsion from the United Kingdom to Jordan, the court initially subsumed lack of fairness of the trial under the preceding torture (and make it subservient to the violation of that peremptory norm) by quoting from the Grand Chamber's judgment in *Gäfgen v. Germany*:[66]

> The use of such evidence, secured as a result of a violation of one of the core and absolute rights guaranteed by the Convention, always raises serious issues as to the fairness of the proceedings, even if the admission of such evidence was not decisive in securing a conviction. Accordingly, the Court has found in respect of confessions, as such, that the admission of statements obtained as a result of torture or of other ill-treatment in breach of Article 3 as evidence to establish the relevant facts in criminal proceedings rendered the proceedings as a whole unfair. This finding applied irrespective of the probative value of the statements and irrespective of whether their use was decisive in securing the defendant's conviction.[67]

Remarkably, the court in *Othman* in a subsequent paragraph noted the autonomous meaning of a fair trial by emphasising the pernicious consequences of the use of tainted evidence on the truthfulness of its outcome:

64 *Al Moayad v. Germany*, supra footnote 56, section 101.

65 We will revisit the Al Moayad case in the next section on assurances.

66 ECtHR, 1 June 2010, App no. 22987/05, *Gäfgen v. Germany*.

67 EctHR, 17 January 2012, Ap. No. 8139/09, *Othman v. United Kingdom*, section 265, quoting from Gäfgen, supra footnote 66, section 165.

> the Court considers that the admission of torture evidence is manifestly contrary, not just to the provisions of Article 6, but to the most basic international standards of a fair trial. It would make the whole trial not only immoral and illegal, *but also entirely unreliable in its outcome*. It would, therefore, be a flagrant denial of justice if such evidence were admitted in a criminal trial.[68]

We will have occasion to revisit this important judgment, in the context of both assurances (Section 9.6) and the required standard of evidence to be procured by the defence in case of extradition proceedings (Section 9.8). Suffice it for the moment to observe that the court acknowledges the significance of a fair trial as an independent value, the potential encroachment whereof might stand in the way of extradition, and not only as a tool to discourage the use of torture. The European Court slightly reproved the British Court of Appeal that still forged a strong link between torture and the subsequent use of its 'fruits' in a criminal trial letting the former prevail over the latter.[69] It raises also the question whether this approach would encourage the European Court or other international human rights institutions to move beyond the particulars of this configuration and balance extradition against the risk of other fair trial incursions in the requesting state. After all, structural iniquities in the procedure or institutional flaws might also affect the legal rights of the fugitive, impair the equality of arms and (hence) jeopardize the reliability of the outcome of the trial.

A comprehensive inquiry into the sustainability of the European Arrest Warrant system in case of serious apprehensions as to the quality and fairness of criminal proceedings in a member state came to the fore after legislative reforms in Poland.[70] The Irish High Court made a reference for a preliminary ruling of the European Court of Justice, inquiring what the consequences of the demise of the rule of law in Poland would be for the execution of EAW's.[71] The immediate cause for the preliminary ruling was a requested person's opposing his surrender to Poland, claiming that he would be exposed to a real risk of a flagrant denial of justice in contravention of

68 *Othman v. United Kingdom*, supra footnote 67, section 267, italics added.

69 Court of Appeal, 9 April 2008, *OO (Jordan) v. Secretary of State for the Home Department*, 2009 WL 833661. The High Court observed that 'the use of evidence obtained by torture is prohibited in Convention law not just because that will make the trial unfair, but also and more particularly because of the connection of the issue with article 3, a fundamental, unconditional and non-derogable prohibition that stands at the center of the Convention protections.'

70 See for the background of the rule of law crisis in Poland: Ewa Zelazna, 'The Rule of Law Crisis Deepens in Poland after A.K. v. Krajowa Rada Sadownictwa and CP, DO v. Sad Najwyzszy,' in 3 *European Papers*, Volume 4 2019, pp. 907–912; http://europeanpapers.eu/en/system/files/pdf_version/EP_EF_2020_I_001_Ewa_Zelazna_0.pdf.

71 European Court of Justice (Grand Chamber), 25 July 2018, Case-216/18 PPU (Minister for Justice and Equality).

Article 6 of the EU Charter. In his submission, he elucidated that the recent legislative reforms of the judicial system in Poland would deprive him of a fair trial, adding that those reforms affected the mutual trust that sustained international cooperation in criminal matters in the European Union and called the operation of the European Arrest Warrant system into question.[72] These submissions were supported by a reasoned proposal of the Commission that had expressed concerns about the ensuing lack of independence of the Polish judiciary. Adopting these findings and making them its own, the Irish court pointed at specific developments like the minister of justice serving as public prosecutor and equipped with disciplinary powers over presidents of courts, which would have a chilling effect on those presidents, the compulsory retirement of members of the Supreme Court and their replacement by political appointees and the interference in the activities of the Constitutional Court, jeopardizing the compliance of statutes with the Constitution.[73]

The crucial issue in the preliminary ruling under scrutiny was whether the executing judicial authority should, in view of the systemic demise of the rule of law and the concomitant infringement of fair trial in the issuing state, still assess whether the individual concerned was exposed to a real risk of an unfair trial. After all, such a 'specific and precise' inquiry was demanded by the *Aranyosi and Căldăraru* scheme.[74] And if such a specific investigation was necessary, what guarantees would the executing authority be expected to obtain? The ECJ elaborated on the eminent value of judicial protection, emphasising its relevance within the context of the operation of the European Arrest Warrant system:

> The high level of trust between Member States on which the European arrest warrant mechanism is based is thus founded on the premise that the criminal courts of the other Member States ... meet the requirements of effective judicial protection, which include, in particular, the independence and impartiality of those courts.[75]

It proceeded by acknowledging that, if the fugitive would be exposed to a real risk of being deprived of his fundamental right to be tried by an independent and impartial court after being surrendered, the executing authorities would, exceptionally, be allowed to refrain from giving effect to the European Arrest Warrant. However, an automatic refusal, on the basis of the general deficiency of judicial protection in the issuing member

72 ECJ, 25 July 2018, supra footnote 71, section 16.

73 ECJ, 25 July 2018, supra footnote 71, section 21.

74 ECJ, 25 July 2018, supra footnote 71, section 25. For this judgment, see supra footnote 46 and accompanying text.

75 ECJ, 25 July 2018, supra footnote 71, section 58.

state, would be too bold a step, that could be taken only after the European Council had decided to suspend the execution of European Arrest Warrants in view of a finding of serious and persistent encroachment in the issuing member state of the principles set out in Article 7 of the Treaty on the European Union, including those inherent in the rule of law. The court thus fell back on its *Aranyosi and Căldăraru* standard, requiring that the executing judicial authority would investigate whether the individual concerned ran a risk of suffering impairment of his fair trial rights. Such inquiry involved two steps. First, it was mandatory to sort out whether the general and structural deficiencies had an impact on the quality of adjudication of the specific court that would be called to conduct the criminal trial. Next,

> If that examination shows that those deficiencies are liable to affect those courts, the executing judicial authority must also assess, in the light of the specific concerns expressed by the individual concerned and any information provided by him, whether there are substantial grounds for believing that he will run a real risk of breach of his fundamental right to an independent tribunal and, therefore, of the essence of his fundamental right to a fair trial, having regard to his personal situation, as well as to the nature of the offence for which he is being prosecuted and the factual context that form the basis of the European arrest warrant.[76]

It goes practically without saying that the ECJ expected the executing judicial authority to enter into a constructive dialogue with its counterparts in order to apprise itself in detail of the parameters as expounded above.

The judgment elicits mixed feelings. On the one hand, one might be surprised and slightly disappointed that the court still adheres to the stringent *Aranyosi* criteria, in view of the severe and structural decline of the rule of law in Poland. Would it be warranted to expose any fugitive to a judiciary that presumably lacked the features of independence due to external influence? However, it is understandable that the court shied away from categorically forestalling the execution of EAW's, issued by Polish authorities and considered this as a measure of last resort, to be taken by the Council, as such a drastic method would bring international cooperation with an EU member state to a virtual standstill.[77] Moreover, one could argue that persistent and critical communication with the Polish judiciary, themselves under siege by political powers, would be instrumental in restoring the rule of law and would sustain those segments in the judiciary that craved

76 ECJ, 25 July 2018, supra footnote 71, section 75.

77 In this sense also Vincent Glerum, 'Reflecties op het Arrest *LM*,' 45 *NTM/NJCM Bulletin* (2020), pp. 85–86, who observes that it is inevitable that courts inquire whether requested persons are *individually* exposed to a real risk of fair trial violations, as a categorical refusal of surrender would involve a suspension of the European Arrest Warrant system and would distort the balance between protection of fundamental rights and law enforcement.

(outside) moral and legal support. On the positive side, one should observe that the ECJ in this important decision charted new areas in the relation between extradition/ surrender and human rights, where both the court itself and the Strasbourg Court had feared to tread. For one thing, it was crystal clear that structural deficiencies, conducive to infringements on fair trial rights in the requesting state, could impede the surrender of an individual. The court moved beyond the rather specific situation in which evidence, obtained by torture, would probably be used at the trial, rendering its outcome unreliable and the trial itself blatantly unfair. Moreover, while the court in *Aranyosi* seemed to favour endless protraction of negotiations on guarantees, without even explicitly mentioning that the executing was permitted at a certain point to refuse the surrender, in this case it was far more dauntless. Although the court still demonstrated much circumspection, employing carefully chosen language, it even held that the executing judicial would be *under an obligation* to refrain from giving effect to the European Arrest Warrant

> If the information ... that was sent to the executing judicial authority does not lead the latter to discount the existence of a real risk that the individual concerned will suffer in the issuing Member State a breach of his fundamental right to an independent tribunal and, therefore, of the essence of his fundamental right to a fair trial.[78]

Finally, the court emphasised the necessity of fair trial proceedings and judicial protection in the context of the operation of the European Arrest Warrant system, thereby issuing a clear message that the observance of the rule of law was a common responsibility of the member states engaging in such close cooperation in criminal matters.

In its most recent judgment, the European Court of Justice adhered to its 'two steps approach' in a preliminary decision on questions of the District Court of Amsterdam, inquiring whether the further demise of the Polish judicial system would compel a categorical suspension of international cooperation.[79] The judgment clarified some further issues. For one thing, the court confirmed that a request for surrender could also be refused if the EAW was issued for the purpose of enabling the requesting state (viz., Poland) to execute a sentence. Apparently, the court reasoned that lack of judicial independence can also easily compromise the fairness of the ultimate sentence. Second, the court, rather than copying the 'flagrant denial

78 ECJ, 25 July 2018, supra footnote 71, section 78. In such a situation 'the executing judicial authority *must* refrain from giving effect to the EAW'; emphasis added.

79 European Court of Justice, 17 December 2020, C-354 PPU and C-412/20 PPU, *L & P*. For an illuminating comment, see S.M.A. Lestrade, ' L&P, HvJ, zaak C-354/20 PPU en C/412/20 PPU – Ondanks aanhoudende rechtsstaatcrisis mogen Poolse EAB's niet structureel worden geweigerd' (Annotatie bij Hof van Justitie van de Europese Unie, 17-12-2020, ECLI:EU:C:2020_1033, *European Human Rights Cases*-2021-0017.

of justice' standard of the European Court of Human Rights, qualified the impendent violation of the right to be tried by an independent court as a nullification of 'the very essence of the right to a fair trial.' It raises the question whether the ECJ harbours a lower standard than its counterpart from Strasbourg. For the case under scrutiny the question has little relevance, as lack of independence meets both standards. [80]

The recent decisions of the European Court of Justice on the consequences of the erosion of the rule of law in Poland for the practical application of the EAW system demonstrate that the court is prepared to accept that mutual recognition in exceptional cases has to yield to the protection of fair trial rights. Simultaneously, this position has its limits, as a categorical denunciation of the Polish procedural system would stifle all cooperation with Poland and be conducive to impunity.[81] The court is sooner inclined to order temporal suspension of the execution of European Arrest Warrants if procedural and institutional flaws, amounting to infringements of the right to a fair trial, can be repaired. It used such suspension as a lever to force member states of the European Union, including Poland, to change their procedure of issuing EAW's by assigning that task to (independent) judicial authorities rather than prosecutors.[82] In case of systemic and pervasive crises in the rule of law, such tactics are unavailable. It raises awkward questions about the sustainability of the principle of mutual recognition and trust as the foundation of international cooperation with such states.

9.6 Assurances

In view of the embarrassment caused by a conflict of treaty obligations, as expounded in Section 9.2, it is understandable that states make attempts to circumvent such a predicament. Two strategies that are applied in particular include the asking of assurances from the requesting state that it will observe the human rights of the surrendered person and an inquiry whether local remedies are extant. While we will address the latter in Section 9.7, this paragraph discusses the former.

The practice of states requesting assurances in respect of human rights protection, deportation or extradition is widespread. There is a paradoxical element in this practice. After all, the urge to request assurances is triggered by the apprehensions in respect of the observance of human rights in the requesting state in the first place. How is one to assess the quality of such assurances and whether they are reliable? The European Court of Human Rights has acknowledged the problem by noting that 'the preliminary

80 In a similar vein, Glerum, supra footnote 77, p. 84.

81 See Lestrade, supra footnote 79, section 9.

82 ECJ (Grand Chamber), 24 November 2020, C-510/19, *AZ* and ECJ (Grand Chamber), 27 May 2019, C-508/18 and C-82/19 PPU, *OG & PI*.

question is whether the general human rights situation in the receiving State excludes accepting any assurances whatsoever,' adding, however, that ' it will only be in rare cases that (such) situation will mean that no weight at all can be given to assurances.'[83] The issues surrounding assurances have yielded ample case law, both from international/regional courts on human rights and from national courts.[84] All the details of the topic need not detain us. We will focus on the quality and veracity of assurances, the manner in which they can be verified and to what extent the cogency of assurances depends on the nature of the potential violations at issue.

The quality and reliability of assurances are largely dependent on their specificity and past experiences with the requesting state. In the case of *Al Moayad v. Germany*, mentioned above, the latter had obtained assurances from the United States – the requesting state – that the applicant would not be transferred to one of the detention facilities outside the USA in respect of which interrogation techniques at variance with Article 3 had been reported. The German authorities had been allowed to attend proceedings against the applicant in the United States and had indeed corroborated that Al Moayad had not been detained in a prison outside the United States prior to or during his trial. The court attached importance to the fact that Germany's confidence in previous dealings with the United States had not been diminished and concluded that, there being no evidence that human rights of terrorist suspects had been compromised in regular detention facilities within the United States, 'the assurance obtained by the German Government was such as to avert the risk of the applicant's being subjected to interrogation methods contrary to Article 3 following his extradition.'[85]

In a similar vein, the ECtHR noted in the *Othman* case that the Memorandum of Understanding, guaranteeing that the applicant would not be ill-treated on his return, was 'specific and comprehensive,' and was approved at 'the highest levels of the Jordanian Government, having the express support of the King himself.'[86] It is interesting to contrast these cases with a situation before the court in which such quality standards were apparently not complied with. In *Saadi v. Italy*, the Italian government had sought diplomatic guarantees from the Tunisian authorities that the applicant, who was deported to Tunisia in order to serve a prison sentence in his home country, would not be ill-treated on his return. After initially having ignored these queries, the Tunisian minister of foreign affairs had merely responded that Tunisian law guaranteed prisoner's rights and that Tunisia had acceded to the relevant international treaties and conventions.

83 ECtHR, 21 October 2010 App. No. 25404/09, *Gafarov v. Russia*, section 138.

84 For a useful survey of EctHR's decisions, see *Othman v. United Kingdom*, supra footnote 67, section 189.

85 *Al Moayad v. Germany*, supra footnote 56, sections 67–71.

86 *Othman v. United Kingdom*, supra footnote 67, sections 194–195.

According to the court, such 'paper practice' did not suffice to refute reliable sources that had reported systematic ill-treatment in Tunisian prisons that were manifestly contrary to the Convention. Moreover, even if the Tunisian authorities had offered more substantial assurances, that would not have absolved the instant court from the obligation to examine whether such assurances provided a sufficient guarantee that Saadi would be protected against ill-treatment.[87]

As suggested in the *Saadi* case, the availability of monitoring mechanisms is indispensable in order to verify the reliability of assurances. In the case of *Gasayev v. Spain*, the European Court, after having noted that a visit of the UN Committee against Torture (CAT) was materially impossible, observed that the Spanish Audiencia Nacional had requested both the CAT and the Russian authorities (the state, requesting the extradition of the applicant) to assume the monitoring functions itself, a request that was granted. The procedure convinced the court that the assurances were genuine and that the applicant would be sufficiently protected against the risk of being exposed to irreversible life imprisonment.[88] At times, the court appears to be rather easily persuaded of the requesting state's good intentions. Contrasting the situation with *Gasayev*, the court avowed that the Slovakian authorities in the case of *Chentiev and Ibragimov v. Slovakia* had not availed themselves of the offer by the Russian authorities to carry out monitoring of the compliance with the assurances, but held that 'by offering that opportunity the Russian authorities undoubtedly gave additional weight to the guarantees previously given.'[89] It is only in the total absence of any monitoring mechanism that international human rights bodies are inclined to call the value of assurances into question. Accordingly, the CAT found in *Agiza v. Sweden* that 'the procurement of diplomatic assurances, which, moreover, *provided no mechanism for their enforcement*, did not suffice to protect against the manifest risk of torture.'[90] In a similar vein, the European Court held in the case of *Ryabkin v. Russia* that

> even accepting that such assurances were given, ... the reports cited above noted that the authorities of Turkmenistan (the requesting state) systematically refused access by international observers to the country, and in particular to places of detention. In such circumstances, the Court is bound to question the value of the assurances that the

87 ECtHR (GC), 27 February 2008, App. No. 37201/06, *Saadi v. Italy*, sections 147–148.

88 EctHR (Admissibility Decision), 17 February 2009, App. No. 48514/06, *Gasayev v. Spain*, section 1.

89 EctHR (Admissibility Decision), 14 September 2010, App. Nos. 21022/08 & 51946/08, *Chentiev and Ibragimov v. Slovakia*.

90 *Agiza v. Sweden*, 24 May 2005, CAT/C/C/34/D/233/2003, section 13.8. Italics added.

> applicant would not be subjected to torture, given that there appears to be no objective means of monitoring their fulfillment.[91]

The final part of this sentence begs the question of whether, and if so, how and to what extent an objective assessment of observance of human rights is feasible at all, especially in the context of extradition. This question is to be understood against the backdrop of the consideration that violations of some human rights are simply easier to verify than others. As long as individuals are not summarily executed, the requested state can ascertain whether a state that gives an assurance that a sentence involving capital punishment will not be enforced lives up to its promises. Guarantees that the authorities of the requesting state will refrain from torture, however, should not automatically be taken for granted. After all, torture is shrouded in a veil of secrecy and rarely openly admitted.

Sensitive to the changing international opinion on the compatibility of capital punishment with basic human rights, the UN Human Rights Committee held in *Judge v. Canada* that countries that had abolished the death penalty were under an obligation not to expose a person to the real risk of its enforcement. As Canada had indeed abolished capital punishment, that state party to the International Covenant on Civil and Political Rights violated the applicant's right to life under Article 6(1) by deporting him to the United States, where he was under sentence of death, *without ensuring that the death penalty would not be carried out*.[92] Canadian courts had already anticipated the findings of the UN Committee. In the case of *United States v. Burns*, the Canadian Supreme Court held that the government must seek assurances, in all but exceptional cases, that the death penalty would not be enforced prior to extraditing an individual to a state where h/she would face capital punishment.[93] While these judgments are laudable, they can nowadays hardly be considered astoundingly progressive. As early as 1957 the European Convention on Extradition allowed states that had abolished the death penalty to condition extradition on 'such assurance as the requested Party considers sufficient that the death-penalty will not be carried out.'[94] The main difference with such optional grounds for refusal is that, in view of the *Judge v. Canada* decision, the requested state would incur responsibility for failing to request assurances.

Guarantees that purport to reassure the requested state that the receiving state will refrain from torture are an entirely different story. To our knowledge, no court has phrased the quandary clearer and more eloquently than

91 EctHR, 19 June 2008, App. No. 8320/04, *Ryabkin v. Russia*.

92 *Judge v. Canada*, 5 August 2002, Un Doc. CCPR/C/78/D/829/1998, section 18.3. Italics added.

93 *United States v. Burns* [2001], 1 SCR 283.

94 Compare supra footnote 395 and accompanying text. See also Dugard and van den Wyngaert, supra footnote 7, p. 197, who note that many extradition treaties contain such a 'death penalty clause.'

the Canadian Supreme Court in the case of *Suresh v. Canada*. The Court pointed to

> the difficulty in relying too heavily on assurances by a state that it will refrain from torture in the future when it has engaged in illegal torture or allowed others to do so on its territory in the past. This difficulty becomes acute in cases where torture is inflicted not only with the collusion but through the impotence of the state in controlling the behavior of its officials. *Hence the need to distinguish between assurances regarding the death penalty and assurances regarding torture. The former are easier to monitor and generally more reliable than the latter.*[95]

It cannot be gainsaid that the European Court has acknowledged the problem of central government wielding insufficient control over local authorities and having them not on a leash. In the case of *Chahal*, a militant Sikh leader who faced deportation to India and against whom security forces bore a vicious grudge, the court did not question the good faith of the Indian government in providing assurances. However, the court continued, 'it would appear that, despite the efforts of that Government, the NHRC and the Indian courts to bring about reform, the violation of human rights by certain members of the security forces in Punjab and elsewhere in India is a recalcitrant and enduring problem.'[96] Against this backdrop, it bears emphasis that careful examination of the value of assurances, depending on the situation at issue, is warranted. Whenever torture or inhuman treatment is endemic and individuals are particularly vulnerable of being targeted because of their political affiliation, or ethnic/religious background, judicial authorities, which have to decide whether people are to be deported or extradited to such a state, should be vigilant that central authorities may lack the power to rein in local authorities or security forces, making their assurances pointless. It goes without saying that assurances from states with centralized detention systems, in possession of transparent and adequate supervisory mechanisms to prevent abuse of prisoners, yield more confidence than assurances from those states that have outsourced the operation of prisons to special forces or private companies.[97] Moreover, it would definitely make a difference whether a well-functioning judicial system is available that enforces the rule of law and sanctions officials that engage in human rights violations. That takes us to our next topic.

95 *Suresh v. Canada (Minister of Citizenship and Immigration)*, 11 January 2002, 1 SCR 3, section 124, italics added.

96 ECtHR (GC), 15 November 1996, App no. 22414/93, *Chahal v. United Kingdom*, section 105.

97 The comment of Dugard and van den Wyngaert, supra footnote 7, p. 208 that 'it would be easy to monitor prison conditions by visiting the extraditee' is too sweeping, as it depends on whether observers would have access to those prisons.

9.7 Local remedies

Whereas assurances serve the purpose of convincing the requesting state that serious violations of human rights will not occur, the availability of local judicial remedies serve to demonstrate that, whenever they take place, the culprits will not get away with it. As indicated in the previous section, the two concepts conflate when the promise that the requested person will have access to a court is part and parcel of the package of assurances.

Both international human rights bodies and domestic courts are indeed inclined to allow extradition, if they are informed that the requested person can obtain redress for a wrong in the requesting state. It raises the question why the availability of a local remedy in the requesting state would absolve the requested state of responsibility. At first blush, the rationale appears to be that a violation of human rights is not complete, as long as the aggrieved person has a legal remedy. To a certain extent, that idea dovetails with the rule that an application is admissible before the European Court or the UN Human Rights Committee only after all local remedies have been exhausted.[98] If an effective local remedy is available, it does not imply, of course, that no infringement of human rights has occurred. However, the local judiciary has apparently been capable of dealing with the violation and it demonstrates that international and regional human rights bodies serve a subsidiary function. Conversely, the absence of an effective local remedy constitutes a separate breach of the European Convention of Human Rights (Article 13), which necessarily coincides with a violation of one or more of the substantive rights of the Convention.[99] In view of the close connection between the right to a fair trial and the access to an effective remedy, the Court does not bother to duplicate its findings, by separately addressing the lack of effective local remedies after it has already concluded that Article 6 has been breached.[100] Although a violation of the right of a victim of human rights violations to an effective local remedy is therefore somewhat implicit and concealed in each assessment of his claims, it is of paramount importance. It does not merely add insult to injury but constitutes the backbone and final piece of each and every inquiry into a complaint that human rights have been impaired.

98 European Convention of Human Rights, Article 35(1); Optional Protocol to the International Covenant on Civil and Political Rights, Article 2.

99 Compare F.G. Jacobs & R. C.A. White, *The European Convention on Human Rights*, Clarendon Press: Oxford 1996 (2nd ed.), p. 336: 'whenever a violation of the Convention has been established, there has necessarily been ... a breach of Article 13.'

100 Jacobs & White, supra footnote 99, p. 338: 'It would be reasonable to assume that if the Court concludes that Article 6 has been violated, a further enquiry into whether there has or has not been an effective remedy under Article 13 would seem unnecessary' observing later on more generally that ' the tendency of the court is ... not to pursue the Article 13 violation where a violation of one of the substantive provisions has occurred.'

Could the same logic mutatis mutandis be applied in an extradition configuration? Would the requested state be correct in feeling assuaged that it can safely surrender the fugitive, in the knowledge that even if his human rights are slighted he will have redress to a national court in the requesting state? There are some reasons to be careful in answering these questions in the affirmative. For one thing, the requested state is in a different legal position. It does not serve as a supervisory instance in respect of the observance of human rights in the requesting state. Second, and more important, the assurance that a victim of human rights violations can ultimately have justice done by a national court does not make up for the fact that the requested state has exposed him to an infringement of his rights in the first place. It would be rather quaint to suppose that the remedy in the requesting state makes amends for the initial wrong of the requested state and would nullify its responsibility on that count. On the other hand, we should recall that the requested state may be under an obligation to comply and that any violation of human rights, though probable, is still prospective. The guarantee that the fugitive will have his rights vindicated by a court will restore the balance of interests.

Against the backdrop of these reflections, we assert that it is necessary to differentiate on the basis of the nature and the (ir)retrievability of the violations at hand. The most easy nut to crack is the situation in which a judicial review can still preclude the infringement of human rights from materializing. The paradigmatic case is the enforcement of life sentence without parole, as discussed in Section 9.4.2. It is therefore completely justified that the UN Human Rights Committee found no violation of Article 7 of the Covenant on the part of the requested state because the applicant still had the option to appeal his life sentence:

> As to whether the State party's extradition of the author to serve a sentence of life imprisonment without possibility of early release violates Article 7 and 10 of the Covenant, the Committee observes ... that the author's conviction and sentence are not yet final, pending the outcome of the resentencing process which would open the possibility to appeal against the initial conviction itself. Since conviction and sentence have not yet become final, it is premature for the Committee to decide, on the basis of hypothetical facts, whether such a situation gave rise to the State Party's responsibility under the Covenant.[101]

A bit more difficult to appraise is the situation in which a fugitive has resort to a court after his fair trial rights have been breached. After all, one might wonder whether the requested state might not have been able to spare the requested person such a fate, especially if the risk is considerable and the

101 *Sholam Weiss v. Austria*, 8 May 2003, UN Doc. CCPR/C/77/D/1086/2002, section 9.4.

flagrancy of the violation is apparent. Nonetheless, the Dutch Supreme Court was satisfied that extradition in such a case was authorized, provided that both the requesting state and the requested state were party to a human rights treaty, in the case under scrutiny: the European Convention:

> In cases in which both the requesting and the requested State are parties to the ECHR, the confidence that the requesting will respect the provisions under this convention implies that it should be taken for granted that the requested person, in case of a violation *of any right* allotted by the Convention, will have, after being extradited, an effective local remedy in the sense of Article 13 ECHR before a court of law in that state. It implies that the contractual obligation to extradite should only yield to the obligation imposed on the Netherlands by Article 1 ECHR to guarantee the rights of the Convention, if (a) the requested person appears to be exposed by his extradition to a flagrant infringement of *his rights to a fair trial*, and (b) it transpires, on the basis of a sufficiently substantiated defence, that he will not have the benefits of local remedy to repair such an infringement.[102]

The judgment is highly interesting and deserves some comments. First of all, the court apparently gives weight to the counterpart being party to the European Convention of Human Rights, beyond and above the trust that is owed to regular extradition partners, on the basis of a treaty on international cooperation. It is not entirely clear whether this 'surplus of confidence' is merely elicited by the fact that the former have committed themselves to observe human rights or by the European Convention specifically providing for a right to obtain a local remedy. Probably, both parameters are relevant. Second, however, the trust is not axiomatic or absolute for it can be rebutted by credible evidence that the requesting state does not afford an effective local remedy. The portent of this conditional confidence is not to be underestimated because it implies that the Dutch courts do not shirk all responsibility by speculating that the fugitive in final instance can always have recourse to the European Court of Human Rights. If indications are strong that the fugitive has no opportunity to have access to local remedies, the requested state is to refuse the extradition forthwith. Finally, the findings of the court appear to be inconsistent, as it initially seems to accept that a remedy against violation of all rights would warrant extradition, whereas it later on tends to confine the salutary effects of local remedies to an infringement of a fair trial. We would argue that the latter – more restrictive – position is correct and the former is too broad and mistaken. In view of the close connection between the availability of a local remedy

102 Dutch SCt. 11 March 2003, NJ 2004, 42; confirmed in Dutch SCt.7 September 2004, NJ 2004, 595; italics added.

and the (general) fairness of trials as expounded above, it is reasonable for the requested state to have trust in the final outcome of proceedings. The presence of a reliable system of judicial appeal bears testimony to a state's general adherence to the rule of law. Violations of due process rights – even flagrant ones – may be accidental and can be rectified by a higher instance.

In contrast, in case of a real risk of irreparable damage – for instance impending torture or inhuman treatment – access to a local remedy is a poor consolation because the harm is already done. We therefore consider the authorization of an extradition by a Divisional Court of the United Kingdom to the United States of two terrorist suspects, in spite of the likely risk that they would face harsh treatment during detention, irresponsible and unacceptably carefree. In the case at hand, the court held that the extradition of the two fugitives would not be contrary to Article 3 of the European Convention, one of the considerations being that 'there was access to the US courts if the prison authorities acted unlawfully.'[103]

There is evidence that the European Court of Human Rights supports such differentiation in the interpretation of the content of Article 13, according to the kind of right the infringement whereof the remedy seeks to redress. In the case of *A. v. the Netherlands*, the court pointed out that

> the scope of the State's obligation under Article 13 varies depending on the nature of the applicant's complaint under the Convention. Given the irreversible nature of the harm that might occur if the alleged risk of torture or ill-treatment materialized and the importance which the Court attaches to Article 3, the notion of an effective remedy under Article 13 requires ... (ii) the provision of an effective possibility of suspending the enforcement of measures whose effects are potentially irreversible.[104]

It bears emphasis that in the case under scrutiny the court addressed the robustness of the judicial system of the state that was on the brink of expelling an undesirable alien, rather than the availability of local remedies in the state of destination (Libya), which was not under an international obligation to afford them. It is submitted, however, that the court suggested that the obligations under Article 13 of the expelling or requested state would require that state to take provisionary measures, suspending expulsion or extradition, even if the other state were to provide for remedies *post facto*. After all, the latter measures would not protect the fugitive sufficiently against irreparable harm.

103 *R. (on the application of Bary) v. Secretary of State for the Home Department*, [2009] EWHC 2068 (Admin) Times, 14 October 2009, Official Transcript.

104 ECtHR, 20 July 2010, App. No. 4900/06, *A. v. the Netherlands*, section 157.

In conclusion, we argue that the availability of local remedies is not a 'one size fits all' solution that relieves the requested state from its obligation to investigate scrupulously what the direct consequences of a surrender will be. If those remedies are capable of forestalling or repairing infringements of human rights, the requested state can rely on the judicial system of the requesting state. If, on the other hand, extradition would expose the fugitive to an immediate and irreversible harm, the requested state should, by refusing or suspending extradition, by proxy afford the legal protection that the requesting state can provide only in retrospect.

9.8 The question of evidence

One of the most delicate issues in the assessment of the question whether extradition is to be refused on the basis of an imminent violation of the fugitive's human rights concerns the amount and quality of evidence that must be adduced to demonstrate such risk and the division of the burden of proof. After all, such a violation is inherently prospective and any refusal is fraught with both legal and political problems.

As each assessment is case specific and the case law yields a *mer à boire,* we will attempt to distill and identify a number of normative guidelines, focusing on the appropriate evidential standard, including the burden of proof, the existence of possible countervailing factors, like the fugitive presenting a danger to the national security, and the source of the risk of human rights violations.

9.8.1 Standard of evidence

As indicated earlier, the European Court of Human Rights has set the evidential standard of an imminent risk of torture or inhuman treatment, precluding extradition in the *Soering* case by holding that the requested state would incur responsibility under the Convention if that state were to 'surrender a fugitive to another State where there were *substantial* grounds for believing that he would be in danger of being subjected to torture.'[105] That standard – substantial grounds- is a rather rough-and-ready parameter that requires further clarification.

In its communications on the question whether deportation or expulsion to a country would amount to a breach of the principle of 'non-refoulement,' in view of the fugitive's risk of being exposed to torture, the CAT has helpfully elucidated the standard. The CAT's consistent starting point is that 'the burden of proof is upon the author of the communication who has to present an arguable case – i.e. to submit circumstantiated arguments showing that the danger of being subjected to torture is foreseeable, present,

105 Soering case, supra footnote 1, section 88. Italics added.

personal and real.'[106] This general rule invites a number of comments. First, one may wonder what standard of evidence is exactly meant in terms of its probability. The CAT has held that the assessment must go beyond mere theory or suspicion, but it denied that the risk needs to be *highly probable*, consistently reiterating the danger *indiciae*, as pronounced in its general comment.[107] Second, it can be gleaned from the general comment that a general pattern of human rights violations prevalent in a state does not suffice:

> the existence of a pattern of gross, flagrant or mass violations of human rights in a country does not as such constitute sufficient reason for determining that a particular person would be in danger of being subjected to torture on return to that country; additional grounds must be adduced to show that the individual concerned would be personally at risk. Conversely, the absence of a consistent pattern of flagrant violations of human rights does not mean that a person might not be subjected to torture in his or her specific circumstances.[108]

While the applicant may thus run a real risk even if torture is not endemic, a 'consistent pattern of flagrant violations of human rights' is usually a crucial first step for the assessment of the danger. Referring to its case law, the CAT provides a non-exhaustive list of parameters that will be indicative of such a consistent pattern:

> (a) widespread use of torture and impunity of its perpetrators; (b) harassment and violence against minority groups; (c) situations conducive to genocide; (d) widespread gender-based violence; (e) widespread use of sentencing and imprisonment of persons exercising fundamental freedoms; and (f) situations of international and non-international armed conflicts.[109]

After the general pattern is established, the applicant must enter into some detail, explaining why he or she considers him/herself to be particularly prone to victimization. Previous bad experiences understandably strengthen his/her case and correspondingly alleviate the burden of proof. The CAT has referred to the applicant being arbitrarily arrested or detained in the past or having suffered brutalities or excessive force from public officials on the basis of discrimination or gender.[110]

106 Committee against Torture, General Comment No. 4 (2017) on the interpretation of Article 3 of the Convention in the context of Article 22, 9 February 2018, 62th session, section 38.
107 See, for example, *Sylvia Bakatu-Bia v. Sweden*, 8 July 2011, CAT/C/46/D/379/2009, section 10.3.
108 *Sylvia Bakatu v. Sweden*, supra footnote 107, section 10.3.
109 General Comment, supra footnote 106, section 43.
110 General Comment, supra footnote 106, section 29.

Even if the applicant has not personally been exposed to prior human rights violations, (s)he may succeed in proving that (s)he runs the risk of falling victim to torture or inhuman treatment, especially if (s)he belongs to a particularly vulnerable political or religious group or is targeted on account of his sexual orientation.[111] Attention for the political affiliation of the applicant, augmenting the risk of being exposed to human rights violations, is a common thread in the case law of human rights courts and bodies, as we already learned from the *Chahal* case of the European Court.[112] As a rule of thumb one can safely assume that the more details the applicant provides on his specific vulnerability, the greater the chance he stands of convincing both international human rights courts and domestic jurisdictions.[113]

A final observation on the general rules of evidence in respect of prospective human rights violations that might preclude extradition or expulsion concerns the burden of proof. While the CAT has held in general that the burden of proof that he runs the risk of being tortured or ill-treated on return is on the applicant, the Committee has acknowledged that the burden may shift to the state authorities:

> when the complainant is in a situation where he/she cannot elaborate on his/her case, for instance, when the complainant has demonstrated that he/she has no possibility of obtaining documentation relating to his/her allegation of torture or is deprived of his/her liberty.[114]

The European Court of Human Rights has elaborated on the problems involved in making a reasonable case for (imminent) torture. In the *Othman* case, the court observed that

> due regard must be had to the special difficulties in proving allegations of torture. ... It is practiced in secret, often by experienced interrogators who are skilled at ensuring that it leaves no visible signs on the victim.

111 General Comment, supra footnote 106, section 24.

112 *Chahal v. United Kingdom*, supra footnote 96, in which the court found that 'it must be borne in mind that the first applicant (Mr. Chahal) is a well-known supporter of Sikh separatism', adding that his high profile position within that political group made him particularly vulnerable.

113 Compare ECtHR, 26 July 2005, App. No. 38885/02, *N. v. Finland,* 43 EHHR 12 in which the court calculated the risk for the applicant – an official within the toppled Mobutu regime – of being exposed to revenge: 'The overall evidence before the Court supported the applicant's account of his having worked in the DSP, having formed part of President Mobutu's inner circle and having taken part in various events during which dissidents seen as a threat to the President were singled out for harassment, detention and possibly execution. There was therefore reason to believe that the applicant's situation could be worse than that of most other former Mobutu supporters, and that the authorities would not necessarily be able or willing to protect him.'

114 General Comment, supra footnote 106, section 38.

> All too frequently, those who are charged with ensuring that torture does not occur – courts, prosecutors and medical personnel – are complicit in its concealment. In a criminal justice system where the courts are independent of the executive, where cases are presented impartially, and where allegations of torture are conscientiously investigated, one might conceivably require a defendant to prove to a high standard that the evidence against him had been obtained by torture. However, in a criminal justice system which is complicit in the very practices which it exists to prevent, such a standard of proof is wholly inappropriate.[115]

The quote displays a fine understanding of the predicament of most applicants to demonstrate that they run the risk of being exposed to torture or ill-treatment and suggests that the burden of proof needs to be reversed, requiring state authorities to invalidate allegations of (possible) torture, especially if torture is widespread and structural.

International courts and human rights bodies have developed a fine-grained framework of assessment that serves domestic courts as normative example. There is no room for complacency though. The very fact that evidence of prospective torture is so difficult to obtain may move courts to raise the threshold for the applicant even higher, making it virtually impossible to reach the mark. That the review – in the context of extradition proceedings – of the existence of a risk that the fugitive will be exposed to inhuman treatment is very demanding was confirmed by the Constitutional Court of the Republic of Slovenia. The review should inquire whether the subjective fear is so objectively concretized that the person is in fact threatened and should include an assessment of the general situation in the requesting state as well.[116]

9.8.2 Balancing risks of torture against national security interests

International human rights courts and bodies have exhibited remarkable resistance to any claims of states that the risk of torture after expulsion or extradition should be balanced against the alleged threat the applicant poses to national security. The standard of proof of impending torture should therefore not be raised, as the supposed dangerousness is simply not part of the equation. In its very principled decision of *Saadi v. Italy*, the ECtHR accordingly held that

> the argument on the balancing of the risk of harm if the person is sent back against the dangerousness he or she represents to the community

115 *Othman case*, supra footnote 67, section 325.

116 Constitutional Court of the Republic of Slovenia, 29 June 2000, *Official Gazette RS*, no. 66/2000, section 15.

> if not sent back is thus misconceived. The concepts of "risk" and " dangerousness" in this context do not lead themselves to a balancing test because they are notions that can only be assessed independently of each other. Either the evidence adduced before the Court reveals that there is a substantial risk if the person is sent back or it does not. The prospect that he may pose a serious threat to the community if not returned does not reduce in any way the degree of risk of ill treatment that the person may be subject (to) on return. For that reason it would be incorrect to require a higher standard of proof, where the person is considered to represent a serious danger to the community, since assessment of the level of risk is independent of such a risk(sic).[117]

The European Court and the UN Human Rights Committee have been consistent and unanimous in 'holding the line' on this topic.[118] It should be observed, however, that most, if not all, of the case law in which this opinion was expressed concerned expulsion or deportation cases. The situation of extradition is different, as both states share a mutual interest in having the fugitive removed and surrendered to the requesting state, an interest that is backed up by the obligation to comply with the request. It is submitted, in view of the absolute prohibition of torture or inhuman treatment and the increased temptation to connive in a risky surrender if the requested state has good reasons to get rid of the fugitive, that domestic courts are to stand firm. The situation should rather serve as an incentive to consider alternatives, like the transfer of criminal proceedings to the requested state, on the basis of the *aut dedere, aut judicare* principle. We will address this possibility in the final section.

9.8.3 The source of the danger

The risk of torture or inhuman treatment need not necessarily derive from the state or public officials. Article 3 of the European Convention also applies where the danger emanates from non-state actors.[119] As such this extension is closely connected to the absolute character of the prohibition of torture and the concomitant positive obligation of states (parties) to shield

117 *Saadi v. Italy*, supra footnote 87, section 400.

118 Compare *Chahal v. United Kingdom*, supra footnote 67, section 151: 'This scrutiny (as required by Article 13) must be carried out without regard to what the person may have done to warrant expulsion or to any perceived threat to the national security of the expelling State.' See also UN Human Rights Committee, 31 July 2008, *Maksudov et al. v. Kyrgyzstan*, CCPR/C/93/D 1461, 1462, 1476 and 1477/2006, section 12.4: 'This principle [that no one should be exposed to torture etc. by way of their extradition, expulsion or refoulement] should not be subject to any balancing of considerations of national security or the type of criminal conduct an individual is accused or suspected of.'

119 ECtHR 22 April 1997, App. No. 24573/94, *H.L.R. v. France*, section 40.

individuals against violence of third persons. In the context of extradition, this obligation shifts to the requested state if it transpires that the requesting state appears to be unable to offer such protection. In the case of *H.L.R. v. France*, the applicant claimed that he would after deportation to Colombia be exposed to the wrath and violence of drug traffickers that might seek revenge because of certain statements that he had made to the French police. In line with its general findings on evidence in case of prospective violations in other states, the court held that a finding of a general situation of violence in Colombia would not suffice. The applicant would have to demonstrate that he would personally be in great danger, showing that 'the risk is real and that the authorities of the receiving State are not able to obviate the risk by providing appropriate protection.'[120] As the applicant was unable to produce documents supporting his claim that his situation would be worse than that of other Colombians, were he to be deported, the court did not find a violation of Article 3 on the part of France.

The Committee against Torture obviously is of the same opinion. In its General Comment it notes that

> States parties should refrain from deporting individuals to another State where there are substantial grounds for believing that they would be in danger of being subjected to torture or other ill-treatment at the hands of non-State entities, including groups which are unlawfully exercising actions that inflict severe pain or suffering for purposes prohibited by the Convention, and over which the receiving State has no or only partial de facto control or whose acts it is unable to prevent nor to counter their impunity.[121]

And domestic courts have followed suit. In the case of *Scattergood v. Attorney General*, the Supreme Court of Cyprus held that extradition should be refused if the threat of torture or inhuman treatment did not emanate from the state, but from non-state actors which the state was apparently unable to control.[122]

9.8.4 Conclusion

The burden of evidence that a fugitive in extradition proceedings has to produce in order to convince the court that his/her human rights are at peril is particularly arduous because the human rights violation is usually still

120 *H.L.R. v.* France, supra footnote 119.

121 General Comment, supra footnote 106, section 30, referring to M.K.M. v. Australia 10 May 2017, 681/2015, section 8.9.

122 Supreme Court of Cyprus, 21 January 2005, *Scattergood v. Attorney General*, Appeal Decision, Civil appeal no. 12/2005, ILDC 921 (CY 2005), comments by Aristotle Constantinides.

to occur and takes place on distant shores. Moreover, both human rights organs and domestic courts must balance that risk against the prerequisites of criminal law enforcement. The European Court of Human Rights, the ECJ and human rights commissions, like the CAT, have been helpful in developing a normative framework that involves a demanding but reasonable standard of evidence, acknowledges that there cannot be a trade-off between human rights and national security and understands that the fugitive can be exposed to violence that emanates from non-state agents.

9.9 Extradition and double jeopardy

As indicated in Section 9.2, states parties to different treaties can prevent collision of those treaties by regulating the hierarchy between them or at least between treaty provisions. Hence, a treaty on extradition may stipulate that surrender will give way to the concern that fundamental rights of the requested person may be compromised due to the extradition. Incidentally, such priority rules are incorporated in extradition treaties, though usually not generically. Treaties on international cooperation contain clauses that extradition can or should be refused if the fugitive is likely to be prosecuted twice for the same act (double jeopardy or *non bis in idem* rule). Similarly, extradition for the purpose of the execution of a sentence may be refused if the convicted person has not been offered the opportunity to attend his trial, nor had the right to challenge his conviction at a review trial on the facts (trials in absentia). This section addresses the former topic, while the intricacies of extradition for the purpose of execution of sentences, rendered in absentia will be discussed in 9.10.

9.9.1 Limited scope of double jeopardy in extradition treaties

Most extradition treaties comprise mandatory grounds for refusal if double jeopardy is at issue. The UN Model on Extradition, for instance, stipulates that 'extradition shall not be granted ... (d) If there has been a final judgement rendered against the person in the requested State in respect of the offence for which the person's extradition is requested.'[123] In virtually similar words the European Convention on Extradition holds that 'Extradition *shall not be granted* if final judgement has been passed by the competent authorities of the requested Party upon the person claimed in respect of the offences for which extradition is requested.' The provision follows by adding an optional ground for refusal: 'Extradition *may be refused* if the competent authorities of the requested Party have decided either not to institute or to terminate proceedings in respect of the same offence or offences.'[124]

123 UN Model Treaty on Extradition, supra footnote 9, Article 3, sub d.
124 European Convention on Extradition, supra footnote 8, Article 9; italics added.

It immediately strikes the eye that the scope of protection against double jeopardy is rather limited, as the fugitive is only safe if the final judgment derives from the judicial authorities of the requested state. Moreover, such immunity is only temporary, for the time that the requested person remains on the territory of that state. After all, other states are not under an obligation to respect the *res judicata* of a foreign state. In other words, the requested person is not shielded against a dual prosecution for the same acts in the requesting state, nor can he invoke a final judgment on these acts in a third state as an impediment for extradition. While the former situation is perhaps not very likely to happen often, because the requesting state would infringe its own rules on double jeopardy,[125] the latter is definitely more serious. The fact that extradition treaties allow or even prescribe requested states to refuse extradition if they have already rendered judgment on the same acts is unspectacular and rather self-evident. Apart from having no interest in the prosecution of those acts, as they have already been dealt with under its own criminal law system, the requested state may likely consider the request for extradition as an insult to its judicial decision-making power, as it puts into question or even disdains the correctness or righteousness of such decision. While there is therefore a superficial semblance between the dual criminality rule and the refusal of extradition in case of double jeopardy, the latter strikes much deeper. Whereas assessment of dual criminality boils down to a formal comparison of criminal law systems, the request for extradition for acts that have already been finally judged in the requested state entails an affront to its sovereign pride. The requested state is in a position and has the power to render extraterritorial effects to its judicial decisions by refusing to cooperate in respect of a criminal prosecution of an act that it considers already set and done. This specific opportunity also explains the broad scope of the discretion of the requested state: not only is it authorized – and by treaty even compelled – to refuse extradition if its courts have reached a final judgment on the case, but it can also reject the request if the Prosecutor's Office has decided, on the basis of lack of evidence or for policy reasons, not to pursue the case or to drop charges. In other words, while the geographical scope of the protection against double jeopardy is extremely limited, its substantive scope is very broad. However, if the requested person decides to leave the territory of the requested state and moves to the requesting state, whose extradition request has been turned down, no rule of international law prevents the latter from starting criminal proceedings in respect of the offence.

This final observation bears evidence to the fact that the rule of double jeopardy applies, in principle, only within a legal system. Neither human rights conventions nor customary international law stipulate that states are

125 Although the rule of non-inquiry would probably under most jurisdictions impede the judiciary to check whether the requesting state would comply with its own law.

under an obligation to recognize foreign *res judicata* because that would entail an encroachment on the state's sovereignty. The European Convention on Human Rights does not explicitly address the topic of double jeopardy, not even within the context of one and the same legal system. On several occasions, the former European Commission on Human Rights has denied the applicability of Article 6 to multiple prosecutions for the same fact, although it did not completely rule out the possibility that, in specific circumstances, a second prosecution might militate against the fair-trial principle of Article 6.[126] Article 4, paragraph 1 of the 1984 Seventh Protocol to the European Convention, however, does contain a provision on *ne bis in idem*. The phrasing of the provision makes it perfectly clear that it does not apply to decisions of foreign courts.[127] Article 14, paragraph 7, of the International Covenant on Civil and Political Rights provides that no one shall be liable to be tried or punished again for an offence for which he has already been finally convicted or acquitted in accordance with the law and penal procedure of each country. The phrasing of the provision is somewhat arcane and doubts have lingered as to the question of whether it would require all states parties to respect the final judgments of other parties. The UN Human Rights Committee, however, has clarified that the article does not apply to foreign *res judicata*.[128]

Against the backdrop of the silence of international law, it is basically up to each state to decide whether, and if so to what extent, they are prepared to render legal effect to foreign criminal judgments. The Dutch criminal law system, for instance, is rather generous in considering final judgments of foreign courts – nearly – on the same par as similar decisions of domestic judicial authorities, for the purpose of *non bis in idem*.[129] The relevant provisions in Dutch law, governing the *ne bis in idem* effect of foreign *res judicata* within the Dutch legal order are Article 68, paragraphs 2 and 3 of the Dutch Penal Code. Article 68, paragraph 2, precludes criminal proceedings in the Netherlands after a final judgment has been rendered by a foreign court in case of acquittal or dismissal of the charges and in case of conviction, if punishment has been imposed, followed by complete enforcement, pardon, or lapse of time. Furthermore, according to paragraph 3 of Article

126 European Commission on Human Rights, 13 July 1970, App. No. 4212/69.

127 Protocol No. 7 to the Convention for the Protection of Human Rights and Fundamental Freedoms, as amended by Protocol No. 11, Strasbourg 22 November 1984, ETS No. 117, Article 4, section 1: No one shall be liable to be tried or punished again in criminal proceedings *under the jurisdiction of the same State* for an offence for which he has already been finally acquitted or convicted *in accordance with the law and penal procedure of that State*'(italics added).

128 UN Human Rights Committee, 2 November 1987, Report 204/ 1986, *A.P. v. Italy*.

129 *Cf.* Peter Baauw, 'Ne bis in idem,' in: Bert Swart & André Klip (eds.) *International Criminal Law in the Netherlands*, Band S 66, Max-Planck-Institut für ausländisches und internationales Strafrecht: Freiburg im Breisgau 1997, p. 79.

68 DPC, criminal prosecution in the Netherlands is barred by the fulfilment of a condition set by the competent authorities of a foreign state to prevent prosecution. The condition that the foreign judgment has to be enforced in order to produce *non bis in idem* effect in the Netherlands has been inserted to counter impunity, in case a Dutch national were to escape from a foreign prison and returned to his home country. After all, as the Netherlands does not allow extradition of nationals for the purpose of the execution of a judgment, it would have no power to execute the remainder of the foreign sentence, if it had no treaty relations with the foreign state, providing for the execution of the foreign sentence. The loophole in Article 68, paragraph 2 enables the Netherlands to prosecute the escapee nonetheless, a construction that can effectively be considered as a transfer of criminal proceedings.

This brief excursus to the regulation of the recognition of foreign criminal judgments takes us back to the *non bis in idem* principle within the context of international cooperation. Interestingly, some instruments on international cooperation in criminal matters that have been concluded within the institutional framework of the Council of Europe contain provisions on international *non bis in idem* that mirror the Dutch regulation, as expounded above. Article 53 of the European Convention on the International Validity of Criminal Judgments provides that

> (1) A person in respect of whom a European criminal judgment has been rendered may for the same act neither be prosecuted nor sentenced nor subjected to enforcement of a sanction in another Contracting State:
> a) if he was acquitted;
> b) if the sanction imposed:
> (i) has been completely enforced or is being enforced, or
> (ii) has been wholly, or with respect to the part not enforced, the subject of a pardon or an amnesty, or
> (iii) can no longer be enforced because of lapse of time;
> c) if the court convicted the offender without imposing a sanction.[130]

The provision continues with identifying a number of exceptions that serve to safeguard the sovereign interests of the state *loci delicti*. They need not detain us here, but we will return to these exceptions in the following section(s). Remarkably, the regulations on *non bis in idem* effect of foreign judgments are detached from international cooperation. Nonetheless, the fact that they have been incorporated in treaties that envisage such cooperation suggests a relationship between these phenomena. A state that has agreed to transfer criminal proceedings or the execution of its own criminal

130 European Convention on the International Validity of Criminal Judgments, Strasbourg, 28 May 1970, ETS No. 70. Article 35 of the European Convention on the Transfer of Criminal Proceedings, Strasbourg, 15 May 1972, ETS No. 73 reads virtually the same.

judgment to another state will have no incentive to start prosecution anew at a later moment and can more easily be persuaded to renounce its claims.

It bears emphasis that a refusal of extradition on account of non-*bis in idem* does not have such salutary effects. It usually leaves the requesting state frustrated and offers the requested person only limited and temporary protection, as we have expounded before. To placate the requesting state, efforts are often made to mitigate the effects of a prior final judgment by a restrictive interpretation of the concept of 'same act' or 'same offence.' Such endeavours can be understood only against the backdrop of differences in legal qualification that are inherent in an international society that consists of a patchwork of legal systems.

The fragmentation of criminal offences to the detriment of the protective function of the double jeopardy principle is further facilitated by the claim that the crime affects the interests of distinct states and can be located on different territories. This line of argumentation came to the fore in the case of *United States v. Doria* which concerned the extradition from Mexico to the United States of an American citizen (Salinas Doria) who was charged with conspiracy to import (into the United States) a controlled substance (narcotics) and conspiracy to distribute, and possess with intent to distribute, a controlled substance.[131] Salinas had opposed his extradition, claiming that it would violate the principle of *non bis in idem,* as he had already stood trial before Mexican courts on charges of similar offences. The Mexican Ministry of Foreign Affairs (MMFR) had rejected his argument, contending that

> the acts for which Salinas is requested for extradition by the government of the United States ... are different from those for which he is being tried by Mexican legal authorities.

In reaching that conclusion, the MMFR held that the extradition request was based on 'acts committed in the United States,' adding that

> Salinas had failed to make any showing that the allegations underlying the extradition request were the same as those underlying his prosecutions ... for various crimes against health, of organized crime, and of transactions with income of illegal origin, being heard before the Mexican courts.[132]

Back in the United States, Salinas made a novel attempt by moving to counter his indictment before the New York District Court, submitting that his

131 *United States v. Doria*, District Court decision, No 01 CR 21GEL), ILDC 1245 (US 2008), 21 October 2008, United States: New York: District Court for the Southern District Court of New York.

132 *United States v. Doria*, supra footnote 132, section 4.

extradition had been in violation of the applicable bilateral treaty. The court was quick in dismissing his claim. Invoking previous case law, the court held that

> it is well-established that 'a foreign government's decision to extradite an individual in response to a request from the United States is not subject to review by United States courts.'[133]

Moreover, even if, for the sake of the argument, the District Court would be prepared to review the decision of the Mexican authorities, Salinas's defence was bound to fail as Salinas

> did not even argue that the crimes for which he was prosecuted in Mexico and those alleged in the instant indictment would constitute the same offence under US double jeopardy law if prosecuted by the *same* sovereign.[134]

In other words: the case of *Doria* was particularly weak for two reasons. First, the court suggested that Salinas had seized the wrong forum. After his application before the Mexican authorities had been rejected, he could not repeat it before the court of the requesting state, as the determination by the surrendering state was final.[135] After all, a review of the requested state's decision would entail the questioning of its assessment of the extradition request, which would not only be preposterous in view of US courts' lack of expertise of foreign (Mexican) law, but also be in contravention of international comity. Second, the New York Court addressed, as an *obiter dictum*, the substance of the double jeopardy issue and concluded that, even if the relator would invoke the principle before a hypothetical court within the same legal system, he would not stand a chance of convincing the court.

We have dwelled upon this case because the New York District Court made the intermittent observation that

> [while] the US Constitution recognizes the prohibition against double jeopardy in principle, … [it] nevertheless permits successive prosecution by different sovereigns.[136]

Whereas this contention is factually correct and in line with the legal assessment of foreign *res judicata*, it displays a misunderstanding of *non bis in*

133 *United States v. Doria*, supra footnote 132, section 7. The New York District Court's quotation is derived from *United States v. Medina*, 985 F. Supp. 397, 401 (SDNY 1997).

134 *United States v. Doria*, supra footnote 132, section 17. Italics in original.

135 See also the Supreme Court's findings in *Johson v Browne*, 205 U.S. 309.316 (1907).

136 *United States v. Doria*, supra footnote 132, section 17.

idem in the extradition context. A state is not allowed to disregard the effects of a foreign judgment if it has obtained custody over a fugitive by virtue of the cooperation of another state.

To obviate the apparent weaknesses of the *United States v. Doria* case, which could quite easily be refuted by the court, we should therefore look for claims in respect of double jeopardy advanced by the fugitive before the courts of the *requested* state, which would, at first sight, stand a higher chance of being accepted. US case law, at least, reveals that such configurations are extremely difficult to identify. The gist of the problem is that any part of the crime that materializes on the territory of the requesting state or otherwise affects the interests of that state is considered as an additional element, distinguishing it from the original offence that has already been adjudicated in the requested state. Whether courts adhere to the conventional and narrow *Blockburger* test – stipulating that the court, for the purpose of determining the 'same act,' is to inquire whether each statutory provision charged requires proof of a fact that the other does not have – or harbor a broader approach, the outcome in international (extradition) cases would often be the same.[137] The correct understanding of what constitutes the 'same offence' has been a matter of controversy in the context of the question of whether, within the federal legal system of the United States, a state prosecution would bar a subsequent federal prosecution for the same acts.[138] Justice Brennan advanced a new take on the issue, arguing that the old-fashioned *Blockburger* test would deprive the constitutional double jeopardy principle of its essence. Instead, he submitted that the double jeopardy clause requires the prosecution to join at one trial all the charges against the defendant that emanate from 'a single criminal act occurrence *or transaction*.'[139] The implication would obviously be that the decision of the criminal court would be final and would preclude any new prosecution.

Both the *Blockburger* test and the wider 'same transaction test' that was introduced by Justice Brennan have been applied in the extradition context. In the case of *Stowe v. Devoy*, the defendant had been convicted in the United States for possession and sale of 100 pounds of hashish. When his extradition was subsequently requested by the Canadian authorities on account of conspiracy to import hashish into Canada, Stowe claimed that the double jeopardy clause in the US-Canada treaty would preclude the extradition. The US Court of Appeals rejected the defence, holding that, for both

137 *Blockburger v. United States*, 284 U.S. (1932), 299, 304.

138 For an illuminating commentary, see Shelley M. Goldstein, 'Extradition and Double Jeopardy: Will the Same Transaction Test Succeed in an International Context?' 6 *North Carolina J. of International Law and Commercial Regulation* (1980), pp. 141, 144.

139 J. Brennan initially made this proposal in his dissenting opinion in *Abbate v. United States*, 359 U.S. 187 (1959) (Brennan, J. dissenting), 200, and repeated it in *Ashe v. Swenson*, 397 U.S., 436 at 453–454 (Brennan, J. concurring); Goldstein, supra footnote 138, 143–145. Italics added.

charges to refer to the 'same offence,' they had to be sustained by the same evidence. That condition was not fulfilled, as the hashish that was imported into Canada was different from the narcotics for the possession and sale whereof Stowe had previously been convicted in the United States.[140]

In the case of *Sindona v. Grant*, the Second Circuit changed its tune and sided with the Brennan approach.[141] The defendant had previously been convicted in the United States on account of a comprehensive fraud operation, including conspiracy, mail fraud and embezzlement. His extradition was sought by Italy for similar fraudulent crimes that originated in the same scheme but had affected the interests of Italian corporations and citizens. The Court departed from the *Blockburger* test and embraced a 'modified and more flexible test of whether the same conduct or transaction underlies the criminal charges in both transactions.'[142] Nonetheless, the court denied defendant's claim that his extradition would contravene the double jeopardy provision in the American-Italian extradition treaty, holding that the crimes for which his extradition was sought were different from the ones for which he previously had been convicted in the United States. Heeding Justice Brennan's prescription that all crimes emanating from the same transaction should be joined at one trial, the court found that US courts would be precluded from doing so, due to lack of territorial jurisdiction over the Italian crimes.[143]

Sindona perfectly illustrates the difficulties of applying even the broader 'same transaction test' in the context of extradition. The requesting state will naturally have an interest in protecting its citizens against crimes that materialize on its own territory. That these interests are not necessarily shared by the requested state is reflected in the absence of criminal jurisdiction to prosecute such crimes. Any expansion of jurisdiction to also cover these extraterritorial crimes that originate in the requested state might be explained as a commitment to counter transnational crime, but it may also be considered as interference in the domestic affairs of a foreign state. The ensuing 'division of labour' that is accomplished by international cooperation inevitably diminishes the protection against double jeopardy in the international realm because each state is expected to deal with the (separate) crimes that affect its interests.

The fact pattern in *Stowe* and *Sindona* is too diverse to draw conclusions on the scope and effects of both tests. *Sindona* involved a comprehensive fraudulent operation, comprising a myriad of separate transactions, whereas *Stowe* concerned a much simpler scheme. Although it is of course a matter of conjecture, it would be interesting to speculate whether the

140 *Stowe v. Devoy*, 588 F.2d 336, 340 (2d Cir. 1978), cert. denied, 442 U.S. 931 91979).
141 *Sindona v. Grant*, 619 F.2d 167 (2d Cir. 1980).
142 *Sindona v. Grant*, supra footnote 141, p. 178.
143 *Sindona v. Grant*, supra footnote 141, p. 179.

application of Brennan's 'same transaction' test would have yielded another outcome in that case. In our view, it is questionable. Because the possession and sale of hashish for which Stowe initially had been convicted related to different narcotics than the commodities he later exported to Canada, one may assume that these crimes were predicated on different transactions. Any subsequent sale of hashish in Canada would most certainly exceed the jurisdiction of US courts, implying that it would not meet the second prong of Brennan's test that such crimes could be addressed during one and the same trial.

The true litmus test that enables us to measure the effects of the *Blockburger* test and the 'same transaction' test in comparative perspective concerns a hypothetical adaption of the *Stowe* case, in which we presume that the defendant has been convicted for possession and exportation of narcotics and whose extradition is subsequently requested for the importation of the very same commodities. Under the 'same transaction' test, the defendant would definitely be protected against extradition and double jeopardy, as importation is merely the mirror image of exportation and the (same) factual event derives from one 'transaction.' Under the *Blockburger* test the outcome is less certain. It depends on whether the prosecutor of the requested state has implicitly heeded the interests of the foreign state by charging the suspect with 'illicit drugs trafficking,' or has issued a more self-serving indictment, charging the defendant merely with possession and exportation of drugs.[144] In the latter case, one might argue that the initial evidence did not encompass the harm inflicted on the other state, implying that the importation would constitute a 'new' offence.

One might object that this result is far-fetched, if not absurd, but it is not merely a scholarly example. Article 36, section 2, sub a, under (i) of the 1961 Single Convention on Narcotic Drugs stipulates that 'Each of the offences enumerated in § 1, if committed in different countries, shall be considered as a distinct crime.'[145] The section referred to reads as follows: 'Subject to its constitutional limitations, each Party shall adopt such measures as will ensure that ... *importation* and *exportation* of drugs, contrary to the provisions of the Convention ... shall be punishable offences when committed intentionally.'[146] Without exaggerating, one might conclude that the Single Convention effectively endorses the *Blockburger* test.

These final observations reveal that *non bis in idem* provisions in extradition treaties have very little relevance and offer hardly any protection to the fugitive. States can simply circumvent the 'obstacle' by breaking down

144 It might be observed that the Brennan approach would require the prosecutor to opt for the broader indictment.

145 Single Convention on Narcotic Drugs, 1961, as amended by the 1972 Protocol Amending the Single Convention on Narcotic Drugs, 1961, New York 30 March 1961, 520 UNTS, 151.

146 Italics added.

the offence in distinct elements, reflecting their respective interests and, by doing so, contend that they are not talking about the 'same offence,' The effects of the provision are confined to *res judicata* in respect of offences that exclusively affect the requested state, in which case the requesting state will have no incentive to ask for extradition in the first place. At least in the realm of the regulation of double jeopardy within the context of extradition relations, states' interests completely prevail over the legal protection of the fugitive. It also demonstrates that international cooperation, in general, and extradition, in particular, are still a rather self-centered affair, triggered by the expectation that the other state will return the favour if asked for. A more visionary approach would require increased interstate consultation, attuned to 'finding the best place for prosecution,' in view of accomplishing criminal law objectives.[147] Within that configuration, due process rights, including protection against double jeopardy, and prospects of rehabilitation would have a more prominent place. Such more ambitious projects, waking states out of their solipsist slumbers, can take shape only with in a framework of more mature and integrated political institutions. This takes us to a discussion of the *non-bis in idem* arrangements in the framework of the European Arrest Warrant.

9.9.2 Double jeopardy and the European Arrest Warrant

The European Arrest Warrant operates within an 'Area of Freedom, Security and Justice,' or 'European Judicial Space,' in which the inner borders have been abolished. The political and social objective underpinning this project is that European citizens should be allowed to move freely within that space, without too many encumbrances. Clearly, the nuisance of being held accountable in respect of the same offence by more EU member states would be an impediment to this freedom. Moreover, the guiding principle of mutual recognition, predicated on mutual trust, encourages a more generous acknowledgement of foreign judicial decisions and serves as an antidote against the pursuit of parochial interests.

These lofty ideals are reflected in the regulation of *ne bis in idem* as a *mandatory* ground for refusal in the Framework Decision on the European Arrest Warrant. Article 3(2) provides that member states are under an obligation to refuse the execution of an EAW

> if the executing judicial authority is informed that the requested person has been finally judged by a *Member State* in respect of the same acts provided that, where there has been sentence, the sentence has been

147 On this topic, see B. De Ruyver, G. Vermeulen & T. VanderBeken, *Finding the Best Place for Prosecution: European Study on Jurisdiction Criteria*, Maklu-Uitgevers: Antwerp 2002.

served or is currently being served or may no longer be served under the law of the sentencing Member State.[148]

It immediately strikes the eye that the effects of *res judicata* barring surrender are no longer confined to those that derive from the requested state but extend to final judgments of all member states. The condition that the sentence must have been served is inserted in order to preclude impunity in case surrender of the fugitive for the purpose of the enforcement of the sentence would not be possible (compare the general elucidation of this construction in the context of international *non bis in idem* above).

Under the heading of optional grounds for non-execution of the EAW, the Framework Decision grants member states leeway to further expand protection against double jeopardy. Some of these provisions are less spectacular, as they accommodate the interests of the executing state and feature in regular extradition treaties as well.[149] Article 4(5) and Article 4(3) second part of the Framework Decision are innovative as they pay attention to further-reaching blocking effects of foreign *res judicata*. Article 4(5) allows the requested state to refuse, with the familiar exceptions, execution of an arrest warrant if final judgment has been reached by a third State, whereas Article 4(3) qualifies a final judgment, passed on the requested person in a member state that prevents further proceedings as an optional ground for refusal. The phrasing of the latter provision begs the question of what is to be understood by a 'final judgement which prevents further proceedings.' The term 'judgment' suggests that the decision must derive from a judicial authority.[150] Could it also encompass, by extension, out of court settlements, proposed by the Prosecution, that relieve the suspect from criminal proceedings, provided he complies with certain conditions, like, for instance, the paying of a fine?

The question was addressed by the European Court of Justice in the case of *Gözütok and Brügge*.[151] Domestic courts in Belgium and Germany had requested the European Court, within the framework of a prejudicial

148 Framework Decision on the EAW, supra footnote 10, italics added.

149 Article 4(2) qualifies pending criminal proceedings in the executing state as an optional ground for refusal, whereas the first part of Article 4(3) allows states to attach a similar consequence to its Prosecutorial Office decision not to pursue charges or to drop proceedings.

150 Blekxtoon, supra footnote 44, p. 235, gives as an example a judgment that confirms the evidence but ends up in a dismissal of the charges since the conduct is not punishable under the law of that member state. He adds that such a situation 'might seriously impede surrender for facts where the double criminality is no longer necessary.' That is a justified concern, although it is not limited to the international cooperation context: a dismissal of the charges in a member state precludes any criminal prosecution in the entire European Union, which means that the requesting state was not authorized to issue the European Arrest Warrant in the first place.

151 ECJ, 11 February 2003, Joined Cases C-187/01 and C 385/01, *Gözütok and Brügge*.

decision, to shed its light on the proper interpretation of Article 54 of the Schengen Convention that regulates *non bis in idem* within the Schengen Area.[152] The issue had emerged in two sets of criminal proceedings, the first in Germany against Gözütok and the second in Belgium against Brügge, for offences committed in the Netherlands and Belgium, respectively, despite the fact that proceedings brought in other member states against the two accused on the same facts had been definitively discontinued after they had paid a sum of money determined by the Public Prosecutor as part of a procedure whereby further prosecution was barred. The case before the court in essence boiled down to the question of whether an out-of-court settlement proposed by the prosecutor in which the accused had complied with the conditions, implied that the trial had been 'finally disposed of' in the sense of Article 54 CISA, precluding a second prosecution in another member state. The court affirmed that an out-of-court settlement, for the purpose of *non bis in idem*, should indeed be considered on the same par as a judicial decision, adding a number of noteworthy observations. First, it pointed out that the principle of mutual recognition had been introduced to accommodate international cooperation in spite of inevitable interstate differences in criminal law and procedure. The principle invited states to pass over such 'procedural and purely formal matters' and rather aim for the broader object and purpose of Article 54, which implied the protection of persons against the hazard of being held accountable multiple times for the same offences. 'Nowhere,' so the court observed, 'is the application of Article 54 of the CISA made conditional upon harmonisation, or at the least approximation, of the criminal laws of the Member States relating to procedures whereby further prosecution is barred.'[153] In respect of the case under scrutiny it implied that

> the application by one Member State of the ne bis in idem principle, as set out in Article 54 of the CISA, to procedures whereby further prosecution is barred, which have taken place in another Member State without a court being involved, cannot be made subject to a condition

152 Convention implementing the Schengen Agreement of 14 June 1985 between the Governments of the States of the Benelux Economic Union, the Federal Republic of Germany and the French Republic on the gradual abolition of checks at their common borders (OJ 2000 L 239, p. 19; hereinafter 'the CISA'), signed on 19 June 1990 at Schengen. Article 54 of the CISA reads as follows: 'A person whose trial has been finally disposed of in one Contracting Party may not be prosecuted in another Contracting Party for the same acts provided that, if a penalty has been imposed, it has been enforced, is actually in the process of being enforced or can no longer be enforced under the laws of the sentencing Contracting Party.' Article 54-58 of the CISA is part of the Schengen acquis and has been incorporated in the Treaty of the European Union.

153 *Gözütok and Brügge*, supra footnote 151, section 32.

that the first State's legal system does not require such judicial involvement either.[154]

Second, the Court forged a direct link between a broad interpretation of the double jeopardy principle and the freedom of movement within the European judicial space. The court reasoned that

> Article 54 of the CISA, the objective of which is to ensure that no one is prosecuted on the same facts in several Member States *on account of his having exercised his right to freedom of movement*, cannot play a useful role in bringing about the full attainment of that objective unless it also applies to decisions definitively discontinuing prosecutions in a Member State, even where such decisions are adopted without the involvement of a court and do not take the form of a judicial decision.[155]

And it drew from this finding the logical inference that any contrary opinion would prejudice the petty offender who would be eligible for out-of-courts settlements when compared with suspects of more serious crimes:

> if Article 54 of the CISA were to apply only to decisions discontinuing prosecutions which are taken by a court or take the form of a judicial decision, the consequence would be that the ne bis in idem principle laid down in that provision (and, thus, the freedom of movement which the latter seeks to facilitate) would be of benefit only to defendants who were guilty of offences which — on account of their seriousness or the penalties attaching to them — preclude use of a simplified method of disposing of certain criminal cases by a procedure whereby further prosecution is barred, such as the procedures at issue in the main actions.[156]

Against this backdrop, the equation of out-of-court settlements with judicial decisions makes perfect sense indeed. While *Gözütok and Brügge* was decided outside the context of surrendering proceedings, it is obvious that the findings of the Court would bar the executing state from complying with a European Arrest Warrant if the offence had already been disposed of by an out-of-court settlement in another member state.

One cannot deny that on the drawing table the regulation of *non bis in idem* within the European Union offers unprecedented protection against double jeopardy. Its practical effectiveness, however, depends entirely on the answer to the question what constitutes 'the same offence.' One would expect the European Court of Justice to offer member states some guidance

154 *Gözütok and Brügge*, supra footnote 151, section 34.
155 *Gözütok and Brügge*, supra footnote 151, section 38. Italics added.
156 *Gözütok and Brügge*, supra footnote 151, section 40.

on this topic, as a narrow interpretation, similar to the practice we encountered in the previous section, would entirely obliterate the lofty principles that have just been expounded. The topic of the concept of the 'same act' has indeed yielded a considerable number of preliminary decisions by the ECJ. A comprehensive discussion of all these cases would obviously exceed the scope of this monograph.[157] It suffices to obtain a general idea of the court's approach, in particular whether the court instructs member states to adopt a common understanding of what constitutes the 'same act.' To that purpose, we will briefly analyse three cases, two of which address the topic in general and one pertaining to the context of the European Arrest Warrant.

The *Van Esbroeck* case concerned exactly the configuration that we, hypothetically, discussed in the previous section, to wit, the exportation of commodities that constitutes the offence of importation of prohibited substances from the perspective of the state of destination.[158] Van Esbroeck had been sentenced by a Norwegian court to five years' imprisonment for illegally importing narcotic drugs into Norway. After having served part of his sentence, he was conditionally released and escorted to Belgium, where he faced proceedings and was sentenced to one-year imprisonment for exporting exactly the same drugs. The question brought before the ECJ was simple: would the importation and exportation of the same narcotic substance, in view of the applicable Article 54 of the CISA, amount to the 'same act'? Noting the difference in terminology between Article 54 of the CISA ('same act') and the corresponding provisions in the International Covenant on Civil and Political Rights and the Seventh Protocol of the European Convention on Human Rights (that refer to the 'same offences'), the court observed that the legal classification in different contracting states could never be decisive in the application of Article 54 CISA.[159] It concluded that

> the relevant criterion for the purposes of the application of Article 54 is identity of the material acts, understood as the existence of a set of facts which are inextricably linked together, irrespective of the legal classification given to them or the legal interest protected.[160]

Applied to the specific topic under scrutiny, the court found that

> punishable acts consisting of exporting and importing the same narcotic drugs and which are prosecuted in different Contracting States to the

157 For a slightly outdated, but seminal analysis, see W.B. van Bockel, *The ne bis in idem in EU law: A conceptual and jurisprudential analysis*, Kluwer Law International: Alphen a/d Rijn 2010.

158 ECJ, 9 March 2006, C-436/04, *Van Esbroeck*.

159 *Van Esbroeck*, supra footnote 158, sections 27 and 31/32.

160 *Van Esbroeck*, supra footnote 158, section 42.

> CISA are, *in principle*, to be regarded as 'the same acts' for the purposes of Article 54 of the Convention, *the definitive assessment in that respect being the task of the competent national courts.*[161]

The outcome of the case invites some comments. On the one hand, the court deserves credit for disentangling the assessment of the same act from legal classifications because a contrary opinion would enable states to circumvent double jeopardy issues by invoking their own legal interests. On the other hand, however, the court nullifies that steadfast approach by leaving the decision ultimately to the national authorities.

In the *Gasparini* case, domestic courts again asked the European Court to shed light on the concept of 'same act' for the purpose of the application of Article 54 CISA.[162] Shareholders and directors of the company Minerva had agreed to import lampante (refined) olive oil from Turkey and Tunisia through the port of Setubal (Portugal), without declaring the provenance of the oil to the customs authorities. Instead, they had used false invoicing to create the impression that the oil came from Switzerland, thereby attempting to evade import taxes. The Supreme Court of Portugal had acquitted two of the defendants (amongst them Mr. Gasparini), finding that the prosecution had been time barred. During subsequent criminal proceedings before the District Court of Malaga against Gasparini, standing trial on charges of marketing smuggled olive oil into Spain, the question arose whether the oil, after having been imported, was in 'free circulation within the European Union' and, more importantly, whether

> the sale of the goods in another Member State following their importation into the Member State where the acquittal was given [could] be regarded as independent conduct which may therefore be punished or, instead, as conduct forming an integral part of the importation.[163]

Before addressing this substantive issue, the court had to decide on the preliminary question whether an acquittal on the basis of statutory limitations could be equated, in light of the *non bis in idem* principle, to an acquittal due to lack of evidence. Briefly referring to its judgment in *van Straaten*, which corroborated – rather superfluously – that an acquittal due to lack of evidence qualified as a 'final judgment,' impeding fresh criminal proceedings in another member state,[164] the court held that it did.[165] The outcome stands to logic. A decision that criminal proceedings

161 *Van Esbroeck*, supra footnote 158, section 42, italics added.
162 ECJ, 28 September 2006, C-467/04, *Gasparini*.
163 *Gasparini*, supra footnote 162, section 20.
164 ECJ, 28 September 2006, C-150/05, *Van Straaten*, section 61.
165 *Gasparini*, supra footnote 162, section 33.

are time barred is even more irrevocable than an acquittal due to lack of evidence which, at least theoretically, could be reversed whenever new evidence pops up. The inquiry therefore centered on the crucial question of whether the sale of goods in Spain after their illicit importation into Portugal could be considered as the same – continuous – conduct. The court suggested that it might:

> the marketing of goods in another Member State, after their importation into the Member State where the accused was acquitted, constitutes conduct which *may* form part of the 'same acts' within the meaning of Article 54 of the CISA.[166]

The court reiterated its previous finding in *Van Esbroeck* that the ultimate assessment of whether the material acts constitute a set of facts that are inextricably linked together in time, in space and by their subject matter was the privilege of the national courts.[167]

Although the court expressed its opinion in extremely cautious terms – even more so than in *Van Esbroeck* – it is nonetheless interesting because the approach reminds us of the 'same transaction' criterion discussed in the previous section.

In the *Mantello* case, the court seemingly adjusted its course by explicitly holding that the understanding of 'same act' could not be left to the discretion of the member states, according to their national laws, as it constituted an autonomous concept of European Union law.[168] The case is especially relevant for this monography, because, different from both previous cases, it concerned the assessment of the double jeopardy principle in the context of the execution of a European Arrest Warrant. The request for a preliminary decision derived from the Oberlandesgericht of Stuttgart, which had received an EAW from the Italian district court of Catania, seeking the surrender of Mr. Mantello on charges of illicit trafficking in cocaine within a criminal organization. Mantello had previously stood trial and was sentenced to imprisonment for the period of 3 ½ years on account of possession of cocaine intended for resale by the very same court. However, the new charge, underpinning the EAW, had a broader ambit, not only in referring to new crimes for which Mantello had not been convicted, but also by putting emphasis on his key role in the criminal organization. In substance, the issue concerned the question of whether a trial and conviction for specific offences precluded a subsequent trial for participation in a criminal organization within the framework of which those offences had been

166 *Gasparini*, supra footnote 162, section 57. Italics added.

167 *Gasparini*, supra footnote 162, section 56.

168 ECJ, 16 November 2010, C-261/09, *Mantello*, section 38.

committed. The *Oberlandesgericht* had framed the preliminary question in a straightforward way, by inquiring whether the existence of ' same acts' within the meaning of Article 3(2) of the Framework Decision had to be decided according to the law of the issuing state, the executing state or according to an autonomous interpretation of 'same act,' on the basis of European Union law.[169] As indicated above, the court confirmed that the latter interpretation was the correct one. However, the court gave a different turn to the discussion by holding that the German court's inquiry involved the content of 'final judgment,' rather than the concept of 'same act.' The heart of the matter was whether the first conviction by the Court of Catania did not relate only to the specific charge of possession and sale of cocaine, but had a broader scope, enabling the defendant to make a clean sweep by atoning for his participation in the criminal organization. In the latter case, the judgment would indeed be 'final' barring the execution of the EAW on the basis of Article 3(2) of the Framework Decision. As the Italian authorities, in an exchange of information in accordance with Article 15(2) of the Framework Decision, had explicitly indicated that they had not intended to discontinue the case, leaving in abeyance whether they had not used evidence for strategic reasons or simply had not been aware of new offences, the German court had no other option than to comply with the request. In an uncommonly laborious wording, the court held that

> In circumstances such as those at issue in the main proceedings where, in response to a request for information within the meaning of Article 15(2) of that Framework Decision made by the executing judicial authority, the issuing judicial authority, applying its national law and in compliance with the requirements deriving from the concept of 'same acts' as enshrined in Article 3(2) of the Framework Decision, expressly stated that the earlier judgment delivered under its legal system did not constitute a final judgment covering the acts referred to in the arrest warrant issued by it and therefore did not preclude the criminal proceedings referred to in that arrest warrant, the executing judicial authority has no reason to apply, in connection with such a judgment, the ground for mandatory non-execution provided for in Article 3(2) of the Framework Decision.[170]

At first blush, the outcome may appear rather surprising and disappointing. The court gave its blessing to the full power of the requesting state's determining what counts as the 'same act.' It thereby possibly condoned a devious (ab)use of *Blockburger*-like constructions, entailing

169 Mantello, supra footnote 168, section 30.
170 Mantello, supra footnote 168, section 51.

that the state would conceal evidence while pretending that it was previously unaware of it. The 'fresh' evidence would sustain new charges that would justify the issue of an EAW. However, on closer scrutiny one may doubt whether the court could have reached a more dauntless conclusion. If the requested state had already a difficult job in unravelling the intricacies of the requesting state's substantive criminal law, how would one expect the European Court, being more detached and dependent on the information provided by the stakeholders, to show a better performance? We encounter here the limitations of the supervisory capacities of the court. Any further inquiry into the particularities of the construction of charges by the Italian authorities would display a lack of confidence, which would run counter to the principle of mutual recognition that governs international cooperation within the European Union.

From a more general perspective, one may wonder how the finding of the court that the understanding of the 'same act' constitutes an autonomous concept of EU law can be reconciled with its earlier opinion that such determination should be left to the national authorities. In view of the obvious tension between these assertions, one should assume that the court can indicate only broad parameters like time, place, similarity of subject matter, that would point at the identity of acts. As long as states do not reduce the assessment of the issue to a formal comparison of legal qualifications, thereby extolling their own legal interests, they still enjoy a wide margin of appreciation.

The pertinent question arises whether, even in the context of sophisticated international cooperation within the European Union, much progress has been made with the push back of international double jeopardy. A skeptic might find sufficient ammunition in the previous deliberations in defence of a negative answer. However, that conclusion would not be entirely correct nor fair. It is no coincidence that many – and important – preliminary decisions have been rendered on the question of what constitutes the same act. National courts are seeking guidance from the court in their struggle to come to terms with the topic, which inevitably implies a confrontation with the opinions and interests of other states. The court has moved cautiously, navigating between the Scylla of imposing its own views and the Charybdis of leaving the states too much leeway. It has subtly expressed its own opinions on the matter, finding that importation and exportation of the same narcotics are the 'same act,' and suggesting that member states should not resort to criminal prosecution of the sale of commodities if a prior illicit importation of those goods has been previously disposed of by final judgment in another member state. If domestic courts follow suit by internalizing such approaches to the problem, the objective of a common European Union–wide legal policy has been achieved. The current practice of national courts' seeking the advice of the court by means of a preliminary judgment bears testimony to their propensity to find common ground.

9.10 Trials in the absence of the accused (trials in absentia)

9.10.1 Introduction to the topic

Any person charged with a criminal offence has a right to be present during the trial that deals with his case and to take part in the hearing. In its landmark decision of *Colozza v. Italy,* the European Court of Human Rights considered that this right was implicit in the notion of a fair trial as such and was presupposed in the accused's right to defend himself in person (Article 6, section 3, sub c ECHR).[171] According to the court, it implied that representation by mandated counsel could not compensate for the absence of the accused and that during the entire criminal proceedings a factual assessment of his guilt could, in principle, take place only in the presence of the accused.

The intrinsic weight and value of this principle must be considered against the backdrop of a criminal trial's primordial truth-seeking function in combination with the respect owed to any accused as an autonomous human being. Being the crown witness in his/her own case, any suspect must at least be offered the opportunity to present his/her own perspective of the chain of events (in accordance with the maxim *audi et alteram partem*). It stands to logic that common law and civil law systems, harbouring different opinions on how the facts of a criminal offence can be best reconstructed, also reveal distinct approaches towards the phenomenon of trials in absentia. Whereas the adversarial system starts from the premise that the 'truth' is provisional and can best be procured by the collision of perspectives of the antagonist parties in the proceedings, the inquisitorial procedure aspires to the determination of the material truth. For common law systems adhering to the adversarial process the presence of the accused is therefore indispensable, while the civil law/inquisitorial system can do without it because the accused is at most the *primus inter pares* amongst various sources of information from which the judge can choose to find the truth.

This brief and perfunctory introduction to a rich and profound topic must suffice for our purposes.[172] The absence of the accused during a trial before the courts of the requesting state will come to the fore in extradition proceedings whenever the surrender is requested for the purpose of the execution of a judgment. As the right to be present is part and parcel of a fair trial, the issue can systematically be classified under the wider compatibility of extradition obligations and prospective violations of a fair trial in the requesting state. In principle, impending conflicts can be resolved by provisions in extradition treaties exempting the requested state from complying

171 ECtHR, 12 February 1985, App. No. 9024/90, *Colozza v. Italy*, section 27.

172 For a probing analysis, deducing the organization of fact-finding procedures in criminal law to the ideal types of state authority, see Mirjan R. Damaška, *The Faces of Justice and State Authority: A Comparative Approach to the Legal Process*, Yale University Press: New Haven 1986.

with the obligation to extradite, whenever the requested person will not be afforded the opportunity to attend the factual assessment of his guilt. However, such exceptions rarely feature in regular extradition conventions. The Framework on the European Arrest Warrant and ensuing case law, on the other hand, have (again) yielded an unprecedented regulation of the topic that addresses the problem in minute detail. This section therefore starts with a concise survey of the state of the art in extradition law and proceeds with a more elaborate discussion of the applicable standards within the framework of the European Arrest Warrant.

9.10.2 Trials in absentia and regular extradition

There is an intriguing contradiction between any well-intended effort to secure the presence of an accused at his/her trial and the average condition and interests of many fugitives. After all, suspects will often travel to foreign countries to escape justice. The entire institution of extradition owes its existence to (wo)man's basic urge to be free. While the *Colozza* case was not tailored to the extradition context, the court acknowledged this predicament. The court started by observing that the right to be present does not have an absolute character and suggested that an accused would be entitled to waive the guarantees of a fair trial.[173] However, if a person charged with a criminal offence had not been notified in person, ' it could not be inferred merely from his status as "fugitive" (*latitante*) ... that he had waived his right to appear at the trial and defend himself.'[174] Moreover, an accused must not be left with the burden of proving that he was *not* seeking to evade justice or that his absence was due to *force majeure*.[175] However, the national authorities should be allowed to demonstrate that the accused failed to show good cause for his absence and that there was nothing in the case file to warrant the finding that he had been absent for reasons beyond his control.[176]

Obviously, the court attempts to find the proper balance of responsibilities in a cat-and-mouse game. The prime obligation is on the authorities to apprise the accused of the imminent trial, an obligation that is intimately related to the right of everyone charged with a criminal offence "to be informed promptly, in a language which he understands and in detail, of the nature and cause of the accusation against him" (Article 6, section 3, sub a ECHR). Ideally, this should be done by summoning the accused and

173 *Colozza v. Italy*, supra footnote 171, section 29. The waiver of the right to appear at trial was not explicitly mentioned in *Colozza* but has been accepted in subsequent case law, see ECJ, 30 November 2000, App. No. 52868, *Kwiatkowska v. Italy*.

174 Colozza, supra footnote 171, section 28, as paraphrased in ECtHR, 1 March 2006, App. No. 56581/00, *Sejdovic v. Italy*, section 87.

175 Colozza, supra footnote 171, section 30; Sejdovic, supra footnote 174, section 88.

176 ECtHR, 14 June 2001, App. No. 20491/92, *Medenica v. Switzerland*, section 57.

serving him the indictment in person. This is an obligation of effort, not of result, because the flight to a foreign country may be inspired by the wish to escape justice and remain untraceable. If summoning in person cannot be accomplished, the next step would be to find out whether the accused is nonetheless abreast of impending proceedings against him. In *Seydović* the court takes some pain to elucidate when such an assumption would be justified, appreciating the difficulties in summoning 'volatile' suspects that choose to remain under the radar:

> The Court cannot ... rule out the possibility that certain established facts might provide an unequivocal indication that the accused is aware of the existence of criminal proceedings against him and of the nature and the cause of the accusation and does not intend to take part in the trial or wishes to escape prosecution. This may be the case, for example, where the accused states publicly or in writing that he does not intend to respond to summonses of which he has become aware through sources *other than the authorities*, or *succeeds in evading an attempted arrest* ... or when materials are brought to the attention of the authorities which unequivocally show that he is aware of the proceedings pending against him of the charges he faces.[177]

While absolute certainty on whether the accused is aware of the proceedings cannot be obtained, unless he is summoned in person or he has explicitly waived his right to be present, the court allows states to presume such knowledge. From that moment on, life becomes much easier for the national authorities because the burden of proof shifts to the accused, requiring him or her to indicate why the authorities are still to blame for insufficiently informing him (or her). If the accused fails to do so, nothing impedes the requested state to surrender the fugitive, as the trial in absentia is caused by his (or her) own (in)activity.

Even if the summoning of the accused has not been 'spotless,' however, the extradition context creates new opportunities to repair the potential infringement of fair trial. For one thing, the default judgment is considered to be covered if appointed counsel has been able to conduct the defence in name of and as a representative of the accused. While in regular criminal proceedings this would not count as a full and appropriate alternative, it would not thwart an extradition for the purpose of the enforcement of a judgment that was rendered in the absence of the accused. Second, the fugitive will usually have the option of his case being reexamined, even if he is allowed to appeal against a conviction in absentia, provided that this entails the possibility of a 'fresh factual and legal determination of the criminal charge, so that the proceedings as a whole could be said to have been fair.'[178]

177 *Sejdović v. Italy*, supra footnote 174, section 99. Italics added.
178 ECtHR, 9 September 2003, app. No. 30900/02, *Jones v. United Kingdom*.

After all, while the fugitive might initially have been untraceable, (s)he is now in the custody of the requested state, so the requesting state can retrieve previous flaws. We will address these modes of reparation in more detail in the next section.

It bears emphasis that the Second Protocol to the European Convention on Extradition – one of the very few international instruments that explicitly acknowledges the optional ground of refusal in case of trials in absentia – provides for the possibility of remedying the default judgment.[179] Article 3, section 1 holds that

> When a Contracting Party requests from another Contracting Party the extradition of a person for the purpose of carrying out a sentence or detention order imposed by a decision rendered against him in absentia, the requested Party may refuse to extradite for this purpose if, in its opinion, the proceedings leading to the judgment did not satisfy the minimum rights of defence recognised as due to everyone charged with criminal offence.

However, it continues by pointing out that

> extradition shall be granted if the requesting Party gives an assurance considered sufficient to guarantee to the person claimed the right to a retrial which safeguards the rights of defence.

The effects of the assumption that a fugitive may well have fled abroad to escape justice, combined with the possibilities to remedy a trial in absentia, make the threshold for refusing extradition on account of the requested person having been denied a fair trial extremely high. In the case of *Stoichkov v. Bulgaria,* the court neatly summarized the stringent requirements by holding that

> the refusal to reopen proceedings conducted in the accused's absence, without any indication that the accused has waived his or her right to be present during the trial, amounts to a 'flagrant denial of justice' rendering the proceedings 'manifestly contrary to the provisions of Article 6 or the principles embodied therein.'[180]

In extradition proceedings, in which the United States features as the requested state, refusal of a request for the purpose of the enforcement of a judgment rendered in absentia is equally rare. Although the adversarial

179 Second Protocol to the European Convention on Extradition, Strasbourg 17 March 1978, CETS No. 98.

180 ECtHR, 24 March 2005, App. No. 9808/02, *Stoitchkov v. Bulgaria.*

procedural system in the United States cannot be reconciled with the accused being absent, the United States has no qualms about cooperating with states that harbour different opinions and practices in this respect. For US courts it is of decisive importance whether the appropriate standard of proof is met in order to allow the extradition. In case of an extradition request for the purpose of the enforcement of a sentence, usually a certified copy of the conviction suffices.[181] However, the common law system's unfamiliarity with, if not disguised disdain for, default judgments resonates in the inclination of US courts to consider a request for extradition for the purpose of the enforcement of a judgment that was reached in the absence of the defendant as if the request was merely lodged for the purpose of prosecution. Consequently, courts sometimes demand additional and independent evidence to sustain the charges.[182] The overarching standard of evidence in extradition proceedings for the purpose of prosecution under US law is 'probable cause,' which is similar to the standard required for a preliminary hearing in a criminal case. It stands to logic that the requirement cannot be more demanding, as the surrender is precisely requested in order to facilitate further investigations into the defendant's involvement in an offence. From that perspective, it would indeed be far-fetched to demand convincing evidence that would sustain a conviction, as such assessment is for the foreign court to make.[183] Precisely because the standard of evidence is rather low, US courts are usually easily satisfied when the requesting state simply transmits the information contained in the foreign judgment that was rendered in the absence of the accused.[184]

The niceties and details of US evidential standards in extradition proceedings need not detain us. What is relevant to observe is that the United States puts the topic of the admissibility of extradition for the purpose of the enforcement of judgments rendered in the absence of the defendant entirely in the key of sufficiency of evidence. Any apprehensions in this respect are not primarily inspired by the concern whether the defendant's rights to a fair trial have been observed or will be observed. By virtue of the (in)famous rule of non-inquiry, courts are not authorized to verify whether

181 *Spatola v. US*, 925 F.2d 615, 618 (2d Cir. 1991): 'A certified copy of foreign conviction obtained following a trial at which the defendant was present is sufficient to sustain a judicial officer's determination that probable cause exists to extradite.'

182 Compare, *Germany v. United States*, No. 06 CV 01201, 2007 WL 2581894, at *7 (E.D.N.Y. Sept. 5, 2007) ("Where a defendant was convicted in absentia, the conviction is merely a charge and an independent determination of probable cause in order to extradite must be made."). For an insightful analysis, see Roberto Iraola, 'Foreign Extradition and In Absentia Convictions,' 39 *Seton Hall Law Review* (2009), p. 843.

183 *Peterka*, 307 F. Supp. 2d at 1349; accord In re Extradition of Chan Seong-I, 346 F. Supp. 2d 1149, 1161 (D.N.M. 2004) ("The evidence showing probable cause need not be sufficient to support a conviction, but need only be sufficient to warrant a finding that there are reasonable grounds to believe the relator is guilty and thus hold her for trial.").

184 For examples, see Iraola, supra footnote 182, 856.

the defendant upon his return to the requesting state would be entitled to apply for a retrial and make extradition dependent upon such a guarantee. In fact, the Second Circuit Court of Appeals in *Galina v. Fraser* corroborated the assumption, just expressed, that foreign trials in absentia for the enforcement of which extradition was sought should trigger the US court's attention whether the evidential standard was met, but did not expect those courts to meddle with the subsequent proceedings in the requesting state.[185]

The approach in *Galina v. Fraser* is remarkable because it confirms our earlier findings that courts of the requested state are utterly reluctant to assess prospective fair trial violations in the requesting state. They endorse a rigid separation of responsibilities, reasoning that the defendant must seek a remedy in the state that has infringed his rights and that the requested state has not the foresight, nor the capacity to protect the defendant against such mischief. Any lingering qualms of conscience that the requested state has exposed the fugitive to that risk are conveniently refuted by the assertion that the state has no other option than to comply with the request. The position is particularly stern if none of the safety valves, such as the asking for assurances or an inquiry into the availability of local remedies, are put into operation. It should be admitted that the *Gallina* dictum has been credited for creating a hypothetical exception to the rule of non-inquiry, where the court suggested that it could 'imagine situations where the relator, upon extradition, would be subject to procedures or punishment so antipathetic to a federal court's sense of decency as to require reexamination of the non-inquiry principle.'[186] As no American court has ventured to put this daring suggestion in practice, the possibility indeed remains a theoretical one.[187]

Defendants who face extradition for the purpose of the enforcement of a sentence that has been rendered in their absence share the same predicament of those relators that oppose their surrender claiming that their fair trial rights will be compromised in the requesting state. The prospect that they will be able to convince the court is bleak if not nihil. This sobering conclusion stands in stark contrast to the abundant attention that has been paid to the topic of in absentia judgments as a potential obstacle to the practical application of the European Arrest Warrant.

185 See Iraola, supra footnote 182, 857, quoting from *Gallina v. Fraser*, 278 F. 2d, 77, 78-79 (2d cir. 1960): 'The court further observed that the case law holding that in absentia conviction should be treated as a charge "[was] not to be construed as a statement that [a] federal court may, as a condition of discharging the writ, require retrial in the foreign country." Rather, what that holding stood for was simply that an in absentia conviction does not preclude a district court from making an independent, probable-cause determination as to whether the evidence presented justifies a reasonable belief that the fugitive committed the crime for which extradition is sought.'

186 *Galina v. Fraser*, supra footnote 185, at 79.

187 Compare the Third Circuit Appeals Court in *Hoxha v. Levi*, 465 F.3d 554, 564 n.14 (3d Cir. 2006) qualifying the *Galina* exception as 'highly questionable and theoretical' because 'no federal court has applied it to grant habeas relief in an extradition case.'

9.10.3 The European Arrest Warrant and trials in absentia

Article 4a of the Framework Decision on the European Arrest Warrant explicitly allows the executing state to refuse to comply with the request to execute a EAW that has been issued for the purpose of enforcing a sentence that was rendered in the absence of the requested person. However, before the court of the executing state can reach that final decision it has to examine a number of factual and legal parameters that basically serve to preclude such refusal. It is not difficult to identify the elements that have been addressed in the previous section.

The first condition for refusal assumes that the defendant has not been properly informed - or at least not in due time – of the impending trial. Second, even if the defendant had been unaware of the scheduled trial, the executing judicial authority would be bound to comply, if he/she had delegated the defence to a legal counsellor who was explicitly mandated by the defendant to conduct such defence and had in fact done so. Whereas these two conditions are backward looking, the next ones allude to the prospect of a reparation by means of a fresh assessment of the case. Article 4(a), section 1 sub c refers to the waiver of the defendant after he has been informed of his right to have a retrial or appeal, in which he will have a right to participate and which will address the merits of the case. And finally, Article 4(a), section 1 sub d mentions the rectification of the unsuccessful summoning, pointing at the assurance of the requesting state that the fugitive, after his/her surrender, will be personally served with the decision and will be informed that (s)he will have a right to a retrial or appeal. Such information should also include the time frame within which he or she must request such a retrial or appeal.

The assessment of the question whether the EAW can be executed, despite the accused's absence during the trial, has the character of a checking procedure. The issuing judicial authority has to 'tick the box' in the EAW in order to facilitate the executing authority to verify the conditions:

- Has the fugitive been summoned in person, or can it be unequivocally established that (s)he was actually aware of the scheduled trial? If not,
- Has (s)he mandated legal counsel to conduct the defence on his/her behalf in his/her absence and has counsel indeed performed accordingly? If not,
- Has (s)he explicitly waived the right to a retrial or appeal, after (s)he has been expressly informed of this right? If not,
- Has (s)he personally been served with the verdict after his/her surrender and been informed of his/her right to obtain a retrial or an appeal, including the time frame within which (s)he can lodge a request for a retrial or appeal?

Only in case all these questions are answered in the negative, the requested state has the option to refuse the execution of the European Arrest Warrant.

We have presented a bird's-eye view of the applicable provision in the Framework Decision to point out the similarities with the extradition context. Later in this section, we will elaborate on the oftentimes subtle differences in approach of trials in absentia within the realms of extradition and the European Arrest Warrant. For now, it is relevant to paint the background of this profuse regulation and understand why the topic has engendered much legal debate, ending in a number of preliminary decisions of the European Court of Justice.

Article 4a was introduced by a Framework Decision of 2009, in order to replace the original Article 5 in the pristine Framework Decision that created the European Arrest Warrant.[188] Recital 4 of the preamble to this Framework Decision defines its overarching objective:

> refining the common grounds for non-recognition of decisions rendered following a trial at which the person concerned did not appear in person, [in order to] allow the executing authority to execute the decision despite the absence of the person at the trial, while *fully* respecting the person's right of defence.[189]

The phrasing suggests a tension between fully-fledged cooperation and the requirements of a fair trial that is compounded by legal and practical differences in the member states. The idea is that harmonisation of the grounds for refusal will be instrumental in reconciling those objectives. The underlying issue is that opinions on the admissibility of trials in absentia differ within the European Union. As astutely observed by Kei Hannah Brodersen et al., the proposal of the Framework Decision is the result of a trade-off.[190] On the one hand, member states favouring a high level of protection of procedural rights are allowed to refuse the execution of an EAW, whenever the criminal proceedings to which the fugitive is exposed does not match their standards. The optional nature of the ground for refusal, on the other hand, introduces a measure of flexibility. Member states are not obliged to refuse surrender, even if none of the conditions enumerated in Article 4a of the Framework Decision has been met. The executing judicial authority is allowed to take into account 'other circumstances that enable it to ensure that the surrender of the person concerned does not entail a breach of his

188 Council Framework Decision 2009/299/JHA of 26 February 2009 amending Framework Decisions 2002/584/JHA, 2005/214/JHA, 2006/783/JHA, 2008/909/JHA and 2008/947/JHA, thereby enhancing the procedural rights of persons and fostering the application of the principle of mutual recognition to decisions rendered in the absence of the person concerned at the trial, OJ 2009, L 81, p. 24.

189 Recital 4 of the preamble: italics added.

190 Kei Hannah Brodersen, Vincent Glerum & André Klip, *The European Arrest Warrant and In Absentia Judgments*, Eleven International Publishing: The Hague 2020, p. 44.

rights of defence.'[191] Moreover, the system allows member states that are less choosy and condone a lesser level of protection to comply with a request to execute an EAW.

The pertinent question is whether the lofty ideals of the 2009 Framework Decision can be accomplished, which boils down to the question to what extent criminal procedural law in respect of pursuing the presence of the accused at the trial lends itself for harmonisation. On the face of it, the criteria and exceptions, mentioned in Article 4a, section 1, a–d of the Framework Decision, are clear enough. However, they refer to several factual and legal practices that have developed over time and are quite state specific.

One of the issues that has proved most controversial is the practice of summoning. In the case of *Dworzecki* the preliminary question arose whether sending the summons to the address that the fugitive had indicated for the purposes of servicing the process and was subsequently collected by his grandfather complied with the procedure as indicated in Article 4a, section 1, sub a. Dworzecki had not appeared at the trial and was sentenced to several separate terms of imprisonment, amounting to three years and two months in total. The practice that was in full conformity with the Polish Code of Criminal Procedure did not find favour in the eyes of the European Court of Justice. As Dworzecki was not literally summoned in person, the court had to ascertain the meaning of the alternative 'by other means actually received information of the scheduled date and place of that trial in such a manner that it was unequivocally established that he or she was aware of the scheduled trial' (Article 4a, section 1(a) sub i). The court indicated that it was not called upon to meticulously prescribe the methods of summoning that would meet the required standard, but held that the provision under scrutiny 'constituted an autonomous concept of EU law and must be interpreted uniformly throughout the European Union.'[192] Although the court did not rule out that the handing of the summons to a third party could incidentally satisfy the requirements of Article 4a, section 1(a), as long as the issuing member state did not provide concrete evidence that the defendant had actually received notice of the impending trial, the procedure was wanting and allowed the executing judicial authorities to refuse execution of the EAW. Therefore, the court concluded that

> a summons, …, which was not served directly on the person concerned but was handed over, at the latter's address, to an adult belonging to that household who undertook to pass it on to him, when it cannot be ascertained from the European arrest warrant whether and, if so, when

191 ECJ, 24 May 2016, C-108/16 PPU, *Openbaar Ministerie v. Dworzecki*, section 50; ECJ, 10 August 2017, C-270/17, *Openbaar Ministerie v. Tupikas*, section 96.

192 *Dworzecki*, supra footnote 191, section 32.

> that adult actually passed that summons on to the person concerned, does not in itself satisfy the conditions set out in that provision.[193]

Apparently, the approach of the ECJ is slightly more exacting than the one adopted by the Strasbourg Court, as the former passes judgment over specific practices of summoning, while the latter is satisfied when evidence is sufficient that the defendant has been aware of the trial.[194]

The European Court of Justice has taken pains to alleviate the complex decision-making process in the assessment of the execution of European Arrest Warrants for the purpose of the enforcement of judgments rendered in the absence of the fugitive that has been aggravated by the patchwork of distinct legal practices. It has resorted to the notion of 'autonomous concept of EU law,' whenever it has seen fit to do so. It should be emphasised, however, that the context in which the preliminary questions on the correct interpretation of Article 4a of the Framework Decision arise sets limitations to these endeavours. While the implicit objective of the provision is to further and improve fair trial standards within the European Union, it essentially leaves the national regulation of in absentia trials untouched. Brodersen et al. therefore correctly observe that 'Article 4a (1) only harmonizes the ground for refusal, not the national rules concerning trials in absentia.'[195]

The European Court has found room to impose its interpretation of the provision on the member states in respect of the questions which 'decisions' in principle required the presence of the accused to qualify as fair (Article 4a, section 1, sub a) and what should be understood by 'the right to a retrial or an appeal' (Article 4a, section 1, sub d). As to the latter topic the bones of contention were whether it implied that a retrial or appeal should actually take place (or whether the defendant had a right only to request this) and what the purport and nature of such a retrial or appeal should be. In view of the observations above, it makes sense that the court took the opportunity to introduce these notions as 'autonomous concepts,' precisely because they lack any reference to the law of the issuing member state.[196]

The same holds true for the 'decision' that resulted in a custodial sentence or detention order for the enforcement of which the EAW had been issued. The court attaches decisive importance to the question of whether such decision yielded a definite outcome, pronouncing on the guilt of the accused, irrespective of whether that outcome was to the detriment or the benefit of the accused. If the fugitive had been ignorant of the trial that ended in this

193 *Dworzecki*, supra footnote 191, section 54.
194 Brodersen et al., supra footnote 190, p. 285.
195 Brodersen et al., supra footnote 190, p. 160.
196 *Tupikas*, supra footnote 191, sections 65–67.

last decision, the judicial authorities would not be allowed to tick the first box, referring to Article 4a, section 1, sub a:

> when the person concerned appeared before the judge responsible for a fresh assessment of the merits of the case, but not at first instance, the provisions of Article 4a of Framework Decision 2002/584 do not apply. Conversely, the executing judicial authority must carry out the checks provided for in that article when the person concerned was present at first instance, but not in the proceedings concerned with a fresh assessment of the merits of the case.[197]

In other words, for the purpose of assessing the applicability of the optional ground for refusal, the fugitive is not merely entitled to being present at any trial that engages in his involvement in the crime, but must have attended the trial that was conducive of the final determination of the case (unless, of course, one of the exceptions enumerated in the subsequent paragraphs applies).

If a decision did not address the substance of defendant's guilt and left the initial quantum and nature of the sentence unaltered, it does not count as a 'decision' in the sense of Article 4a, section 1, sub a, requiring an investigation into the defendant's attendance of the procedure resulting in that decision. If the defendant was initially sentenced to provisional imprisonment and the court subsequently ordered the enforcement of this sentence because he had flouted one or more conditions, it was immaterial for the assessment of Article 4a, section 1, sub a that the defendant had not attended that revision procedure. In the *Ardić* case the European Court assessed such suspension revocation decisions in the light of the requirements of Article 6 of the European Convention of Human Rights and concluded that

> the concept of 'decision' referred to in Article 4a(1) of the Framework Decision does not cover a decision relating to the execution or application of a custodial sentence previously imposed, except where the purpose or effect of that decision is to modify either the nature or quantum of that sentence and the authority which adopted it enjoyed some discretion in that regard.[198]

In view of the underlying rational of the defendant's right to be present at his trial, it makes sense to confine the concept of 'decision' to a determination of his/her guilt or involvement in the offence, as (s)he should have the opportunity to contest that assumption.

197 *Tupikas*, supra footnote 191, section 86.
198 ECJ, 22 December 2017, C-571/17 PPU, *Ardić*, section 77.

Article 4a, section 1, sub d of the Framework Decision refers to a situation in which the authorities have been unable to reach the fugitive, either because (s)he has succeeded in escaping justice or for other reasons.[199] It explains why Article 4a, section 1(d) is the most frequently 'ticked box': the surrender provides the first opportunity for the authorities of the issuing state to effectuate criminal justice and simultaneously offers a second chance for the fugitive to have his/her case assessed in court. After the surrender, the person concerned will still be served in person of the decision and will be expressly informed of his/her right to a retrial or an appeal. Such retrial or appeal should afford a reexamination of the merits of the case, including fresh evidence, and may lead to the original decision being reversed. The explicit mentioning of the *right* of the fugitive to a retrial or an appeal suggests that such retrial will actually occur, whenever the person concerned so desires. It cannot be made dependent upon other conditions than that the initial decision was not serviced in person and that the request is lodged within the applicable timeframe.[200] In a somewhat roundabout way, the Irish High Court has confirmed that Article 4a, section 1(d) requires a factual assessment of the case, including the examination of fresh evidence. The applicant had claimed that he had not been present at a trial before the Supreme Court of Lithuania during which that court had assessed whether the law had been correctly applied to the facts as determined by the lower courts. Denying that the applicant, as a prerequisite for his surrender, would have a right to be present at such an 'appeal in cassation' during which only points of law would be addressed, the Irish Court implicitly endorsed the finding of the ECJ in *Tupikas* that Article 4a, section 1(d) of the Framework Decision referred to a trial in which both facts and law were reexamined.[201]

It must be emphasised that the right to a retrial or appeal in a way serves as a measure of last resort that makes amends for the fugitive not having been able to be present in person at the trial. Different from the approach of the European Court of Human Rights, the ECJ is not interested in the question of whether the fugitive is him- or herself to blame for this inability. If (s)he has not been summoned in person or if it is not clear beyond any shadow of a doubt whether the person concerned has been aware of the impending trial in any other way – and if the two other exceptions mentioned under

199 Recital 12 of the Preamble to the 2009 Framework Decision notes that this fourth exception applies in cases in which the authorities have been unable to contact the person concerned 'in particular because he or she sought to evade justice.'

200 Brodersen et al., supra footnote 190, pp.166/167 observe that there is no full consensus on this point, some experts holding that it merely refers to a right to ask for a retrial, leaving the authorities the discretion to still grant or deny it. That interpretation is contrary to the clear words of the provision, which does not speak of a 'right to request' but to a 'right to a retrial.'

201 Irish High Court, 8 April 2019, *Minister of Justice and Equality v. Jefisovas* [2019] IEHC 248, section 68.

Article 4a, section 1, sub b and c do not apply – (s)he must have access to a retrial or appeal procedure, period. It follows, however, that the executing judicial authority must inquire whether the preceding conditions, enumerated under a-c have been met, or, rather, have *not* been met. In other words, the executing member state is not allowed to offer a *higher* level of protection by sidestepping those conditions. It is, for instance, not authorized to make the execution of a European Arrest Warrant dependent on the availability of a review in the issuing state, even if the requested person had been properly summoned in person. Nor would the absence of such a right of review be an impediment to surrender if the fugitive had been properly represented by assigned counsel who had actually defended him/her in multiple instances.

The situation and the accompanying legal question came to the fore in the case of Mr. Melloni, charged in Italy with bankruptcy fraud, who, while being aware of his trial from the outset and having deliberately absconded to Spain, had appointed two lawyers to represent him in all proceedings.[202] In a *recurso de amparo* (petition for constitutional protection), Melloni challenged the authorization of his surrender by the Audiencia Nacional, invoking the Spanish Constitution that provides for a full-fledged and unconditional right of retrial in case of in absentia judgments. The Constitutional Court of Spain asked the European Court to indicate whether Article 4a, section 1, of the Framework Decision precluded states from making the execution of an EAW conditional upon the conviction being open to review and, if so, whether states were not allowed to offer a greater level of protection of fair trial rights than EU law. The court answered the first question affirmatively, explaining once more the system of Article 4a that requires a verification of conditions in a (chrono)logical order:

> Article 4a(1) (a) and (b) of Framework Decision 2002/585 provides in essence that, once the person convicted *in absentia was aware, in due time, of the scheduled trial and was informed that a decision could be handed down if he did not appear for the trial or, being aware of the scheduled tria*l, gave a mandate to a legal counsellor to defend him at the trial, the executing judicial authority is required to surrender that person, with the result that it cannot make that surrender subject to there being an opportunity for a retrial of the case at which he is present in the Issuing Member State.[203]

In addressing the second question, the court admitted that Article 53 of the Charter of Fundamental Rights of the European Union, in principle,

202 ECJ, 26 February 2013, C-399/11, *Melloni v. Ministerio Fiscal*, section 17.

203 *Melloni* case, supra footnote 202, section 42. Italics are added and refer to the conditions that both were met in the case under scrutiny.

afforded member states leeway to offer a higher level of protection of due process rights, provided that this did not jeopardize the primacy, unity and effectiveness of EU law. In essence, the court held that Article 4a contained a balanced system, which 'reflected the consensus reached by all the Member States regarding the scope to be given under EU law to the procedural rights convicted in absentia who are the subject of a European Arrest Warrant.'[204] Any initiative on the part of member states to attach more conditions to the surrender, in pursuit of heighten procedural safeguards, would question the soundness of that system, making international cooperation more cumbersome.

9.10.4 Some interim conclusions

We have dwelled upon the highly complex issue of the compatibility of the execution of EAW's with the enforcement of trials in absentia at length because it perfectly illustrates that the reconciliation of international cooperation and respect for fair trial rights is an arduous affair. The main stumbling blocks are differences in legal and factual practices and distinct opinions on the degree of protection in respect of fair trial rights between states. A tension between efficiency and protection of fair trial rights is, of course, inherent to every criminal law procedure, but the problems multiply in case of international cooperation in criminal matters. Mutual unfamiliarity with each other's practices, procedures and standards is arguably the main cause of the – often unintentional – elimination of defendant's fair trial rights on the cross section of multiple criminal law systems. In case of mutual assistance in criminal matters, this risk is probably most acute, as the products of criminal procedural activities of a foreign state must be integrated into the legal tissue of the state conducting the trial.[205] In case of extradition/surrender the requested state can remain more aloof because it is 'merely' enabling the requesting state to obtain physical power over the fugitive. However, the requested state's distance from the arena where the action is incites it to shun responsibility for whatever happens after it has carried out its part of the job. It is this very attitude that the European Court of Human Rights censured in the *Soering* case.

Although the practice of the European Arrest Warrant is far from perfect, it may provide guidance on achieving fair(er)administration of justice within a community of states that have reached an advanced level of

204 *Melloni* case, supra footnote 202, section 62.

205 See on this issue, the perceptive, if not visionary, observations of A.M.M. Orie, 'De verdachte tussen wal en schip of de systeembreuk in de kleine rechtshulp,' in: E. André de la Porte et al. (eds.), *Bij deze stand van zaken: Bundel opstellen aangeboden aan A.L. Melai*, Gouda Quint: Arnhem 1983, pp. 351–361.

political integration.[206] From this perspective, the European experience may serve as a model for other states engaging in international cooperation on a regional scale. As evident from the previous sections, two elements are relevant for the attainment of this objective. First, states should engage in a certain degree of harmonisation or approximation of their criminal procedural and substantive law. It should be emphasised in this context that harmonisation and mutual recognition are not mutually exclusive concepts; they are rather complementary. States are not inclined to blindly trust their counterparts if they have not reached some common ground on the organization of their criminal law system.[207] However, harmonisation of criminal law has its (natural) limitations. States are generally reluctant to sacrifice ingrained practices and legal constructs in the realm of criminal law that reflect specific traditions and culture to the (rather elusive) 'common good' of harmonised or even unified criminal law. From this perspective, it seems a wise decision to aim at harmonisation of the conditions for the execution of the European Arrest Warrant, while leaving the internal criminal law and procedures of the EU member states largely intact, as has been elucidated in the previous section in respect of trials in absentia. This takes us to the second element. The project of the European Arrest Warrant has benefited from a supervisory mechanism that oversees international cooperation in criminal matters, making sure that fair trial rights receive maximum attention. The European Court of Justice has performed this function, cautiously navigating between furthering cooperation between states that harbour different levels of protection of fair trial rights and respect for the idiosyncrasies of individual states. Wherever the court has found room to do so, it has introduced 'autonomous concepts of EU law' in which principles of due process rights are incorporated.

Whereas such a supervisory mechanism reflects a top-down approach, intended to impose an authoritative interpretation of European Union law, it must be supplemented by initiatives at the grassroots. The often-quoted project on *The European Arrest Warrant and In Absentia Judgments* (see previous section) has created a platform for the exchange of practices and opinions between representatives of judicial authorities from several members states on the successes and failures of the European Arrest Warrant. The discussions have culminated in a number of recommendations to improve international cooperation with due regard for the position of the requested

206 Political integration is probably indispensable for a system of international cooperation in which criminal law enforcement and respect for due process are given due and equal attention. Cyriel Fijnaut has coined the term 'laboratory for international cooperation,' referring to such cooperation on an even smaller scale between kindred states; C. Fijnaut and A. Spapens, 'The Meuse-Rhine Euroregion: A Laboratory for Police and Judicial Cooperation in the European Union,' in: F. Lemiueux (ed.), *International Police Cooperation: Emerging Issues, Theory and Practice*, Uffculme: Wilan 2010, pp. 101–125.

207 See A.H.J. Swart, *Een ware Europese Rechtsruimte*, ACIL-publications: Amsterdam 2001.

person. The details of these recommendations need not detain us here. What interests us is the choice of methodology, fueled by a desire to reach practical solutions for daily problems. Mutual understanding of each other's legal systems and practice is key to the success of such projects. Concern for the fate of the requested person underpins the enactment of such projects, while the engagement in these initiatives enables a lasting commitment to that noble cause.

9.11 Final reflections

The preceding sections have demonstrated that, within the context of the European Union, the fundamental rights of the requested person have drawn heightened attention. At first sight that may appear somewhat paradoxical. After all, the principle of mutual recognition that underpins the European Arrest Warrant system is predicated on the assumption that the members of the European Union will observe the human rights of criminal suspects, obviating the necessity of further review.

On closer scrutiny, however, the sharper supervision of both the European Court of Justice and national courts makes sense. Reliable information that the human rights record of some member states leaves much to be desired undermines the legitimacy of the entire system that defends the simplified procedure with the argument that the compliance with the rule of law and protection of fundamental rights in the requesting state can be taken for granted. The discovery that this supposition might be incorrect should prompt the European Union to reconsider the assumptions sustaining the project and ponder the remedies to resolve the quandary. A prudent approach favours a tightened control of the performance of law enforcement and criminal courts in the realm of due process as a precondition for the execution of European Arrest Warrants beyond a radical abolition of the entire system.[208]

As has been elucidated in Section 9.2, the tension between mutual trust and concern for the fugitive's fundamental rights pervades the concept and practice of extradition in general, although in a more diluted manner. If states maintain less frequent and cordial relations and are therefore less informed about the quality of each other's administration of justice, mutual trust serves at most as a presumption that can be rebutted. From that perspective, one might expect states to be more circumspect in exposing

208 See on the choice between both options also M. Wendel, ' Mutual Trust, Essence and Federalism – Between Consolidating and Fragmenting the Area of Freedom, Security and Justice after LM', *EUConst* 2019, p. 27 and Jannemieke Ouwerkerk, 'Mutual Trust in the Area of Criminal Law,' in: Hemme Battjes, Evelien Brouwer, Paulien de Morree and Jannemieke Ouwerkerk, *The Principle of European Asylum, Migration and Criminal Law: Reconciling Trust and Fundamental Rights,* Meijers Committee; Standing Committee of Experts on International Immigration, Refugee and Criminal Law, December 2011.

fugitives to foreign justice than within the context of the European Union. However, as was noted in Section 9.3, extradition treaties usually require states parties to oblige. States therefore prefer to evade a direct treaty violation and take a prospective and uncertain risk of human rights infringements into the bargain.

Over the last 30 years – triggered by the decisions of human rights bodies like the European Court of Human Rights and the UN Human Rights Committee – states have endeavoured to resolve the predicament. The proliferation of human rights clauses in extradition treaties, enabling states to refuse extradition whenever they have serious concerns about the imminent fate of the fugitive, bears witness to that change of heart. Moreover, standard *aut dedere, aut judicare* provisions that feature in the so-called sectorial conventions, which serve to counter terrorism or organized crime, equally offer states having qualms about the observance of human rights in the requesting state an appropriate alternative. We identify here a second function of the maxim, alongside the possibility of the prosecution of nationals in the event states are reluctant to extradite their own citizens (as discussed in Chapter2).[209]

The salient question that emerges at the end of this chapter is whether all these good intentions have borne fruit. Have states in the extradition practice outside the regional context of the European Union become more vigilant in scrutinizing the fugitive's prospects of being sheltered against torture or inhuman and degrading treatment and obtaining a fair trial? As this monograph does not aim to present a systematic and comprehensive overview of extradition law and practice around the world, the following analysis is merely illustrative and can give only a rough impression. I have opted to briefly discuss three extradition practices, dispersed over three different continents (Africa, Asia/Oceania and Latin America) that reveal the ongoing struggle with the topic.

The first case study concerns the immediate follow up of a fairly recent extradition treaty that was concluded between Malawi and Rwanda.[210] The background to the agreement was the diaspora of Rwandan genocide perpetrators who had escaped to African countries – some of them to Malawi – in an attempt to evade justice. Rwanda made efforts to obtain custody over these individuals who were suspected of serious international crimes in order to put them on trial. The bilateral treaty contains human rights clauses that are copied verbatim from the UN Model Treaty on Extradition (referred to

209 See Harmen van der Wilt, 'Après Soering; The Relationship between Extradition and Human Rights in the Legal Practice of Germany, the Netherlands and the United States,' 42 *Netherlands International Law Review* (1995), p. 78.

210 See, for a lively discussion, Mwiza Jo Nkhata, 'The Malawi-Rwanda Extradition Treaty of February 2017: An Arrangement of Convenience or a Convenience of Arrangement?' 17 *International Criminal Law Review* (2017), pp. 844–879.

in Section 9.3).[211] Moreover, the treaty acknowledges double jeopardy and trials in absentia without recourse to review as potential grounds for extradition.[212] Both these (potential) legal impediments were raised in the notorious case of Vincent Murekezi, a Rwandan businessman accused of having participated in the genocide of 1994.[213] Rumour had it that Murekezi had already stood trial before and had been convicted in absentia by a Gacaca court, the indigenous dispute resolution mechanism that has been found wanting in terms of fair trial and is considered unsuitable for pursuing genocide cases.[214] The primary question was whether the trial and conviction in the Gacaca court would count for the purpose of assessing the double jeopardy issue. Next, the extradition court of Malawi would have to address the legal consequences of the trial in absentia. Nkahata suggested that the two issues would best be lumped together to reach, for all practical intents and purposes, a satisfactory outcome: the promise of the Rwandan authorities to retry all those who were convicted in absentia by Gacaca courts would technically perhaps amount to an infringement of the double jeopardy rule but would offer the accused the comfort of a full trial in his presence and would also serve to remedy other due process shortcomings of the previous Gacaca proceedings.[215] Murekezi was ultimately extradited to Rwanda in January 2019, after he had served a five-year sentence in Malawi for fraud-related offences.[216] The outcome reveals that the state parties involved struck a fair balance between criminal law enforcement and human rights: Murekezi contends that he received a fair trial and that he has been decently treated in Rwanda. One might conclude that Malawi and Rwanda succeeded in reaching this satisfactory solution in spite of the legal venues provided by

211 Article 3(f) of the Extradition Treaty obliges the requested state to refuse extradition 'if there is sufficient reason to believe that the person whose extradition is sought for, has been or would be subjected in the requesting State to torture or cruel, inhuman or degrading treatment or punishment or if that person has not received or would not be accorded a fair trial as contained in the International Covenant on Civil and Political Rights, Article 14.' In addition, Article 4(d) precludes extradition in case the offence for which the extradition is sought carries the death penalty (unless there are assurances that it will not be imposed), a provision that has lost practical relevance, since Rwanda has abolished capital punishment.

212 Treaty, Article 3(d) and 3(g), respectively.

213 The *State and the Minister of Foreign Affairs and International Cooperation and the Minister of Home Affairs and Internal Security Ex Parte Vincent Murekezi* Miscellaneous Civil Cause No. 265 of 2017 (source: Nkhata, supra footnote 210, p. 867).

214 See especially Avocats Sans Frontières (Lawyers Without Borders), *Monitoring of the Gacaca Courts: Judgment Phase; Analytical Report, March–September 2005*, ASF, December 2005; and Anganile Mwenifumbo, 'Eradicating Delay in the Prosecution of Crimes of Genocide in Rwanda through Gacaca Courts: Will Any Form of Justice Do?' 13 *East African Journal of Peace and Human Rights* (2007), pp. 309–320.

215 Nkhata, supra footnote 210, p. 874.

216 *New Times*, 13 January 2020; https://www.newtimes.co.rw/news/photos-genocide-convict-murekezi-laughs-death-claims.

the treaty. After all, the extradition treaty displays major flaws because the different treatment of trials in absentia by civil law systems (Rwanda) and common law systems (Malawi) has been completely glossed over.[217]

Extradition relations between China and several Western countries, including Australia and Canada, have triggered heated political debates on the domestic front.[218] The incentive for the Chinese government to conclude extradition treaties with a range of Western countries was the large-scale anticorruption campaign, colloquially known as 'Operation Fox Hunt.' Initially, the Chinese government had relied on ad hoc arrangements to obtain surrender of tainted officeholders who had found refuge abroad. However, as such arrangements are by their nature volatile, China sought a higher success rate for its efforts by prompting (Western) states to conclude bilateral extradition treaties. Several states, including Spain, France and Portugal, obliged. Ratification of the treaty with Australia that was signed in 2007 turned out to be highly controversial, pitting the Law Council of Australia, which represents the legal profession, against the Attorney's General Department (AGD). The Law Council's objections to ratification covered the entire gamut of human rights concerns that were identified in this chapter. The council lamented 'corruption within the Chinese judiciary, political interference, prejudgment, and bias in trials; denials of procedural fairness ..., such as the preventing of challenges to evidence by not providing it to defendants; physical abuse of prisoners; use of torture to extract confessions; and poor prison conditions.'[219] Moreover, the Law Council pointed out that the treaty's 'no evidence rule' implying that the request need not be sustained by evidence, such as, for instance, witness statements, would be acceptable in extradition relations with states that abide by the rule of law but would likely compromise the human rights of the fugitive after his or her return to China. Assurances that the death penalty would not be imposed or that the suspect would not be tortured would be of questionable value in view of the critical observations of Amnesty International on the lack of transparency surrounding Chinese detention conditions and the existence of capital punishment. The Law Council therefore insisted on the inclusion of effective monitoring proceedings as a precondition for ratification. The AGC retorted that the extradition treaty contained a 'range of human rights safeguards' and that the formal framework would enable courts and

217 Nkhata, supra footnote 210, p. 875: 'While Malawi's legal system is common law, Rwanda has a civil law system and the possible implications of marrying these two systems for purposes of extradition seem to have been completely ignored by the negotiators of the Treaty.'

218 Compare the fascinating analysis by Asif Efray and Marcello Tomasina, 'Value-Free Extradition? Human Rights and the Dilemma of Surrendering Wanted Persons to China,'17 *Journal of Human Rights* (2018), pp. 605–621.

219 Efray & Tomasina, supra footnote 218, p. 611.

executive to ascertain the risk and gravity of human rights violations on a case-by-case basis. If necessary, they could always ask for additional guarantees. It added that extradition should not serve as an instrument to impose domestic standards on other states that may have (slightly) different opinions on the matter.[220] These arguments sound all very familiar as we came across them in the previous sections. Efrat and Tomasina conclude that the

> Australian debate over extradition to China demonstrates the tension between the competing imperatives: human rights and crime suppression,

adding that the opinions were divided along the fault lines that one might expect: the legal profession emphasising human rights and the institutional actors focusing on crime control.[221] In between the lines, the authors, however, suggested that the advocates of formalised extradition relations with China were also inspired by extra-legal motives. China has gradually expanded its political and economic power in Southeast Asia and Oceania. The demonstration of goodwill to assist in the 'repatriation' of suspects of corruption would be instrumental in soothing a major trade partner.

An illustration of the Latin American posture towards extradition and human rights is, perhaps surprisingly, borrowed from the famous criminal prosecution of former Peruvian president Alberto Fujimori, who was wanted in his home country on charges of embezzlement of public funds and human rights violations. Interpol had circulated an international arrest warrant that was initially refused by Japan, claiming that its domestic law precluded the extradition of Japanese citizens.[222] When he arrived in Santiago, Chile, his extradition was requested by the Peruvian authorities. One of the arguments that Fujimori submitted in an attempt to fight his surrender was that the extradition proceedings did not conform with due process. The Chilean Supreme Court made short shrift of that claim, responding that the proceedings complied with the principles of a fair trial because the president had been informed of the charges, was able to submit evidence and was assisted by legal counsel, both in Peru and in Chile.[223] Interestingly, however, Fujimori also pleaded that he would be exposed to the risk of double jeopardy in Peru. The Chilean court refuted the argument, holding that within

220 'Extradition relationships in no way require equivalence between justice systems ... there is no requirement that another country apply the same standards as Australia.' Quoted in Efray & Tomasina, supra footnote 218, p. 613.

221 Efray & Tomasina, supra footnote 218, p. 614.

222 Fujimori had double, Peruvian and Japanese, nationality and had fled to Japan to evade prosecution.

223 *Peru v. Chile, Appeal Decision, Ro! No 2242-06, ILDC 1443 (CL 2007), 21 September 2007, Chile Supreme Court*, Comments by Nicole Gamble, Camila Rodriguez Maldonado.

extradition proceedings there was no room to raise this issue as it had to be decided during the full trial in Peru. The case reveals some fascinating differences with the European approach. On the one hand, the Chilean court, by substantially addressing the applicant's claims, acknowledged that the extradition proceedings themselves had to be tested against the principles of a fair trial. That position deviates from the findings of the European Court of Human Rights that extradition is not within the remit of Article 6 of the European Convention. The purport of this approach is, on the other hand, somewhat diluted by the Chilean court's holding that issues of double jeopardy had to be decided by the criminal courts of the requesting state. As has been extensively discussed before, within the framework of the European Arrest Warrant, double jeopardy may serve as an optional or even mandatory ground for refusal. Admittedly, the reluctance of the courts of the requested state to anticipate (potential) procedural flaws that compromise the suspect's rights does not formally affect the fairness of the extradition proceedings as such. However, the outcome of the case sheds an interesting light on the Chilean court's proclivity to neatly separate between the sequential phases of the criminal procedure, reflecting a refusal to consider the human rights of the fugitive as a common responsibility of the cooperating states.[224]

Obviously, these cases provide no more than snapshots into the emergence of human rights issues in extradition cases in non-European states. However, they demonstrate the commonalities we identified in this chapter. First of all, the question to what extent the requested state can be held responsible for human rights violations that – potentially – occur in and at the hands of another state is a recurrent theme and the core issue of the topic. With the exception of highly predictable, flagrant violations of fundamental human rights – torture, inhuman treatment, trials without defence counsel – one can understand the predicament of the requested state. After all, apart from the fact that infringements of due process usually are prospective, they are often inextricably intertwined with the criminal law system of the requesting state. As no criminal (procedural) law system is inherently superior to another, states will be reluctant to impose their own standards and will shun responsibility when things go awry. The decision of the Chilean court in the Fujimori case should be considered against this background.[225] Second, lack of familiarity with each other's criminal procedure in case of cooperation

224 It is interesting to add that Judge Ballesteros, in a dissenting opinion, held that the extradition had to be denied, because Fujimori was not charged in Peru for the crimes for which extradition had been sought (Gamble et al., supra footnote 223, H 8). The anticipatory reference to the violation of the specialty principle (see Chapter 4) displays a broader view on the shared responsibility of cooperating states, requiring some concern for the fate of the fugitive after extradition.

225 My criticism concerns the rather categorical nature of the finding, implying that double jeopardy issues should always be decided at the criminal trial in the requesting state.

between states hailing from the civil law and the common law system is likely to aggravate the problem just identified, as the Rwandan example has demonstrated. Insufficient insight in the reasons why adversarial systems consider trials in the absence of the accused anathema or, reversely, in the way civil law systems compensate for the absence of the accused during the trial may not only hamper international cooperation in criminal matters, but may also infringe due process rights of the fugitive if the requested state relies too much on its own solutions. Finally, the reluctance of states to engage in a scrutiny of the human rights record of the requesting state does not only derive from respect of its sovereignty and a concomitant acceptance of its legal system, but may be inspired by (extra-legal) political and economic motives as well. The strained relations between Australia and China that originated in cumbersome international cooperation in criminal matters make abundantly clear that this can have a backlash on domestic politics.

It would be preposterous to claim that a sophisticated regional framework of international cooperation, as exhibited in the European Arrest Warrant system, would cure all these ills. However, intensified and regular contacts between judicial authorities in the realm of criminal law increase mutual understanding of each other's procedures and legal practice. This is likely, in turn, to sharpen the attention of courts to impairments of due process rights that the fugitive will sustain when compared with the applicable standards in the requested state. While it is generally acknowledged that the requested state is not to check whether the conduct of the trial would be in full conformity with its own conception of a fair administration of criminal justice, familiarity with its counterpart's legal practice precludes the requested state from asserting that it could not have foreseen the violations of due process. Mutual trust must be corroborated by previous experience and the principle of confidence should not serve as a convenient cloak to cover ignorance or lack of interest.

10 Conclusions

The positions of the stakeholders in extradition revisited

In the introductory chapter it was announced that the concept of extradition would be examined from the prism of its stakeholders, to wit, the states involved, the fugitive and the international community. The underlying hypothesis is that the nature of the device could best be understood against the backdrop of the interaction of the legal and political interests of these entities/persons which is conducive to shifting alliances and determines the outcome of proceedings. Belonging to the realm of international criminal law, extradition law combines the complexities of international relations and the tension between law enforcement and due process. In the subsequent chapters, the dynamics that were just mentioned have been further elaborated.

10.1 States involved in extradition

At first blush, one may presume that states share a common interest in cooperating for the purpose of repressing crime. The reasons are easy to understand. They may both be equally vulnerable, especially in the case of transnational and organised crime. Besides, the appetite to assist each other is triggered by the perfect symmetry of performances (at least in theory or on the drawing board): each state can expect that its counterpart will return the favour. Reciprocity is the bedrock of extradition law. However, as became manifest in Chapters 2 through 5 in particular, there are limitations to the degree states are prepared to engage in extradition, which are rooted in concerns over sovereignty reflecting political, moral or cultural predilections.

States belonging to the civil law tradition have been reluctant or downright adamant (not) to surrender their own nationals, considering this an affront to the historically developed mutual bonds between the state and its citizens (Chapter 2). The proposal, by way of compensation, to engage in criminal proceedings on the basis of the active nationality principle (*aut judicare*) may strike common law states as inappropriate because they consider the alternative as second best or even as no option at all.

The dual criminality rule extensively discussed in Chapter 3 connotes the idea that states are adverse to cooperating in respect of the suppression

DOI: 10.4324/9780429956683-10

of conduct that they do not consider reprehensible or unlawful themselves. Apart from practical considerations – 'why would we bother to apply our enforcement system for such trivial purposes?' – the refusal on the basis of lack of (dual) criminality may reflect a deeper and more principled stance of liberal states that people are entitled to lead their own lives and that the application of the harsh instrument of criminal law should be reserved for those inflicting serious harm.[1]

From the perspective of the requested state, refusal of extradition for political offences (Chapter 5) may be based on several considerations. The state may wish to keep aloof from internal political disturbances in the requesting state, it may have sympathy for the dissidents' cause or, more realistically, it may welcome the weakening of another state as a result of political cleavage. The abstract nature of the political offence exception in extradition law saves the state from having to elaborate the particular reason for its negative decision. As political institutions and choices constitute the essence of sovereignty, it is self-explanatory that states will differ from each other more broadly on politics than on crime. In the context of extradition, this translates into the requested state's power and prerogative to define the difference between the two.[2]

As discussed in Chapter 8, the most palpable derogation of sovereignty is a state's trespassing on another state's territory to obtain custody over a fugitive from justice. In its landmark decision in the *Lotus* case, the Permanent Court of International Justice famously held that

> the first and foremost restriction imposed by international law upon a State is that – failing the existence of a permissive rule to the contrary – it may not exercise its power in any form in the territory of another State. In this sense jurisdiction is certainly territorial; it cannot be exercised by a State outside its territory except by virtue of a permissive rule derived from international custom or from a convention.[3]

Attempts to vindicate such infringements by invoking the *male captus, bene judicatus* maxim have been denounced as outrageous, both in academia and

1 See the highly interesting digressions of Joel Feinberg, *The Moral Limits of the Criminal Law, Volume I, Harm to Others,* New York: Oxford 1984, pp. 3–27. The introduction of 'qualified dual criminality' requiring a minimum prison sentence of one year in both the requesting and the requested state has its roots in the maxim *de minimis non curat praetor* and serves as an antidote against the abuse of extradition procedures for the prosecution of misdemeanours.

2 It may be noted that this prerogative works both ways. In national criminal law, offences against the state and the political order – high treason, assault on the head of state, sedition – count among the most serious crimes. In the political offence exception, that hierarchy of gravity is reflected invertedly.

3 Permanent Court of International Justice, 7 September 1927 (*France v. Turkey*), the Case of the S.S. *Lotus*, Series A No. 10, section 18.

in later case law (see the discussion of the *Alvarez Machain* case and its aftermath in paras. 8.2.3 and 8.2.4). Apart from constituting a blatant infringement of international law from which the culprit should not reap the benefits, the underlying assumption is that such actions are to be condemned because extradition is the exclusive way to obtain physical power over the fugitive. That perspective acknowledges the sovereign rights of states to determine whether, and if so under what conditions, they are prepared to engage in international cooperation in criminal matters with other states, allowing them to balance the propriety of such a commitment against other interests.

10.2 Rights of the requested person

In a conception that considers states as the main – or even the only relevant – actors and agents within international (legal) society, the rights of human beings can only be secondary to and derivative of states' interests. Of course, the human rights discourse that burgeoned after, and in response to, World War II challenges that position. However, that development cannot detract us from an analysis of the timeless quandary posed by the relationship between order and justice. Recent conflicts, such as the Arab Spring demonstrations, make the issue even more urgent or compelling.

An extensive investigation of theories of international relations in which the topic features prominently would clearly exceed the scope of this book, which has focused on law and legal practice. Incidentally, clashes between the maintenance of order and the pursuit of justice have come to the fore when the background of conflicting interests was addressed. It suffices to make some observations on the dichotomy between order and justice that partially aligns with the collusion of the interests of states and the right of the requested person involved in the extradition procedure. For a proper understanding of the repercussions for extradition law and practice, it is necessary to understand that the tension surfaces at different levels.

As Hedley Bull has pointed out, the orthodox and 'conservative' international law assumption that only states are subjects of international law stemmed initially from the inability to reach consensus on the content of human rights and how to uphold them:

> order was best founded on a system of international law of which states alone were subjects, and from which the divisive issues of the rights and duties of individuals and groups other than the state were excluded.[4]

Bull is quick to add, however, that the human rights discourse 'carried to its logical extreme' is subversive of the fabric of the society of sovereign

4 Hedley Bull, *The Anarchical Society: A Study on Order in World Politics*, Columbia University Press: New York 1977, p. 146.

states, as it jeopardises the unfaltering loyalty/allegiance of its citizens on which that sovereignty is built. It does not imply that the efforts to establish human rights in international law are to be discredited because order is not 'the only or commanding value .... It is simply to observe that in our times the international discussion of human rights and duties in international law is more a symptom of disorder than of order.'[5]

In discussing the priority between order and justice, Bull obviously acknowledges the potential of conflict, but avows that 'demands for the preservation of order and for the promotion of just change in world politics are not mutually exclusive, and that there is sometimes scope for reconciling the one with the other.'[6]

As the inherent tensions between the search for order and the pursuit of justice for individuals pervade the entire gamut of international law and international relations, it naturally does affect extradition law and practice as well. However, in this particular area the problem is compounded because justice in criminal law is not a monolithic concept (leaving aside the question of whether it ever is in *any* discipline). The claim that criminal law should administer justice immediately begs the question: 'justice for *whom*'? (Organised) crime affects the rights and well-being of other people. Criminal law enforcement serves not only to restore order, but also to right the wrong and redress injustice. The paradigm change in both domestic and international criminal law entailing the heightened attention to the position of victims is exemplary.[7] When victims are increasingly allotted influence over decisions whether prosecutions should be started, on the basis of which charges and where the trial should take place, the balance will soon tip in favour of criminal law enforcement, implying – if necessary – extradition.[8] As justice is not an unequivocal concept in criminal law, the clear-cut

5 Bull, supra footnote 4, p. 147.

6 Bull, supra footnote 4, p. 91.

7 The bibliography on the topic is abundant. Suffice to mention, amongst many others: Kerstin Braun, 'Giving Victims a Voice: On the Problems of Introducing Victim Impact Statements in German Criminal Procedure,' 14 *German Law Journal* (2013), pp. 1889–1908; M. Heikkilä, *International Criminal Tribunals and Victims of Crimes*, Turku: Institute for Human Rights, 2004; C. Hoyle & C. Ullrich, 'New Court, New Justice? The Evolution of Justice for Victims at Domestic Courts and at the International Criminal Court,' 12 *Journal of International Criminal Justice* (2014), p. 681; B. McGonigle Leyh, *Procedural Justice? Victim Participation in International Criminal Proceedings*, Cambridge: Cambridge University Press 2011.

8 Interestingly, in a case of manslaughter that recently took place on the Spanish island of Mallorca, the agreement of the Spanish and Dutch authorities that the latter would take over the criminal proceedings was based on the fact that both the perpetrator(s) and the victim had Dutch nationality. The additional weight of the passive nationality principle was thus decisive in the determination of the place of prosecution and trial. See https://www.nu.nl/binnenland/6148305/experts-dat-nederland-de-mallorca-zaak-overneemt-is-opvallend-maar-logisch.html.

equation of order and justice as presented by Hedley Bull is distorted to the detriment of the legal position of the requested person.

The assumption that classic grounds for refusal in extradition law, discussed in Chapters 2 through 5, were created to serve the interests of the requested state and that the fugitive could only indirectly benefit from them is not far-fetched. It is confirmed by the fact that states can often renounce invoking these grounds, or at least mitigate their effects, whenever they see fit. In general, it is certainly in the interest of the accused to be prosecuted and tried in his/her home country, rather than to be exposed to foreign justice. However, even states belonging to the civil law tradition are increasingly prepared to surrender their own nationals, provided that they have a right to return to their home country to serve their sentence.[9] Similarly, a fugitive from justice can – at least for the time being – take advantage of the fact that his conduct is not a criminal offence in the state of sojourn. However, as we have noticed in par. 3.3, states have made attempts to get around the obstacle by focusing on the narrow legal question of whether the conduct in any way could be covered by a criminal provision under their own law, without bothering whether the foreign equivalent protected the same legal interests. Moreover, kindred states within the European Union had no qualms in even partially abolishing the rule of dual criminality. Such a move is inconceivable within a perspective that presents dual criminality primarily as protection of the rights of the fugitive by forging a, somewhat contrived, link with the *nullum crimen* principle.[10] Finally, while the humanitarian rationale underpinning the political offence exception in extradition law has certainly risen in prominence, states have found ways to circumvent the hurdle by raising the bar of application and requiring that the fugitive would be entitled to the exception only if he had refrained from violent action. Again, the exception has become obsolete within the framework of cooperation between political allies on the presumption that they share the same friends and foes.

The brief summary of prior findings demonstrates that in the traditional extradition exceptions the requested person's rights are largely subsidiary to the requested state's interest. Even in case of abduction by foreign officials, acting without authority in another state, that entails a blatant infringement of the right to personal liberty, the fugitive is often dependent on the aggrieved state's lodging a protest against the violation of its territory. That state can afterwards condone the unfriendly act and even conspire with the other state in an unlawful rendition.[11]

9 The legal device of transfer of prisoners obviously serves to alleviate the fate of persons who have been tried and convicted abroad. So it can be considered as a halfway house reconciling criminal law enforcement with humanitarian interests.

10 See for a critical discussion of that view, par. 3.3.1.

11 See for an analysis of the phenomenon of disguised extradition, par. 8.4.

In Chapter 9 of this book, the attention shifts completely to the human rights of the fugitive. The length of the chapter is justified by, and reflects the relevance of, the development. In the opinion of the author, the spectacular proliferation of human rights in extradition law that started some 30 years ago with *Soering*, served to remedy the rather deplorable position of the requested person in surrender proceedings. As the topic has been discussed at length, some general conclusions suffice.

The quintessential question is in what cases extradition should yield to concerns for the violation of fundamental rights of the fugitive. The bottom line is that extradition should be refused forthwith if credible evidence reveals that the fugitive will face capital punishment or will likely be tortured or exposed to inhuman or degrading treatment. Beyond that extreme situation, the outcome hinges on the probability that the infringement will actually occur and the seriousness of the violation, the two parameters functioning as communicating vessels. In case of a relatively mild violation of procedural rights, for instance, a trial in absentia by a court of appeal without the accused having been properly summoned, surrender or extradition could still be refused, provided the incursion cannot be repaired, as the certainty of the infringement can easily be determined. Reversely, the seriousness of a potential violation of a person's bodily integrity and right to liberty, for example, the risk that the fugitive will be exposed to dismal prison conditions, compensates for the lack of certainty that the risk will materialise. It should prompt the court of the requested state to insist on further assurances that dispel the concern, on pain of a refusal to comply with the request to transfer the fugitive.

It has been observed that the subtle balancing of law enforcement through international cooperation and due process rights has taken shape primarily within the framework of the European Union.[12] However, increased attention to the human rights of the fugitive within the framework of extradition proceedings is a universal phenomenon. Whether it is deplorable that refusals of extradition, emanating from concerns for the human rights of the fugitive, impede criminal law enforcement obviously depends on one's personal opinions on the merits of crime repression, when weighed against countervailing values of the rights of criminal suspects and cannot be answered in the abstract. Criminal law enforcement is not an end in itself and its capacities to cure all societal ails are often overrated.[13]

12 It is the personal experience of the author, serving in his capacity as an ad litem judge in the Special Chambers for international cooperation in criminal matters in Amsterdam, that the vast majority of legal issues arising in the assessment of European Arrest Warrants concern due process rights and prison conditions that await the fugitive after his surrender.

13 In his highly critical assessment of the virtues and effectiveness of (international) criminal law, Friedrich Kratochwil observes, when discussing the well-known dilemma of the choice between fighting impunity and trusting truth and reconciliation commissions, that 'we need a variety of policy options that have to be carefully weighted, but which will entail hard

While such sobering notions are certainly apposite, it cannot be gainsaid that some crimes are considered to be so serious and devastating in their effects that the question of whether and how they are to be suppressed cannot be left solely to the decisions of individual states that seek to serve their parochial interests. It is in this area that the international community at least attempts to put its weight on the scale, prompting states to cooperate to counter threats and crimes that are of concern to humankind. This phenomenon takes us to the final sub-section of this book.

10.3 International community

The interests of the international community as a stakeholder in international cooperation, in general, and extradition, in particular, have come to the fore at points in this book. It surfaces most prominently in the claim that the obligation to prosecute or extradite (*aut dedere,aut judicare*) in respect of specific, very serious crimes (war crimes, crimes against humanity, genocide) has obtained the status of customary international law. This opinion is generally included in resolutions of the United Nations that propound such a claim.[14] In his seminal analysis of the nature of the obligation to extradite or prosecute, Raphaël van Steenberghe notes that 'the weight in the formation of a customary international obligation to extradite or prosecute is remarkably strong, especially given that no state voted against the resolutions and the reasons for abstention were not concerned with the recognition of an obligation to extradite or prosecute.'[15] Nonetheless, the influence of the maxim on classic prerogatives of the state is (far) less strong than meets the eye, as van Steenberghe is quick to point out. For one thing, he observes that some states, including the most powerful such as the United States and Russia,

choices. It is exactly in this context that we have to see that professions of mere faith in the virtues of criminal law are neither convincing nor responsible. Here the dangers of an "ideal discourse of justice" ... become obvious, particularly if, in addition, it gets monopolized by the fascination with "punishment" as the *via regia* of social order.' F. Kratochwil, *Praxis: On Acting and Knowing*, Cambridge University Press: Cambridge 2018, p. 308.

14 See the General Assembly Resolution (GA) (XXVI), 18 December 1971 ('Question of the punishment of war criminals and of persons who have committed crimes against humanity'). Section 1 of the resolution urges all states to put an end to and prevent war crimes and crimes against humanity and to ensure the punishment of all persons guilty of such crimes, *including their extradition* to those countries where they have committed such crimes' (italics added). For similar wordings, with a bit stronger emphasis on the duty to cooperate, GA Resolution 3074 (XXVIII) titled 'Principles of International Cooperation in the Detection, Arrest, Extradition of Persons Guilty of War Crimes and Crimes against Humanity.'

15 Raphaël van Steenberghe, 'The Obligation to Extradite or Prosecute; Clarifying Its Nature,' 9 *Journal of International Criminal Justice* (2011), p. 1100.

> oppose a customary obligation because they consider that such an obligation would render extradition or extraterritorial jurisdiction mandatory and that such an obligation would be contrary to the freedom of action that normally characterizes the regulation of both these state competences.[16]

The tensions between the position of the international community and the sovereign interests of individual nations are succinctly and poignantly expressed! Van Steenberghe seeks to resolve the contradiction between unanimous support for the maxim and such objections by suggesting a conceptual distinction between the obligation to extradite or prosecute as a 'rule' and as 'a system'. 'As a rule' – or perhaps more precisely ' in principle' – states are compelled to choose between the two alternatives, but that action only serves as a tool to accomplish the wider purpose or aspiration, to wit, the construction of a watertight 'system' of criminal law enforcement that prevents perpetrators of international crimes from escaping to safe-havens. In actual practice, this implies that a state may be relieved from the obligation to choose either option, if national law or sovereign concerns preclude it from doing so. Second – and for the purpose of this treatise more relevant – van Steenberghe claims that the intrusion into the discretion of a state to grant or refuse extradition is even less dramatic because it is generally acknowledged that such decisions belong to the sovereign realm.[17] He refers to the ILC Commentary on the Articles of the Draft Code of Crimes against the Peace and Security of Mankind that would support this contention.[18] He concludes therefore that 'conditions under which extradition may be granted remain *almost* entirely dependent upon the national law of the custodial state.'[19] At this point, van Steenberghe is probably too rash. The devil is in the details and the qualifier '*almost*' is crucial here. Van Steenberghe - implicitly or explicitly – acknowledges no less than three exceptions to his assertion that extradition is a sovereign affair, on which the obligation to extradite or prosecute has no bearing. First of all, treaties that embody the principle urge states to consider international crimes as extraditable offences. Second, some treaties on the suppression of terrorism stipulate that the prohibited conduct shall never be qualified as a political offence.[20] And finally, the *aut dedere, aut judicare* maxim obliges states to

16 Van Steenberghe, supra footnote 15, p. 1103.

17 Van Steenberghe, supra footnote 15, p. 1103.

18 ILC Commentary on the Articles of the Draft Code of Crimes against the Peace and Security of Mankind, UN Doc. A/51/10. 1996, §§ 28-29: 'extradition is always to be considered as a sovereign act *even as a component of the obligation to extradite or prosecute* ... the full implementation of this obligation depends upon the alternative obligation to prosecute' (italics mine).

19 Van Steenberghe, supra footnote 15, p. 1104 (emphasis added).

20 To his credit, van Steenberghe mentions this in footnote 59 of his article.

submit a case to its competent authorities that should decide on surrender, if it chooses not to prosecute itself, thus depriving the state of its sovereign right to reject the request forthwith. In view of these exceptions, the conclusion seems more correct that the rise of customary status of the *aut dedere, aut judicare* obligation, while certainly not sounding the death knell to discretionary powers of the state in the realm of extradition in respect of suspects of international crimes, exerts a subtle but incontrovertible influence.

The indirect enforcement system that is predicated on the *aut dedere aut judicare* principle and the supranational International Criminal Court (ICC) are aligned in their common purpose to end impunity.[21] While the ICC was created to compensate for the failures of interstate cooperative efforts to suppress international crimes, both systems are supposed to work in tandem through the principle of complementarity. It is well known that the ICC, after a short-lived honeymoon, faces mounting criticism. The gist of the critique is that the institution does not live up to the – admittedly gigantic – expectations placed on it. Its underachievement is commonly attributed to a lack of resources, the unwillingness of states to cooperate and the rather naïve assumption that the institute can brace itself against political manipulation by strictly adhering to the law.[22] Torn between the necessity to be selective and make hard choices and the political pressure of those powers on whose cooperation the court is dependent, the court has been tempted to opt for easy targets, inviting the reproach of bias.[23] On an even more fundamental level, questions have been raised in asking on behalf of whom the ICC, lacking a constituency, is actually speaking: who are the 'we' from whom it derives its legal and moral authority?[24] In line with criticism of the questionable legitimacy and poor performance of the ICC, some wonder

21 For the terminology, see Bassiouni, quoted in Chapter 6.

22 Compare William Schabas, *Unimaginable Atrocities: Justice Politics and Rights*, Oxford University Press: Oxford 2012; see also Tor Krever, 'International Criminal Law: An Ideology Critique,' 26 *Leiden Journal of International Law* (2013), pp. 701, 705–706, who accuses the triumphalism surrounding international criminal law of 'shaping passive acquiescence in the status quo and discouraging more thoroughgoing efforts to address the systematic forces underlying instances of violence.'

23 See on the anti-Africa bias, for instance, Max du Plessis, Tiyanjana Maluwa & Annie O'Reilly, *Africa and the International Criminal Court*, London: Chatham House Report 2013.

24 Compare for a general discussion on the legitimacy of international courts: Armin von Bogdandy & Ingo Venzke, 'In Whose Name? An Investigation of International Courts: Public Authority and Its Democratic Justification,' 23 *European Journal of International Law* (2012), pp. 7–41; specifically in relation to the ICC and international criminal law: Immi Tallgren, 'Who Are "We" in International Criminal Law? On Critics and Membership,' in: Christine E.J. Schwöbel (ed.), *Critical Approaches to International Criminal Law: An Introduction*, Abingdon: Routledge, 2014, pp. 71–95.

whether the ICC is the proper forum in which to adjudicate international crimes at all, or they suggest alternative justice mechanisms.[25]

The choir of critical voices is large, still increasing and their arguments are multifarious. As this work deals with interstate cooperation in criminal matters and it has touched only ephemerally on the supranational system, the continuing debate need no longer detain us. In two respects, the brief excursion to the International Criminal Court and its critical assessment informs our quest into the influence of the international community on extradition. First of all, it raises the question of whether the establishment of a permanent international court has strengthened the role of the international community in international cooperation between states when compared with the indirect enforcement system. The answer to this query can be rather brief: there are no indications that it has. Obviously, domestic criminal law enforcement in respect of international crimes is influenced by the existence of the International Criminal Court through the complementarity principle. And that may include (the lack of) international cooperation. A state may be unable to prosecute and try suspects because of another state's 'unwillingness' to surrender the fugitive. In such a case, both parameters for the threshold of the admissibility of a case before the ICC are spread over several states. The ensuing activation of the ICC's jurisdiction, however, is merely a consequence of the failure to perform. It does not create new obligations that exceed the ones that states are already bound to observe under the indirect enforcement system. If the court proceeds to investigate and prosecute crimes within its jurisdiction, states are under an obligation to cooperate fully with the court, which includes the duty to surrender persons.[26] The cooperation system in the Rome Statute hardly affects the interstate framework of extradition. Apart from the fact that the obligation, in principle,[27] pertains only to states parties – implying state-consent – the cooperation system in the Rome Statute is governed by specific rules and functions that largely parallel the indirect enforcement system.[28]

Second, one may wonder whether the criticism directed at the performance of the International Criminal Court also includes the indirect enforcement system of international criminal law and, in particular, whether it criticises the increasing impact of the international community on extradition.

25 See, for instance, Sarah M.H. Nouwen & Wouter G. Werner, 'Monopolizing Global Justice,' 13 *Journal of International Criminal Justice* (2015), p. 157.

26 Part 6 (articles 86-102) of the Rome Statute. Articles 89–92 specifically address the duty to surrender.

27 'In principle,' because all states may be forced to cooperate if a situation is referred to the ICC by a resolution of the Security Council and the resolution contains a provision expressly stipulating such an obligation.

28 See for a more comprehensive discussion, Chapter 6.1. It bears emphasizing that, in case of competing requests, hailing from the ICC and 'any other State,' the requested state party is not even under an obligation to always give priority to the court: Article 90 Rome Statute.

The issue is definitely more complex because the answer depends on what aspect of the ICC's presumed failure is addressed. If the objections concern the unimaginative obsession with criminal law solutions, the states acting within the indirect enforcement system are equally in the dock. The system is more impervious, however, to the constitutionally, ideologically or politically tainted remonstrations against the ICC that have been briefly set out above. The authority to enforce criminal law is vested in the state's sovereignty and states do not even have to bother to conceal dependence on political actors, potentially resulting in bias, behind a mask of righteousness and legal impartiality. States are openly involved in politics and prejudiced in serving the interests of their institutions and citizens. Any concerns of the international community must be factored into that overarching interest.[29]

The ultimate question before us is therefore whether the – slightly – increased influence of the international community on extradition law and practice is to be considered as a good development or whether it upsets the equilibrium of interests to the detriment of the states involved and maybe at the expense of the fugitive's rights. In this book, some rather modest and tentative arguments have been advanced to sustain the former position. For one thing, Chapters 6 and 7 further substantiate the already well-established rule in international law that fugitives who are suspected of war crimes or terrorism should not benefit from the political offence exception. One of the most convincing reasons is that they intentionally flout the distinction between combatants and non-combatants by targeting civilians for calculated or ideological purposes. By doing so, they violate one of the core principles of international humanitarian law, which reserves a mutual license to kill to those who are directly and actively participating in hostilities. War criminals and terrorists thus forfeit the privileged, though precarious, status of combatants or political offenders and become ordinary criminals, subject to punishment but also – crucially – entitled to a fair trial.

Second, in Chapter 8 it is argued that a state's claim to territorial integrity dwindles in case of forceful abductions or luring of suspects of international crimes. That position has been advanced by international criminal courts and tribunals, partially for practical reasons, because they lack the enforcement power to effectuate their decisions. However, the partial acceptance of the *male captus, bene judicatus* principle in these extraordinary cases has a broader bearing in that it presents the rejection of sovereign claims as a consequence of the state's prior defaulting on its obligation to bring perpetrators of international crimes to justice.

29 As acknowledged by van Steenberghe, supra footnote 15, p. 1106, who, in discussing the attitude of states towards the *aut dedere, aut judicare* obligation, comments that 'Generally, a choice must be made between protection of the international community and the protection of sovereignty.'

It is clear that in both cases the international community sets its sight on the extradition configuration that has traditionally been monopolised by states and expects (or implores) both states and individuals to make their interests – albeit in the limited area of international crimes – subservient to its program and aspirations. It is equally obvious that this development directly follows from the project to advance international criminal justice that has come to fruition after World War II. However, acknowledging the logical coherence of these phenomena does not shed light on the project's necessity or desirability. Such a value judgment would require a profound and comprehensive inquiry into the essence of international crimes, the status and characteristics of perpetrators and the features of an international community that claims powers of legislation and adjudication in the realm of criminal law. This Herculean task exceeds the capacities of the current author and is most certainly beyond the scope of this book.[30] It must suffice to give some brief and tentative reflections on the last-mentioned element, to wit, the nature and evolution of the international community, because its decision to engage in criminal justice reveals its transformation into an incipient moral community.[31] The international community has, at least partially, transcended the dichotomy of enemy versus friend that is inherent in the Hobbesian state of nature and, according to Carl Schmitt, the essence of the political, and has exchanged it for the concept of crime. While the former is devoid of moral connotations, criminal punishment is suffused by it. This development entails, in a way, a certain rapprochement between the international community and the state and not only explains, but also justifies why the international community has an interest in getting involved in interstate cooperation in criminal matters.

The question of why the international community should direct its attention to war crimes, crimes against humanity, genocide and aggression – in other words: what makes these crimes so special? – and whether the concept is in need of extension cannot be answered in detail, as earlier indicated. I tend to agree with the observations of David Luban, who, in my opinion, has offered one of the most profound and lucid accounts on this topic.[32] According to Luban, the essence of international crimes, in general, and

30 For further reading on these fascinating issues, I suggest the recently published *Oxford Handbook of International Criminal Law*, Kevin Jon Heller, Frédéric Mégret, Sarah Nouwen, Jens David Ohlin & Darryl Robinson (eds.), Oxford University Press: Oxford 2020, that combines contributions from a political science, history, culture, law and international relations perspective.

31 Antony Duff, 'Authority and Responsibility in International Criminal Law,' in: Samantha Besson & John Tasioulas (eds.), *The Philosophy of International Law*, Oxford University Press: Oxford 2010, pp. 600–601 uses the term 'embryonic moral community,' which finds favour in the eyes of David Luban, 'The Enemy of all Humanity,' in: Heller et al. (eds.), supra footnote 30, p. 580.

32 David Luban, 'A Theory of Crimes against Humanity,' 29 *Yale Journal of International Law* (2004).

crimes against humanity, in particular, is that they strike at the efforts by human beings to enter political society and live, more or less, peacefully together.[33] Usually, this happens when a state turns against and attacks its own citizens – the paradigmatic case, according to Luban – sometimes when the state is too weak to protect its people against rival powers either from abroad or from within. Where I do not follow Luban is when he still adheres to the qualification of international criminals as *hostes humani generis,* by analogy with Cicero's depiction of pirates.[34] It implies that this person is beyond the human pale and becomes fair game to a 'vigilante jurisdiction in which the criminal becomes anyone's and everyone's legitimate enemy.'[35] Ultimately, Luban is not willing to accept that consequence, where he argues that perpetrators of heinous crimes are called to account to humanity and by this communicative mechanism, while enemies of humanity are simultaneously acknowledged as members of humanity.[36] He attempts to defend that position by presenting the emergence of criminal accountability as a step in the gradual progress towards a moral community and tries to reconcile the contradictory spatial positioning of perpetrators of 'radical evil' beyond and within humanity by drawing a separation between the act and the person.[37] I find that distinction rather contrived because the pejorative qualification of 'enemy' smacks of permanency and may be conducive to casting that person into the state of nature, where all rights are mere illusions.[38] According to Anthony Duff, the term *hostis humani generis* is an anachronism and, in view of the pretensions of the international community to uphold the rule of law, an oxymoron. In my opinion Duff is right. To hold someone to answer for his/her crimes is tantamount to considering him/her as a member of a normative community that calls that person to account.[39] That attitude and process is incompatible with the denouncement of people as 'enemies

33 Luban uses the term 'politics gone cancerous,' supra footnote 32, pp. 116–119.

34 Luban, supra footnote 31.

35 Luban, supra footnote 32, pp. 120–123.

36 Luban, supra footnote 31, p. 581.

37 Luban, supra footnote 31, pp. 579–581.

38 Luban himself acknowledges that risk when he rhetorically asks 'why, given its amazing potential for abuse, not expunge the inflammatory concept of an enemy of all humanity from our moral vocabulary?' He immediately gives his answer 'it is that no other term quite captures the twin nature of atrocity and persecution crimes that makes the idea of international criminal justice imperative: that they are radically evil and that they are everyone's business,' Luban, supra footnote 31, p. 579. Point taken, but he merely repeats his laudable explanation why these crimes are 'anybody's concern' and has an insufficient eye for its dark and potentially disastrous consequences.

39 Duff, supra footnote 31, p. 603: 'to put someone on trial and to punish him for his wrongdoing, is to treat him as a member of the normative community under whose laws he is tried and punished.'

of mankind' because it calls into question or even destroys the common ground on which the idea of a moral community is predicated.[40]

We have dwelled upon the nature of international crimes, the ambiguous approach towards international criminals and the relatively recent decision of the international community to engage in criminal law enforcement to argue that the latter, by taking that step, shows its aspirations to become a moral community. Clearly, that project has achieved its provisional pinnacle in the establishment of the International Criminal Court, but its judicial activities were never intended to be more than the tip of the iceberg. The paradigm change was heralded in Principle 1 of the Nuremberg Principles of International Law, which stipulates that

> Any person who commits an act which constitutes a crime under international law is responsible therefore and liable to punishment.[41]

The silent assumption was that states were expected to do the bulk of the job and that any international institution was to intervene only whenever they appeared to be unfit to the task. As a new competitor in the realm of criminal law enforcement, claiming a superior position in the political and moral hierarchy, the international community wields indirect control over both domestic criminal trials and international cooperation, including extradition, in respect of international crimes.

10.4 Final chord

At the end of this book we conclude that extradition has grown infinitely more complex, reflecting the increased globalisation and mutual interdependence of international society. Initially an interstate affair that afforded states, on a mutual basis, to obtain physical power over a fugitive from

40 See also the acidic comments of Kratochwil, supra footnote 13, p. 259: 'The "enemy" is ... no longer one, as in traditional societies, with whom one duels and to whom one pays respect by accepting his challenge, even if it means a fight to death. ... Instead as the servant of evil he now becomes the enemy of God – most obviously for the fundamentalist, but also for some more "enlightened" representatives of "humanity."' Kratochwil attributes this unhappy state of affairs to a revival of the concept of the 'sacred': 'parallel to the normal (citizen) criminal law, an "enemy criminal" emerges, featuring ... the former *hostis humani generis*, who is beyond the pale, even though he comes in a new garb. The appeal to the "sacred" seems then, despite all the secularism and progressivism of the Enlightenment project, to be just around the corner.' That Kratochwil's admonitions are not merely the nightmares of a brilliant and disillusioned scholar is abundantly demonstrated by the Guantanamo Bay detention camp.

41 *Principles of International Law Recognized in the Charter of the Nuremberg Tribunal and in the Judgment of the Nuremberg Tribunal, Adopted by the International Law Commission and Published in the Yearbook of the International Law Commission*, 1950, Vol. II, section 97.

justice, it has gained a prominent place within multilateral treaties, initiated by the United Nations, its specialised agencies or regional organisations, that have as their exclusive purpose the suppression of transnational crime. Whereas that development had started before World War II, it accelerated thereafter. While it is both a tautology and a truism that transnational (organised) crime does not stop at borders and that criminal law enforcement must accommodate and also become 'borderless,' it cannot be gainsaid that organised crime benefits hugely from the current design of international society. Not only does it exploit the spatial separation between supply and demand for (illegal) goods and services, but it also takes advantage of the windfall of impunity that is created by the absence of an international system of law enforcement. In this respect, transnational crime has something in common with international crime *stricto sensu* because perpetrators of those crimes get off scot-free through the protection of the state whose primary duty is to punish them. Impunity of these serious – transnational and international – crimes is a grave problem because it enables the perpetrators to pursue their nefarious activities that make people vulnerable and ruin their lives. Criminal law enforcement is certainly not a panacea, but it cannot be denied that it is the most robust instrument in the toolbox of the state. However much one may deplore this fact, we simply have not been able to invent a more satisfactory alternative. If states agree on the reprehensibility of conduct, they have good reasons, if they are not under a (moral) obligation, to assist each other. In defending a fierce stance against highly pernicious actions one may recall the words of Machiavelli, who, reflecting on the religious revival of his time with a mixture of respect and apprehension, noted that

> the 'new orders,' which by 'saving religion from being destroyed by the licentiousness of the prelates and heads of Church,' teach people to be good and not 'to resist evil' with the result that 'wicked rulers do as much evil as they please.'[42]

While the legal configuration just outlined reflects the 'sword' function of criminal law, its 'shield' component is represented by the increased attention given to the position and fate of the requested person. Obviously, that concern is related to a general awareness that criminal law owes its 'robust' reputation to the harsh consequences for the suspect standing trial. However, it is intensified by the notion that no two criminal justice systems are alike, that the fugitive may be exposed to a sub-standard trial or punishment in the requesting state and that such treatment is largely beyond the control of the requested state once the fugitive is surrendered. Inevitably,

42 Machiavelli, *Discourses*, book III, chapter I. The quote is taken from Hannah Arendt, *The Human Condition* (2nd ed), University of Chicago Press: Chicago 1998, pp. 77–78.

that attitude impedes, at least to a certain degree, the smooth functioning of the system, but that is the price that is calculated in the venture and that one has to be prepared to pay. The interaction among states, fugitives and the international community, all having their own legal interests that sometimes coincide and more often collide, produces a shaky system of 'checks and balances.' And that is perhaps the most we can hope for in a divided world that is far from perfect.

Index

Note: references following "n" refer to notes

For Product Safety Concerns and Information please contact our EU representative GPSR@taylorandfrancis.com
Taylor & Francis Verlag GmbH, Kaufingerstraße 24, 80331 München, Germany

www.ingramcontent.com/pod-product-compliance
Lightning Source LLC
LaVergne TN
LVHW022204200926
848481LV00006B/1842
9781032257730